THE SUPPLY MANAGEMENT LEADERSHIP PROCESS

Anna E. Flynn
National Association of Purchasing Management

Sam Farney
Supply Chain Advisors

Published by: National Association of Purchasing Management, Inc.
Paul Novak, C.P.M., A.P.P., Chief Executive Officer

© 2000 National Association of Purchasing Management, Inc.
P.O. Box 22160 Tempe, AZ 85285-2160 USA
www.napm.org

INTRODUCTION

Supply management professionals provide many valuable and important contributions to organizations throughout the world, whether they are public, for profit, or non-profit, and across all sectors. The field is quickly evolving and changing, reflecting the evolution of technology, the Internet, heightened professional standards, and increased collaboration between different internal departments, between suppliers, between customes, and between organizations. Supply management is affecting the bottomline more than ever before, and is "value added" for all companies and their financial success.

This new environment, however, requires all supply management professionals to stay on top of the tools, practices, policies, and knowledge relevant not only to supply management, but to the business environment as a whole. NAPM is dedicated to building the professional through education and professional development. The NAPM Supply Management Knowledge Series (previously known as the NAPM Professional Development Series) was developed to assist the supply management professional do this.

The Series has been updated to include an analysis and discussion of newly emerging trends and the new tools, practices, policies, and knowledge that have developed from these trends. Our goal in publishing the Series is to encourage and support your professional growth and contribute to the image of the profession, and to assist you with learning about and mastering these new skills . . . basically, to help you do your job the best you can.

In addition, the books are a resource for preparing for the C.P.M. and A.P.P. certification exams. The exams were also recently updated and many of the topics addressed in this four-volume series appear on these new exams.

It is my intention that NAPM will not only continue its efforts to support and build the supply management profession, but will also add to it. The NAPM Supply Management Knowledge Series is a part of these efforts.

Paul Novak, C.P.M., A.P.P.
Chief Executive Officer
NAPM
August 2000

NAPM – Your Source for Supply Management Resources

Since 1915, the National Association of Purchasing Management (NAPM) has served thousands of supply management professionals from around the world. Domestically, NAPM works with affiliated associations across the country to continually keep its members well informed, and trained on the latest trends and developments in the field.

The information available from NAPM is extensive. One of the greatest resources is the NAPM Web site, www.napm.org. In addition to general information, this expansive site features a vast database of supply management information, much of which is available solely to members. Information includes a listing of general supply management references as well as an extensive article database, listings of products and seminars available, periodicals listing, an Online Career Center with job listings and resumes posted, contact information for NAPM affiliate organizations nationwide, and links to other related Web sites.

The monthly Manufacturing and Non-Manufacturing *NAPM Report On Business®*, including the Purchasing Managers' Index (PMI) in the manufacturing survey, continues to be one of the key economic indicators available today. NAPM members receive this valuable report in the pages of Purchasing Today® magazine, one of the many benefits of membership.

The quarterly publication *NAPM InfoEdge* is also included in membership. *NAPM InfoEdge* provides unique, how-to approaches on single supply management topics.

NAPM also publishes *The Journal of Supply Chain Management*, a one-of-a-kind publication designed especially for experienced supply management professionals. Authored exclusively by accomplished practitioners and academicians, this quarterly publication targets purchasing and supply management issues, leading-edge research, long-term strategic developments, emerging trends, and more.

Members also enjoy discounts on a wide variety of educational products and services, along with reduced enrollment fees, for educational seminars and conferences held throughout the country each year. Topics cover the entire supply management spectrum.

For executives interested in professional certification, NAPM administers the Certified Purchasing Manager (C.P.M.) and Accredited Purchasing Practitioner (A.P.P.) programs. Members receive discounts on test preparation/study materials and C.P.M./A.P.P. exam fees.

To provide a forum for educational enhancement and networking, NAPM holds the Annual International Purchasing Conference. This is a unique opportunity for members and non-members alike to learn from each other and share success strategies.

To learn more about NAPM and the many ways it can help you advance your career, or to join online, visit NAPM on the Web at www.napm.org. To apply for membership by telephone, please call NAPM customer service at 800/888-6276 or 480/752-6276, extension 401.

THE NAPM SUPPLY MANAGEMENT KNOWLEDGE SERIES

Volume 1
THE SUPPLY MANAGEMENT PROCESS
Alan R. Raedels

Volume 2
THE SUPPLY MANAGEMENT ENVIRONMENT
Stanley E. Fawcett

Volume 3
SUPPLY MANAGEMENT FOR VALUE ENHANCEMENT
Lisa M. Ellram and Thomas Y. Choi

Volume 4
THE SUPPLY MANAGEMENT LEADERSHIP PROCESS
Anna Flynn and Sam Farney

SERIES OVERVIEW

In the past decade, purchasing has moved to the center stage of the organization as it has become increasingly clear that purchasing and supply management can make a significant contribution to organizational success. Beyond simply reducing prices for purchased goods and services, purchasing can add value to organizations in many ways, including supporting organizational strategy, improving inventory management, forging closer working relationships with key suppliers, and maintaining an active awareness of supply market trends. The ability of purchasing to significantly contribute to organizational success is the core of this four-book series.

While differences exist among various types of organizations, industries, business sectors, regions of the world, and types of items purchased, these books provide an overview of current issues in purchasing and supply management. The topics covered in this series range from the basics of good purchasing practice to leading-edge, value enhancement strategies. These four books provide an excellent survey of the core principles and practices common to all sectors within the field of purchasing and supply management.

These four volumes were designed to support the National Association of Purchasing Management (NAPM) certification program leading to the Accredited Purchasing Practitioner (A.P.P.) and Certified Purchasing Manager (C.P.M.) designations. They also provide practical and current coverage of key topics in the field for those interested in enhancing their knowledge. They also can serve as useful textbooks for college courses in purchasing.

The textbooks are organized around the four modules of the C.P.M. exam as follows:

1. *The Supply Management Process* (for C.P.M.s and A.P.P.s)
2. *The Supply Management Environment* (for C.P.M.s and A.P.P.s)
3. *Supply Management for Value Enhancement Strategies* (for C.P.M.s only)
4. *The Supply Management Leadership Process* (for C.P.M.s only)

Volume 1, *The Supply Management Process*, focuses on the overall purchasing process and its major elements. It looks at the requisitioning process, sourcing, bidding, and supplier evaluation, and offers an overview of cost and contract management. This volume also examines how technology has changed procurement techniques and provides a summary of the key legal issues facing purchasers.

Volume 2, *The Supply Management Environment*, explores how the ever-changing environment in which purchasers operate is affecting their roles today and in the future. Volume 2 provides an overview of purchasing's role in strategy and looks at how globalization, just-in-time/mass customization are affecting purchasing. This volume also explores issues related to negotiations, quality, reengineering, and supply chain management. It examines the increased role and impact of information technology on purchasing, and looks at what skill sets will be required for success in purchasing in the future.

Volume 3, *Supply Management for Value Enhancement Strategies*, explores a number of traditional and leading-edge approaches for increasing purchasing's contributions to organizational success. The volume begins by looking at outsourcing and lease versus buy issues. It then delves into the many issues associated with inventory management, including inventory classification and disposal. Specific value enhancement methods, such as standardization, value analysis, early supplier involvement, and target costing, are also presented. The volume closes with a discussion of developing and using forecast data, and offers an overview of specific strategies to apply in various purchasing situations.

Volume 4, *The Supply Management Leadership Process*, provides an overview of key general management issues specifically applied to purchasing activities and purchasing's role in the organization. It begins with an overview of strategic planning and budgeting processes, and continues by presenting specific issues related to effectively recruiting, managing, and retaining good employees. Volume 4 then discusses the role of operating policies and procedures, tools to manage workflow, and performance monitoring. It ends with a presentation of how to most effectively present purchasing performance results within the organization.

It has been a privilege to edit this series for NAPM and to work with an excellent group of authors. The authors' practical and theoretical knowledge has contributed to the quality of these books. I hope you find them both useful and interesting.

Lisa M. Ellram
Series Editor

PREFACE

Many books have been written about the art and science of management, and the skills and attributes of successful managers. This book focuses on some of these concepts and practices as they relate specifically to the management of the supply function. As more organizational time, attention, and resources are devoted to supply management, it is increasingly important for those in the profession to develop strategic as well as operational management skills. While it is impossible for one book to address every relevant topic in management, we have attempted to touch on some of the areas of greatest immediate concern to supply managers. We strongly encourage readers to see this book as merely a starting point for continual growth through reading, study, and practice. If this book stimulates interest in any aspect of managerial development, then it will have served its purpose. If it also assists the reader in attaining the certified purchasing manager (C.P.M.) designation, then all the better.

Any inaccuracies or omissions are solely the responsibility of the authors.

Anna E. Flynn
Sam Farney

ACKNOWLEDGEMENTS

I am grateful to the authors of the previous C.P.M. study guides and professional books who provided the foundation for this work. I am also indebted to the managers in many companies who provided real world examples. I would also like to thank Lisa Ellram, the series editor; Cynthia Zigmund, the technical editor; Scott Sturzl, the content-based editor, for their hard work and dedication to this series. Each provided guidance and assistance that improved this volume.

Anna E. Flynn

As a practicing supply management professional, I was honored to be asked to contribute to this publication. The contents of this and the other three volumes of this series should provide great value to the supply management practitioner during a truly exciting period for the profession.

Just as the role of the purchasing person is based upon inter-company relationships, my knowledge of the field is founded in many rich personal relationships. The earliest and most influential of these was the mentoring of Victor Pooler, C.P.M. and NAPM Shipman Medal winner, when I joined the function at Carrier Corporation. Many others have contributed greatly toward my greater understanding of the complexities of optimizing the supply chain in nearly three decades in this profession. Among the most significant of those individuals, listed alphabetically, are John Burlew, John Cologna, Hal Fearon, Frank Haluch, George Harris, Dennis Kdurna (dec.), Bob Monczka, Dave Nelson, and Ken Stork.

As any author can attest, the patience of loved ones is also essential to this work. I am truly thankful for the valued support and sacrifice of my wife Denni during the long hours and late nights at the keyboard.

Sam Farney

To Harold E. Fearon and Michiel R. Leenders. In gratitude for your support, encouragement and friendship.

Anna E. Flynn

To my wife, Denni and sons, Glen and Kevin.

Sam Farney

CONTENTS

Chapter 1: Introduction

Chapter 2: The Strategic Planning Process

Chapter 3: Budgets and the Budgeting Process

Chapter 4: Leading, Managing, and Supervising

Chapter 5: Selecting, Recruiting, and Retaining Personnel

Chapter 6: Operating Policies, Guidelines, and Procedures

Chapter 7: Tools to Manage Work Flow

Chapter 8: Performance Tracking and Improvement

Chapter 9: The Reporting Process

Appendix: Equal Employment Opportunity Laws and Regulations

CHAPTER 1

INTRODUCTION

Why is management of the supply function worthy of study?

Chapter Objectives

- To demonstrate the importance of the supply management function in an organization
- To explain how purchasing makes direct and indirect contributions to the organization

Supply Management in a Changing Business World

Many changes in the way business is conducted have had an impact on the purchasing function, from what the function is called to the way it is managed. Whether producing revenue or managing costs, all organizations must effectively manage the acquisition of goods and services. An argument for allocating resources, time, and attention to the supply function is the significance of the dollars spent on goods and services. In 1995, *Fortune* magazine reported that, "What used to be a corporate backwater is becoming a fast-track job, as purchasers show they can add millions to the bottomline."[1] According to the 1996 "Annual Survey of Manufactures" published by the U.S. Bureau of the Census, materials account for 53 percent of the sales dollars in the average manufacturing company.[2] If new capital expenditures are included, this figure increases to 57 percent. The purchase dollar-to-sales ratio varies greatly depending on the indus-

1

try. For example, in the printing and publishing industry, the material-to-sales ratio is 33 percent (36 percent if capital expenditures are included), but in the petroleum and coal products industry the ratio is 82 percent (85.5 percent with capital equipment). These numbers are strong indicators of the importance of the management of the purchasing and supply function. The purchase-to-sales ratio figures provided by the U.S. Bureau of the Census exclude the cost of services, such as advertising, insurance, telephones, research, developmental work, and consulting. Figure 1.1 shows the purchase-to-sales ratio for several industries.

FIGURE 1.1
Purchase Dollars as a Percentage of Sales

Industry	Material/Sales Ratio	Total Purchase Sales Ratio
Printing and publishing	33	36
Electronic and electrical equipment	43	49
Chemical and allied products	47	53
Primary metal industries	61	65
Petroleum and coal products	82	85.5

Source: 1996 U.S. Bureau of the Census "Annual Survey of Manufactures"

Implications for the Name of the Function

The term *purchasing* has long been used to describe the functional role of those who own the process by which such outside inputs are controlled. Global competition, demands for higher productivity, and tighter controls over cost have increased this function's strategic value to the organization. While people in this function have worked to increase their value and strategic importance in their organizations, many have tried to differentiate the work of today from that of the past. The term *supply management* is now often used to capture this more strategic role. This text will use *purchasing* and *supply management* interchangeably while attempting to describe the changing role of people engaged in this vital work.

Implications for Strategy

To capture the value of the supply function, top management, including chief purchasing officers, must align the purchasing management strategy with the organizational strategy. According to the authors of a Center for Advanced Purchasing Studies (CAPS) report, *The Impact of Purchasing on Financial Performance*, organizations achieving higher financial performance have appropriately matched their purchasing management strategy and their product strategy.[3] The key findings of this study were:

- Pairing a decentralized structure with relatively unique products, or a centralized structure with relatively common or commodity products, leads to better financial performance.
- Pairing a relatively wide scope of purchasing activities with relatively unique products, or a relatively narrow scope with commodity products, leads to better financial performance.

Overall, the researchers found that product uniqueness had to be considered in the equation for the purchasing organization's structure or scope of activities to affect financial performance. This finding reinforces the notion that the supply function does not operate in a vacuum. The supply function must be structured, organized, managed, and led in conjunction with the strategy and direction of the organization.

Technology Implications

Technology allows organizations to automate and streamline many activities that were historically considered to be part of purchasing. Even given the delays and problems that can occur with the implementation of new technologies, changes in the way that goods and services are bought and sold have allowed the purchasing function to move from a transaction-oriented activity to a knowledge- and relationship-oriented role. In *Reducing the Transactions Costs of*

Purchasing Low Value Goods and Services, Trent and Kolchin reported that three of the seven most highly rated methods for managing
low value purchases involve technology.[4] These methods are:

- Online ordering through electronic catalogs
- Electronic commerce through the Internet
- Automated accounts payable systems

The growth of e-commerce and the adoption of Enterprise Resource
Planning (ERP) systems, which are discussed in Chapter 7, will continue to alter the way buyers and sellers interact. Technology will also
affect decisions regarding hiring, retaining, and training employees,
because the skill sets needed in this rapidly changing, high-technolo-
gy environment differ from those previously sufficient for high performance in purchasing.

Implications for Supplier Relationships

The alignment of purchasing strategy to organizational strategy,
the focus on the value chain starting with the needs and desires of the
end customer, and the drive to identify and focus on core competencies have all led to the realization that the purchasing function must
be managed differently than it has been in the past. If the supply function is to make strategic and operational contributions to the organization, how the function is organized, managed, and evaluated matters. The objective of supply management is to capture the contribution of the supply base to the organization. Suppliers carry influence.
Therefore, the management of suppliers is critical to the success of
the organization.

According to *A Multi-Country Study of Strategic Topics in
Purchasing and Supply Management*, published by CAPS, "Probably
most important is the trend of major structural overhauls toward
'integrated supply chains' or 'networks' that both smooth and quick-
en the flow of materials and information, both up and down the supply and demand chain."[5] These findings support the results of a 1997
A.T. Kearney study of senior executives' most pressing concerns,
which identified the following five issues: customer relationships,
supplier relationships, common goals/common barriers with suppliers, building trust in relationships, and leveraging supplier relation-

ships.[6] Another CAPS study focused on supplier development in the automotive and electronics industries in United States, South Korea, Japan, and the United Kingdom. The authors reported on the degree of improvements that can be attributed to supplier development. As shown in Figure 1.2, the firms surveyed reported the greatest supplier contribution in the areas of on-time delivery, quality, new product development time, and order cycle time.[7]

FIGURE 1.2
Degree of Improvement Attributable to the Firm's Supplier Development Effort

Area of Improvement	Estimated Percent Improvement
Order cycle time (from order placement with supplier to receipt of item)	19
Quality (reduction in parts per million defective, warranty returns, and so on)	24
On-time delivery (ability of supplier to deliver within the buying company's specified delivery window)	39
Percentage price change for this item (from this supplier)	3
Shared price reduction (cost savings shared with this supplier)	7
New product development time (from concept to volume production)	19
Access to new technology	15

Source: Krause, D.R. and R.B. Handfield, *Developing a World Class Supply Base*, Center for Advanced Purchasing Studies, Tempe, AZ, 1999.

A key role for supply managers is to develop processes and procedures that optimize the contribution of suppliers, measure the results, and manage these relationships over time. The attention top executives give to suppliers puts the supply function in the spotlight and increases the expectations and opportunities placed on supply managers.

Implications for Supply Leadership

Because suppliers are influential to an organization's success, they are too important to leave to just one department. As the purchasing or supply side of the organization comes into the spotlight, those in the function must drastically change their orientation to internal customers, suppliers, and end consumers. Linking the contribution of the supply function and the suppliers to the overall mission of the organization is critical if the supply function is to make the greatest contribution to the organization. To make this linkage, supply management leaders must share the vision of the organization and translate that vision into strategy and results at the supply management level. The leaders must also be able to communicate the results attained by supply management to multiple, and often competing, constituencies, such as top management, end customers, employees, investors, and suppliers. Today's demands placed on the leaders in an organization's supply function require skills, knowledge, and expertise unlike that of purchasing managers of the past. In the CAPS study *The Making of the CPO: The Mobility Patterns of Chief Purchasing Officers*, it was reported that 60 percent of the CPOs surveyed had spent most of their careers outside of the purchasing function, primarily in operations, marketing, or engineering.[8]

Implications for Internal Relationships

Working with, not against, internal customers is also a necessity. Interdependence among functions — such as accounting, finance, marketing, and engineering — requires purchasers to cross function boundaries and forge alliances within the organization, as well as outside of it. Research conducted at Michigan State University in the 1990s revealed that almost 80 percent of the U.S. firms surveyed planned to use of cross-functional teams to support procurement and sourcing decisions.[9] A 1999 CAPS multi-country study — which included more than 400 companies in Belgium, Canada, France, Hungary, Germany, the United Kingdom, and the United States — also reported that multifunctional teams continue to be an important organizational structure.[10] The ability to work in a team environment, especially a cross-functional one, is a challenging and daunting task for many people.

Implications for Measurement

Focusing on the results, rather than on the activities, is the difficult, but essential, task of those managing and assessing the purchasing and supply function. In fact, a strong argument for devoting managerial resources to the supply function is the contribution that a well-managed purchasing function can make to the organization. Measuring this contribution is, however, difficult. While organizations use many different metrics, Leenders and Fearon describe an approach to measurement that captures the multiple contributions of the purchasing function. They suggest three ways that this contribution can be viewed: operational and strategic; direct and indirect; and negative, neutral, or positive (see Figure 1.3).[11]

FIGURE 1.3
Purchasing's Contributions to the Organization

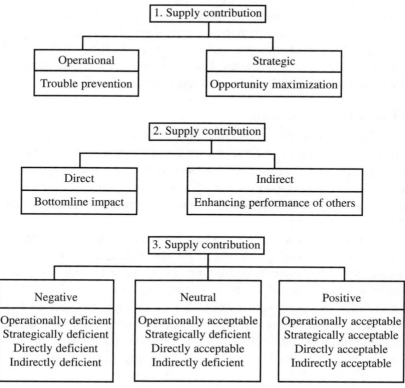

Source: Leenders, M.R. and H.E. Fearon. *Purchasing and Supply Management*, 11th ed.,
Richard D. Irwin, Chicago, IL, 1997. Reprinted by permission of the McGraw-Hill Companies.

Operational and Strategic Contributions

The supply function has long been recognized as being in a prime position to impact the operational side of the organization. Getting the seven Rs — the right (quality) goods and services, in the right quantity, at the right time, in the right place, from the right source, at the right service, and at the right price — has historically been the role of purchasing personnel. The seven Rs are typically depicted as transactional, day-to-day operations. If they are not performed optimally, the results of these purchasing actions might be less than ideal. Many organizations have focused time and resources on streamlining the operational side of purchasing, primarily by applying technology to reengineered processes. While this operational side cannot be ignored, it is not where purchasing personnel and purchasing departments will make their greatest contributions.

Supply management personnel can contribute to the organization strategically when they consider the broader perspective of the supply chain when they make individual supply decisions. The seven Rs take on a new meaning when they are considered in light of the long-term interests of all supply chain members — starting with the end customer and including internal customers, other functional areas of the organization, and the external supply environment.

Direct Contributions

The supply function can contribute directly and indirectly to the organization. Direct contributions are the results that can be linked to the organization's bottomline profitability. The profit-leverage effect and the return-on-assets effect are the two ways purchasing can contribute directly to the bottomline. These effects are discussed in the following paragraphs.

Profit-Leverage Effect – The idea behind the profit-leverage effect is to apply savings on purchased materials and services, which are generated by better purchasing practices, apply directly to the pre-tax bottomline of an organization's profit and loss statement. A similar increase in sales revenue would have a smaller effect on the bottomline. For example, a $100,000 savings on purchased goods would go directly to the bottomline, whereas a $100,000 increase in sales revenue would contribute much less, depending on the pre-tax profit margin. If the profit margin was 5 percent, only $5,000 of the $100,000 increase would go to the bottomline. Many people use the profit-leverage effect as evidence that purchasing is a profit center, not just a cost or service center.

Return-on-Assets Effect – The return-on-assets effect is the inverse relationship between the dollar value of the inventory asset base and the return on assets. If the dollar value of inventory can be reduced while generating the same profit, this will, in turn, lead to a greater return on assets. Purchasing personnel can influence the inventory base through better purchasing practices.

Indirect Contributions

Purchasing's indirect contributions to the organization occur when supply managers' actions influence the performance of others. Many believe that these indirect contributions add more value to the organization than direct contributions. However, as will be discussed in Chapter 8, measuring the results of these actions is often difficult and imprecise.

There are a number of ways that purchasing personnel can enhance the performance of others, thereby making indirect contributions. Working with suppliers to improve the quality of incoming materials will result in less rework, fewer rejects, less downtime, fewer returns, and fewer dissatisfied or lost customers. These results of the purchaser's and manager's work with the supplier will be felt throughout the process — all the way to the end customer. Similarly, if the chief purchasing officer initiates a supply base rationalization program, which leads to a reduction in the size of the supply base and an increased focus on improvement efforts for key suppliers, then the whole organization can benefit from the expertise of the key suppliers. Carrying this a step further, if the chief purchasing officer initiates an early supplier involvement (ESI) program with key suppliers, the results may include shorter leadtimes, shorter cycle times, as well as cost and value improvements in new product designs and on existing products.

Positive, Neutral, or Negative Contributions

The supply function makes a positive contribution to the organization when supply personnel focus on both operational and strategic outcomes. When purchasing personnel focus solely on the operational side of supply management, their contributions can be viewed as neutral. The purchasers are not hurting the organization, but neither are they helping it all that much. If purchasing cannot manage day-to-day, operational tasks in an efficient and effective manner, they are, in fact, hurting the organization and making a negative contribution, and there is little chance that they will be in a position to make strategic contributions.

This approach to assessing the contribution of the supply function may be useful when deciding where and how to improve purchasing performance.

How This Book is Organized

Ideas, concepts, and techniques that can be used to maximize the direct and indirect contributions of the supply function through efficient and effective management will be discussed throughout this volume. Here's a rundown of how this information will be presented:

- Chapter 2 discusses strategic planning. It provides a big picture view of the role of the purchasing function in the achievement of corporate goals and objectives.
- Chapter 3 covers the budgeting process and the role of budgeting in achieving the goals established during the planning process.
- Chapter 4 addresses management theories and styles, as well as the application of the theories to managing the supply function for operational and strategic results.
- Chapter 5 addresses the skill sets needed by purchasing and supply personnel to meet the operational or strategic needs of the supply organization. It covers hiring, training, and retaining employees who can make plans happen within their budgets.
- Chapter 6 discusses operating policies, guidelines, and procedures to automate many important processes.
- Chapter 7 looks at information management tools and the documentation needed for the efficient and effective performance of the supply function.
- Chapter 8 focuses on developing and implementing an appraisal and reward system for individuals, departments, or the supply

function itself. It covers methods of tracking and measuring performance to ensure that the goals and objectives of the supply function align with those of the organization.

- Chapter 9 looks at the communication of vital information throughout the supply management process.

Key Points

1. The average U.S. manufacturing firm spends about 57 percent of its sales revenue on materials and capital expenditures. Any part of an organization that is responsible for decisions of this magnitude deserves the allocation of resources and attention.
2. Purchasing and supply management can contribute directly to the bottomline of an organization through the profit-leverage effect and the return-on-assets effect.
3. Purchasing and supply management can contribute indirectly to the bottomline of an organization through actions that influence and enhance the performance of others. Examples include higher quality inputs, improved processes and procedures, and earlier purchasing and supplier involvement in recognizing and addressing customer needs.
4. The purchasing function can make a positive, neutral, or negative contribution to the organization depending on the actions taken by supply management personnel.

Questions for Review

1. What is the profit-leverage effect of purchasing?
2. How can purchasing personnel affect an organization's return on assets?
3. List several examples of indirect contributions that supply personnel can make to the organization?
4. What does an organization's ratio of purchased goods to sales indicate about the importance of the purchasing and supply management function? How can a supply manager use this information to convince management to allocate resources and attention to the supply function?

Endnotes

1. Tully, S. "Purchasing's New Muscle," *Fortune*, Feb. 20, 1995, p. 75.
2. U.S. Bureau of the Census, "Annual Survey of Manufactures, Statistics for Industry Groups and Industries, M96(AS)-1," www/abs/industry.html
3. David, J.S., Y. Hwang, B.K.W. Pei, H. Reneau, and M. Ruzicka, *The Impact of Purchasing on Financial Performance*, Center for Advanced Purchasing Studies, Tempe, AZ, 1999, p. 5.
4. Trent, R.J. and M.G. Kolchin. *Reducing the Transactions Costs of Purchasing Low Value Goods and Services*, Center for Advanced Purchasing Studies, Tempe, AZ, 1999, p. 11.
5. Arnold, U., et. al. *A Multi-Country Study of Strategic Topics in Purchasing and Supply Management*, Tempe, AZ: Center for Advanced Purchasing Studies, 1999, p. 18.
6. *The Future of Purchasing and Supply: A Five- and Ten-Year Forecast*, "A.T. Kearney 1997 CEO Global Business Study Key Findings," Center for Advanced Purchasing Studies, Tempe, AZ, 1998, p. 19.
7. Krause, D.R. and R.B. Handfield. *Developing a World Class Supply Base*, Center for Advanced Purchasing Studies, Tempe, AZ, 1999, p. 10.
8. Buchko, A.A. *The Making of the CPO: The Mobility Patterns of Chief Purchasing Officers*, Tempe, AZ: Center for Advanced Purchasing Studies, 1998, p. 6.
9. Monczka, R.M. and R.J. Trent. *Cross-Functional Sourcing Team Effectiveness*, Center for Advanced Purchasing Studies, Tempe, AZ, 1993, p. 7.
10. Arnold, 1999, p. 8.
11. Leenders, M.R. and H.E. Fearon. *Purchasing and Supply Management*, 11th ed., Richard D. Irwin , Chicago, 1997, p. 15.

CHAPTER 2

THE STRATEGIC PLANNING PROCESS

How does purchasing contribute to the business plan?

Chapter Objectives

- To show how the purchasing/supply function can contribute to overall organizational objectives
- To identify the steps in the strategic planning process at the organization, business unit or agency, and functional level
- To describe vision, mission, and goal statements and the importance of aligning these statements at all three planning levels
- To present key areas and activities in the strategic planning process at the purchasing/supply management level

Levels of Strategic Planning

The word strategy is derived from the Greek word *strategos*, which means the "art of the general." Strategic planning is a process in which the long-range direction of an organization is determined, and the means of reaching that goal are established. This process can be applied to businesses, agencies, organizations, and to virtually any situation where people are pursuing collective achievement. Developing a strategic plan for an organization is partly an art and partly science. The ability to look ahead and create a shared vision of where the organization is going is at the heart of organizational strategic planning. Taking that vision and putting specific plans together to determine how resources will be found and allocated to achieve that vision is the focus of the next level of planning, business planning. Figure 2.1 shows how Deere & Company describes what the company is, where it is going, how it plans to get there, and how it will measure its performance.

FIGURE 2.1
Deere and Company Alignment of Vision, Mission, Strategy, Goals, Objectives, and Measurement System

Genuine Value at Deere & Company

Who Are We?

John Deere has grown and prospered through a long-standing partnership with the world's most productive farmers. Today, John Deere is a global company with several equipment operations and complementary service businesses. These businesses are closely interrelated, providing the company with significant growth opportunities and other synergistic benefits.

Where Are We Going?

Deere is committed to providing Genuine Value to the company's stakeholders, including our customers, dealers, shareholders, employees, and communities. In support of that commitment, Deere aspires to:

- Grow and pursue leadership positions in each of our businesses
- Extend our pre-eminent leadership position in the agricultural equipment market worldwide
- Create new opportunities to leverage the John Deere brand globally

How Will We Get There?

By pursuing the broader corporate goals of profitable growth and continuous improvement, each of the company's businesses is expected to:

- Achieve world-class performance by attaining a strong competitive position in target markets
- Exceed customer expectations for quality and value
- Earn in excess of the cost of capital over a business cycle

By growing profitably and continuously improving, each of the company's businesses will benefit from and contribute to John Deere's unique intangible assets:

- Our distinguished brand
- Our heritage of integrity and teamwork
- Our advanced skills
- The special relationships that have long existed between the company and our employees, customers, dealers, and other business partners around the world

How Will We Measure Our Performance?

Each business will make a positive contribution to the corporation's objectives in the pursuit of creating Genuine Value for our stakeholders. Our "scorecard" includes:

- Human Resources: Employee Satisfaction, Training
- Customer Focus: Loyalty, Market Leadership
- Business Processes: Productivity, Quality, Cost, Environment
- Business Results: Return on Assets, Sales Growth

Source: Deere & Company.

Strategic plans are typically developed at three levels within an organization: organization or corporate, business unit or agency, and function (see Figure 2.2).

FIGURE 2.2

Hierarchy of Strategies

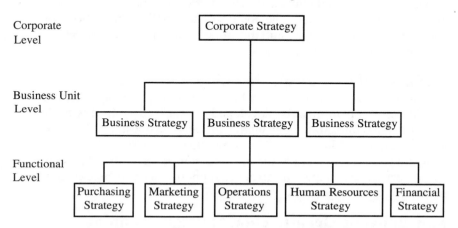

Source: Ellram, L.M. and L.M. Birou. *Purchasing for Bottom Line Impact*,: Irwin Professional Publishing, Chicago, IL, 1995, p. 43.

Organizational or Corporate Strategic Planning

Strategic plans are usually prepared by corporations, government agencies, and organizations of all types and sizes. Typically, the strategic plan is developed by a team of top-level managers, and it answers the following questions:

- What business(es) is the organization in?
- How should resources be allocated among these businesses?
- Where should they operate geographically?
- What acquisitions or divestitures should be pursued?
- What are the goals for growth?

These decisions directly relate to the allocation of internal resources at all levels of the organization and to the management of external resources, such as suppliers.

Purchasing managers historically have not participated in the development of the organization's strategic plan. However, the top management of the purchasing function has played an increasing role in strategic planning since the early 1980s. According to several studies conducted by the Center for Advanced Purchasing Studies, there is a recognized need to link an organization's strategy to its supply strategy, but the means of doing this are often lacking. At Florida Power & Light (FPL) a procurement strategy board comprised of key purchasing and supply managers from each of the organization's business units was created. The board sets core policies that allow for consistency and leverage, but the policies are flexible enough to accommodate individual business unit needs.[1]

Business Unit Strategic Planning

Once it has been decided what business(es) the organization should be in, a plan must be developed for succeeding in that business. Business unit strategic planning answers the question, "How do we compete in this industry?" The corporate strategy should drive the strategic planning process at the business unit level so that the goals and objectives developed at this level support and contribute to corporate goals and objectives.

Functional or Departmental Strategic Planning

The business unit plan, in turn, drives the strategic planning process at the functional level, for example, supply, marketing, finance, operations, accounting, human resources, customer service, and research and development. Functional level strategies answer the question, "How can this function contribute to the business strategy and consequently to the corporate strategy?" Some organizations today are organized by process as well as by function. Strategies should be considered at the process level in the same way. Because the supply chain is vital to the success of business processes, purchasing has a key role in two key business processes: product or service creation as well as product or service delivery. According to Stewart L. Beall, director of sourcing management at Cyprus Amax Minerals Company (a unit of Phelps Dodge):

> Sourcing processes were developed to deal with global business issues when making purchasing and supply decisions. Our core process is an annual sourcing plan that is developed around our company's strategic and operating plans. Each location develops a business plan that is reviewed. Companywide deci-

sions are made to determine size, geographical, or companywide activities. The plan then assigns priorities, timelines, goals, and individual accountability. The plan is reviewed, and results and activities are reported to the company on a quarterly basis.[2]

Keeping all levels of strategy in alignment is critical to the overall success of the organization. In addition to carefully aligned strategic plans, the entire corporate structure, including the performance measurement and reward system, must be congruent with the strategy for long-term organizational success. In developing strategic alignment, it may be useful to view purchasing's role as the management of all resources, not including resources owned or controlled by the organization, that are needed to meet organizational objectives.

Issues in Strategic Planning at the Functional Level

A number of issues in strategic planning at the function or supply level are of critical importance. The key challenge for purchasing and supply executives is to ensure that the supply strategy is aligned with, and contributes to, the success of business unit level and corporate level strategy.

Support for Organizational Strategy

How the top management of the supply function will develop and align supply strategies, goals, and objectives to effectively and efficiently support overall organizational goals and objectives is the key. Supply managers must understand the business unit plans and objectives, ideally through involvement in their development. Then, using that knowledge, they must develop a supply strategy that best supports the organizational strategy. The alignment of supply strategy and objectives with organizational strategy and objectives requires two-way communication during the planning process at all three levels of planning. Purchasing receives input from the corporate and business unit strategy process that enables the development of a supply strategy. Equally important to the success of the organization is input from purchasing about supply opportunities and challenges that may influence the development and direction of the corporate and business unit level strategy.

If supply management is to play a more strategic role in the organization, it must anticipate and guide, rather than react to, internal user requests for goods and services. The analysis and involvement in advance of formal purchase requests should fit within four strategic areas: organizational, operational, financial, and marketing strategies.[3] The purchasing function's boundary-spanning role means that it can directly impact these strategic areas.

Organizational Strategies – Requisitions and buying plans should match the annual needs of the organization as well as the longer-term goals of the organization. This will help to ensure that purchasing contributes to the organization's strategic plan by directly affecting profitability and indirectly enhancing the performance of others. Supply management must fully understand these strategies in order to position the supply base to respond quickly and effectively to specific requirements.

Operational Strategies – Reviewing requisitions helps to maximize purchasing's contribution to operations. In an efficient acquisition process, goods and services are received or performed in a timely manner to ensure smooth running operations. Poor coordination and timing between operations and purchasing may mean organizational losses in terms of competitive position, time-to-market, or profitability. Purchasing inefficiency may have many causes, including process problems and internal customers' or purchasing personnel's lack of understanding of purchasing's role and contribution. If purchasing does not adequately prepare the suppliers, the result may be higher total cost of ownership, special production runs, or premium transportation costs, which may adversely affect the final customer.

Financial Strategies – How and when an organization commits its funds depends on market trends, market and organizational forecasts, and risk assessments. At the need recognition and description stages, the purchaser or sourcing team should analyze the buying plan to determine its appropriateness given economic factors and overall organizational goals. Deciding to buy in advance, because of anticipated price increases or supply shortages despite increased carrying costs, may be an excellent decision if cost analyses indicate a lower total cost of ownership. Reviewing the decision to buy against financial and economic circumstances allows purchasing to make the best contribution to the organization.

Marketing Strategies – Requisitions and buying plans should fit with marketing strategies. Because sales forecasts often originate in marketing, the actual needs or purchase requirements of the organization flow down from sales forecasts. If supply management is able to track forecasts as accurately as possible and transmit this information to suppliers in a timely fashion, the suppliers will be able to plan and execute their fulfillment process effectively. Buying organizations drive up costs unnecessarily when their forecasts are inaccurate and suppliers must rush to meet their demands.

Because purchasing typically manages the acquisition process with the supplier community, the requisitioner, and other internal customers (for example, engineering, quality, finance, and legal), early purchasing involvement is essential in the strategic planning process, as well as in the acquisition process itself. An effective supply strategy contributes to the short- and long-term strategic objectives of the organization when both current and future elements are addressed in the functional- or process-level planning. Developing a supply strategy that is congruent with organizational strategy is a critical challenge for supply executives.

Planning Process and Objectives

From the corporate and business level strategies, the purchasing officer should seek congruence of both short- and long-range goals. The supply strategy can have a profound effect, positive or negative, on customer satisfaction, cost structure, and returns to owners. The high-level planning process contains the following steps:

1. Review corporate and business level strategies for areas impacted by the supply chain or the supply management function.
2. Determine how the supply chain or supply management function can contribute to the higher level strategies, either to maximize the outcome or to reduce risk of failure.
3. Identify opportunities to make specific changes to the existing supply chain or to the acquisition process that will improve the outcome of the higher level strategies.
4. Create specific goals and strategies for addressing the change opportunities identified.
5. Review implementation factors.
6. Gain commitment and then implement improvements.
7. Evaluate the outcomes and the process for improvements.

Figure 2.3 depicts the high-level purchasing planning process.

FIGURE 2.3
Strategic Purchasing Planning Process

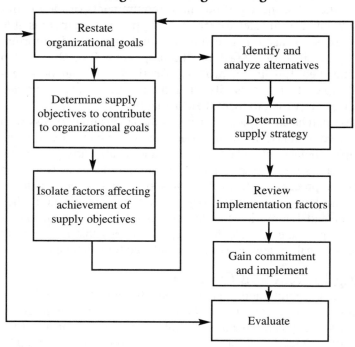

Source: Leenders, M.R. and H. E. Fearon. *Purchasing and Supply Management*, 11th ed., Richard D. Irwin, Chicago, IL., 1997, p. 644. Reprinted by permission of the McGraw-Hill Companies.

Strategic Goal of the Supply Function

The strategic goal of the supply function is to lead or manage supplier relationships for goods and services in support of the organization's overall mission and vision. The extent to which suppliers can be integrated with the organization's own operations will determine how much the supply base can contribute to the success of the enterprise. An effective strategic plan provides the purchasing organization with a mission that it can further define for its own purposes. Purchasing can then use its strategic plan to help suppliers and internal customers understand the contributions that the supply function can make. The challenge is to break this mission into the various elements that can successfully bring goods and services into the organization while minimizing the resources required. Figure 2.4 lists typical questions and alternatives that may apply when developing a supply strategy.

FIGURE 2.4
Supply Strategy Questions

1. What?	High versus low supplier turnover
Make or buy	Supplier relations
Standard versus special	Supplier certification
	Supplier ownership
2. Quality?	
Quality versus cost	8. How?
Supplier involvement	Systems and procedures
	Computerization
3. How much?	Negotiations
Large versus small quantities	Competitive bids
(inventory)	Fixed bids
	Blanket orders/open orders
4. Who?	Systems contracting
Centralize or decentralize	Blank check system
Quality of staff	Group buying
Top management involvement	Materials requirements planning
	Long-term contracts
5. When?	Ethics
Now versus later	Aggressive or passive
Forward buy	Purchasing research
	Value analysis
6. What price?	
Premium	9. Why?
Standard	Objectives congruent
Lower	Market reasons
Cost-based	Internal reasons
Market-based	1. Outside supply
Lease/make/buy	2. Inside supply
7. Where?	
Local, regional	
Domestic, international	
Large versus small	
Multiple versus single source	

Source: Leenders, M.R. and H. E. Fearon. *Purchasing and Supply Management*, 11th ed., Richard D. Irwin, Chicago, IL., 1997, p. 644. Reprinted by permission of the McGraw-Hill Companies.

Fundamental Objectives of the Supply Function

The fundamental objective of the supply function is to provide the highest value at optimum cost to the organization. To restate, the overall objective of purchasing is to acquire materials and services that maximize the organization's ability to meet customer requirements as well as maximize returns to the stakeholders. From a management viewpoint, the key objectives are:

1. To buy at the lowest total cost to the organization, consistent with required quality and service levels
2. To attain a high rate of inventory turnover, thereby minimizing excess storage and carrying costs as well as inventory losses as a result of deterioration, obsolescence, and pilferage
3. To maintain continuity of supply to prevent interruptions in the flow of materials and services to users
4. To attain the highest material and service quality level with minimal variability, which permits efficient and effective operations
5. To develop and maintain good supplier relationships in order to ensure that suppliers will furnish the organization with new ideas and products as well as provide continuous improvement in prices and service levels
6. To participate in strategic "make versus buy" (outsource) evaluations
7. To promote a competitive atmosphere in performance and pricing
8. To minimize the total cost of ownership by identifying and removing non-value-adding activities throughout the supply chain
9. To hire, develop, motivate, and train personnel, and to provide a reservoir of talent
10. To achieve a high degree of cooperation and coordination with user departments
11. To maintain good records and controls that provide an audit trail and ensure efficiency and honesty

Additional objectives support other functions in the organization. These are:

1. To search for effective new products and services that are relevant to the organization's operations, which can be called to the attention of users
2. To suggest to users specific materials or components and services that may improve the organization's products, services, or operations
3. To strive to introduce standardization in requirements to simplify specifications and reduce the costs of materials and inventory

4. To furnish data for forecasting or to assist in forecasting the availability of materials and trends in prices
5. To serve sales personnel by providing an understanding of contemporary purchasing practices and bringing to their attention effective methods and techniques used by the sales forces of suppliers

Because purchasing has the leadership role in managing the acquisition process, it must establish a network of internal and external organizations for all types of procurements. This includes suppliers (external), requisitioners, and other stakeholders in the buying organization (internal) who are supporting the process.

Purchasing personnel become the "communicator" during any procurement. Thus, the first step in the process is to ensure that all organizational elements understand their roles. Second, purchasing professionals need to understand their organization's strategic objectives. Third, they must understand the plan from an operating point of view.

The network will work well if a bond of trust is established. In developing a purchasing strategy, trust can be the most important element. Many redundant purchasing activities are eliminated once trust between the organizational functions is established. For example, development of long-term supply relationships reduces many sources of non-value-adding activity, because terms and conditions, written offers and counter offers, expediting, inspection, late payments, and so forth can be reduced or eliminated. When the supplier and the customer trust each other, their respective organizations can establish communication at all levels. The supplier can become an important resource for new ideas, especially early in the acquisition process.

Commodity Plans and Strategies

Commodity segmentation is one way to distinguish among different commodities and their relative importance to the organization. Commodity segmentation strategies should be driven by the overall corporate strategy, and they should be an integral part of both the business unit plan and the purchasing department functional plan. It is nearly impossible to have too much information when constructing a commodity plan. Commodity segmentation is discussed in greater detail in Chapter 6 of this volume.

Prior to making a commodity plan, the purchaser should consider such elements as:

- The past usage patterns and the forecast of requirements for the commodity over certain time periods
- The source(s) of the commodity (both current and potential)
- The type of market for the commodity (for example, buyers or sellers? Is it traded on an exchange? Can it be purchased from the manufacturer or through a distributor?)
- In what form it is purchased (for example, raw material, refined, or converted)
- The total supply availability
- The geopolitical control of the commodity
- The costs of acquisition

When developing commodity plans, purchasing also needs to consider issues pertaining to source selection, logistical considerations (such as transportation distance and methods, customers, tariffs, free trade zones, and the use of agents and brokers), communication options (such as the use of EDI), and financial issues (such as exchange rates and payment modes).

Commodity plans usually are developed best in a cross-functional team environment to ensure that the knowledge and expertise of all stakeholders is brought to the commodity planning process. This involvement in the planning process can also help ensure buy-in from the stakeholders for the final plan.

Supplier Strategies

It is difficult to distinguish between commodity strategies and supplier strategies because they are closely related. *Commodity strategies* are created to determine how the organization will plan to meet its needs for a specific group of goods or services (the commodity). Such a group of goods or services is normally defined by similar processes used by all suppliers, and commodities are generally available from a common group of suppliers. In contrast, *supplier strategies* are aimed at determining how various suppliers will be positioned, addressed, and developed within the supply chain for the commodity. Supplier strategies will attempt to take advantage of the relative strength of various suppliers to meet the objectives of the commodity strategy. Both strategies address such issues as whether to buy from a manufacturer or from a distributor, or how to acquire new product technology, for example.

Supplier strategies require breaking the high-level commodity down into more narrowly defined sourcing groups, and sometimes down to the part number or line item level. Each subgroup must be evaluated for its impact on the buyer's organization and the relative ease of obtaining supply (see Figure 2.5). The best choice for the source and method of supply will typically be determined by a number of specific technical requirements. Supplier strategies should answer many, if not all, of the following questions:

1. Which supplier(s) offer the best value or combination of lowest total cost, highest quality, shortest leadtime, and best delivery performance?
2. What is the continuous improvement potential in each of these areas?
3. Which supplier(s) offer access to new technology?
4. What is the relative financial strength of each potential supplier?
5. What are the relative risks associated with each possible choice (for example, work stoppage, stability of management team, transportation damage or loss, facility located in a flood zone, and so on)?
6. What resources are required to implement any planned changes?

FIGURE 2.5

Sourcing Group (Commodity) Strategy

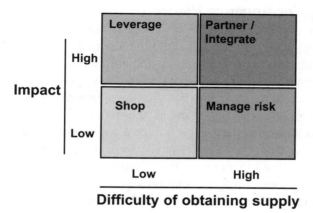

Review of the Plan and Decisionmaking

The strategic plan for managing each sourcing group must be reviewed with the stakeholders in advance. This will ensure that no vital considerations have been overlooked and that these stakeholders have buy-in to the strategic direction. The higher the level in the organization where the review is held, the better the connection to the organization's strategy. During the review process, it is not uncommon for the supply management team to learn vital information from top management. Considerations involved in the decisionmaking process include the following:

1. What resources are required for implementing the plan? These may be financial, human, social, physical, technological, and/or organizational resources.
2. Who has the authority to review/authorize the plan?
3. Who will decide how the plan is to be implemented? Will the decisions be made using team input? What decisions will be made solely by management? Will there be customer or supplier input?
4. What is the timeframe for the plan?
5. What are the qualifications of those implementing the plan?
6. Are there any models or prototypes for the plan being implemented?
7. What is the follow-up plan and schedule for tracking progress against the plan?

Developing Contingency Plans

In the event that the commodity or service is not available in the desired quantity, quality, or cost, what are the alternatives? And how can they be managed to satisfy the customer? Depending on the volatility of the market, the risk level associated with the acquisition, and its importance to achieving a strategic organizational goal, contingency plans may be as important as the actual plan. Chrysler Corporation, for example, may single source a commodity for a particular model of car, but they usually have two or three suppliers per commodity. This allows them to get the advantages of single sourcing, while putting competitive pressure on suppliers to continue producing world-class technologies and competitive pricing.[4]

Profit Planning

Profit planning begins with strategic and operational plans. Supply can influence these plans and the financial results for the organization by considering a number of strategic elements that will affect profitability. These include market acceptance of the product(s) offered, the product life cycle, cost targets, total cost of desired quality, cost reduction opportunities, supplier input into the procurement of the product, competition, and factors that can influence the cost of the commodity.

Advanced Acquisition Planning

Advanced acquisition planning is performed when the business plan has been finalized. Specific factors that a purchaser should consider when performing such planning include:

- Whether the product or service is a new or existing product or service
- The dynamics of the market for the item or service
- The competition among suppliers of the item or service
- The general availability of the product or service
- The best method of scheduling and tracking delivery of the item
- The costs of carrying inventory (if the item is a product)
- The readiness of possible suppliers to produce the needed product or to provide the service
- The projected leadtime for the material or needed human resources
- The degree of standardization of this item with existing items

In summary, detailed information concerning the needs of the organization, alternatives available in the marketplace, and the potential contribution of the suppliers' capabilities is vital to effective strategic planning. An informed and organized procurement specialist can become a valued contributor to organizational strategy formulation. This can earn the supply management function an important role in strategy development and ensure that the supply chain's potential to contribute to the organization's success is realized.

Departmental Strategies

There are two important dimensions to the supply management department's contribution to the enterprise. The first is getting the most from the acquisition of goods and services, and the second is reducing costs and the opportunities for errors in the acquisition process. The purchasing department is uniquely positioned within an organization to ensure that value exists in the goods and services required to meet the organization's mission. The success of the organization may be determined or dramatically enhanced by its ability to maximize the value of its purchases. Purchasing is also expected to control the expenditure of the entity's funds. This includes conformance to laws, cash flow, and record keeping. The departmental or functional strategy must be directed at these contributions.

The Typical Organization's Vision, Mission, and Goals Statements

Each organization should create its own vision, mission, and goals statements representing different levels of the planning process. A generic example as well as company examples are included for illustration purposes.

Vision

A vision statement should be a broad statement that captures the overarching purpose of the organization. A generic vision statement for a purchasing/supply organization might be: "A supply management team and process that produces supplier contributions to the business and is seen as the world-class benchmark of performance." IKEA, the Swedish home furnishings company, has a simple, yet encompassing, vision statement: "A better everyday life." Maho Bay Resorts, which combines eco-tourism with sustainable technology (solar power, composting toilets, and so on) has this vision statement: "Environmental sensitivity, human comfort, responsible consumption." Jade Mountain, Inc., a supplier of more than 7,000 products, including solar electric, micro-hydro, wind generators, and super energy-efficient appliances, describes its vision as, "the fulfillment of appropriate technology — less is more." The Boeing Company's vision is, "People working together as one global company for aerospace leadership. Boeing — the future of flight."

Mission

The mission statement of an organization should flow from the vision statement. It may be as short as a sentence or as long as a paragraph. It should answer fundamental questions such as:

- Who are we?
- Whose needs do we want to meet?
- What needs do we want to meet?
- How do we intend to meet these needs?
- What are our central values?

For example, a supply organization might state its mission as, "Establish supplier relationships that bring maximum value to the customers, owners, and employees of the enterprise. Achieve a level of supply chain integration that allows materials, services and information to flow uninterrupted and at continuously lower total cost year after year." The U.S. Department of Education's mission is, "To ensure equal access to education and to promote educational excellence throughout the nation."[5]

Some organizations create a value statement as well as a mission statement. The notion of establishing the guiding values of the organization may seem strange to some. However, whether stated or implied, these values drive the behavior of all members of the organization, and the values contribute to the corporate culture of the organization. The mission statement tells where the organization wants to go, and the value statement describes the means that the organization will use to get there. The values of an organization have tremendous implications for many aspects of the organization, from hiring and measuring performance to the treatment of suppliers and employees. Figure 2.6 shows the value statement for the Boeing Company.

FIGURE 2.6
The Boeing Company Values

In all our relationships, we will demonstrate our steadfast commitment to:

Leadership. We will be a world-class leader in every aspect of our business — in developing our team leadership skills at every level; in our management performance; in the way we design, build, and support our products; and in our financial results.

Integrity. We will always take the high road by practicing the highest ethical standards and by honoring our commitments. We will take personal responsibility for our actions and treat everyone fairly and with trust and respect.

Quality. We will strive for continuous quality improvement in all that we do, so that we will rank among the world's premier industrial firms in customer, employee, and community satisfaction.

Customer Satisfaction. Satisfied customers are essential to our success. We will achieve total customer satisfaction by understanding what the customer wants and delivering it flawlessly.

People Working Together. We recognize our strength and our competitive advantage is — and always will be — people. We will continually learn and share ideas and knowledge. We will encourage cooperative efforts at every level and across all activities in our company.

A Diverse and Involved Team. We value the skills, strengths, and perspectives of our diverse team. We will foster a participatory workplace that enables people to get involved in making decisions about their work that advance our common business objectives.

Good Corporate Citizenship. We will provide a safe workplace and protect the environment. We will promote the health and well-being of Boeing people and their families. We will work with our communities by volunteering and financially supporting education and other worthy causes.

Enhancing Shareholder Value. Our business must produce a profit, and we must generate superior returns on the assets entrusted to us by our shareholders. We will ensure our success by satisfying our customers and increasing shareholder value.

Source: The Boeing Company. Used with permission.

Boeing also describes its core competencies as:

- **Detailed Customer Knowledge and Focus**. We will seek to understand, anticipate, and be responsive to our customers' needs.
- **Large-Scale System Integration**. We will continuously develop, advance, and protect the technical excellence that allows us to integrate effectively the systems we design and produce.
- **Lean, Efficient Design and Production Systems**. Our design and production systems will be among the best in the world, characterized by efficient use of assets, short time-to market, short flow times, short cycle times, high quality and high inventory turns.[6]

Goals and Objectives

Goals flow from the mission statement, and they are specific statements about what the organization intends to accomplish. Objectives are usually written for each goal, and they are typically specific, measurable, attainable, and time bound. For example, one of the goals of the U.S. Department of Education's strategic plan for 1998 to 2002 is, "Build a solid foundation for learning for all children." Figure 2.7 shows how this goal flows from the mission statement and is followed by specific objectives.

Some sample goal statements at the supply management level are:

1. Supplier generated defect rates are less than 100 ppm.
2. On-time delivery by all suppliers is greater than 99 percent.
3. Flexibility in the supply chain allows all products to be built to customer order with no more than five days inventory in the supply chain.

Resources must be allocated to each objective based on the objective's importance. Figure 2.8 shows the dollar appropriations for one of the goals of the Department of Education.

FIGURE 2.7
U.S. Department of Education Framework of Strategic Plan Goals and Objectives

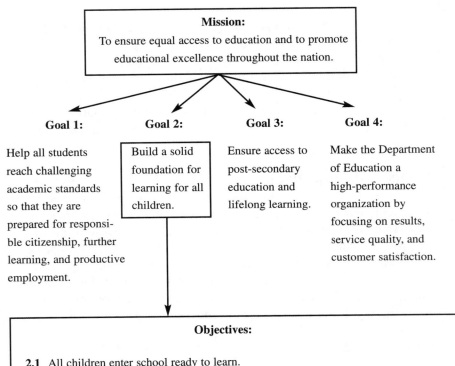

Mission:
To ensure equal access to education and to promote educational excellence throughout the nation.

Goal 1:

Help all students reach challenging academic standards so that they are prepared for responsible citizenship, further learning, and productive employment.

Goal 2:

Build a solid foundation for learning for all children.

Goal 3:

Ensure access to post-secondary education and lifelong learning.

Goal 4:

Make the Department of Education a high-performance organization by focusing on results, service quality, and customer satisfaction.

Objectives:

2.1 All children enter school ready to learn.

2.2 Every child reads independently by the end of the third grade.

2.3 Every eighth-grader masters challenging mathematics, including the foundations of algebra and geometry.

2.4 Special populations receive appropriate services and assessments consistent with high standards.

Source: U.S. Department of Education Web site, www.ed.gov/pubs/StartPln/.

FIGURE 2.8
Support for Strategic Plan Goals and Objectives

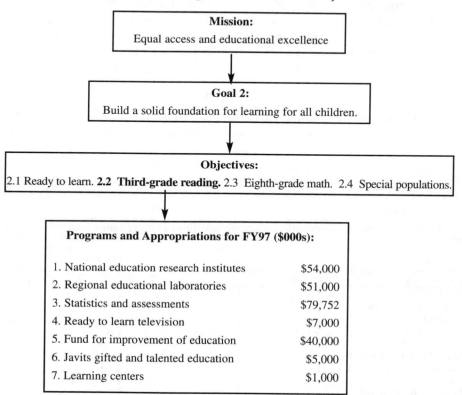

Mission:
Equal access and educational excellence

Goal 2:
Build a solid foundation for learning for all children.

Objectives:
2.1 Ready to learn. **2.2 Third-grade reading.** 2.3 Eighth-grade math. 2.4 Special populations.

Programs and Appropriations for FY97 ($000s):

1. National education research institutes	$54,000
2. Regional educational laboratories	$51,000
3. Statistics and assessments	$79,752
4. Ready to learn television	$7,000
5. Fund for improvement of education	$40,000
6. Javits gifted and talented education	$5,000
7. Learning centers	$1,000

Source: U.S. Department of Education Web site, www.ed.gov/pubs/StartPln/.

One can speculate on how the mission, goals, and objectives of the Department of Education might influence the goals and objectives of its purchasing function. For example, to achieve Objective 2.2, "Every child reads independently by the end of the third grade," under Goal 2, "Build a solid foundation for learning for all children," $51 million has been appropriated for regional educational laboratories. Purchases could conceivably include facilities, computer hardware and software, office furniture, and supplies.

Periodic Review

All strategic plans should include feedback loops for managing the various elements of the plan. Organizational assignments and resources should be part of the review process, as well as progress toward milestones and goals. Figure 2.9 provides several examples of performance indicators and feedback loops for the U.S. Department of Education's strategic plan. This example shows the objective data sources (for example, the National Assessment of Educational Progress in Reading and Math) that will be used to assess performance as well as the timelines given to achieve the goals.

FIGURE 2.9

U.S. Department of Education Strategic Plan, 1998-2002 — September 1997
Excerpt from Appendix A: Supplemental Information on Performance Indicators

This section lists all strategic plan performance indicators in the order they appear in the strategic plan; identifies current or planned data sources; and provides examples of baseline data, or if baselines are not available, related data that may inform the issue. Where data sources have not been specified, the department will work during the next year to set up new data collections or redirect current ones to provide data for all indicators in the plan.

Supplemental Information on Strategic Plan Performance Indicators			
Goals and objectives	Indicators	Illustrative baseline or related data	Data sources and year(s) to be collected (1997-2002)
Goals 1 and 2: K-12 key outcome indicators			
Goal 1. Help all students reach challenging academic standards so that they are prepared for responsible citizenship, further learning, and productive employment. **Goal 2. Build a solid foundation for learning for all children.**	1. Increasing percentages of all students will meet or exceed basic, proficient, and advanced performance levels in national and state assessments of reading, math, and other core subjects.	• *60% of 4th-graders, 70% of 8th-graders, and 75% of 12th-graders scored at or above the basic level in reading in 1994 (National Assessment of Educational Progress, 1994).* • *64% of 4th-graders, 62% of 8th-graders, and 69% of 12th-graders scored at or above the basic level in mathematics in 1996 (NAEP, 1996).*	• National Assessment of Educational Progress (NAEP) Reading, biennially, 1996 • NAEP Math, biennially, 1998 • State Assessments, annual
	2. Students in high-poverty schools will show continuous improvement in achieving proficiency levels comparable to that for the nation.	• *32% of 4th-graders from families with low educational attainment scored at least at the basic proficiency level in reading compared to 70% of children with college-graduate parents (NAEP, 1994).* • *39 % of low-income 8th-graders scored at least basic proficiency in mathematics compared to 71% of other 8th-graders (NAEP, 1996).*	• NAEP Reading, biennially, 1996 • NAEP Math, biennially, 1998

Source: U.S. Department of Education Web site, www.ed.gov/pubs/StartPln/.

Strategic Plan Elements

The departmental or functional plan must address the issues of resources, processes, controls, and deliverables (that is, budget, organization, personnel, and systems). A typical departmental plan would include:

- Planned organizational changes with impact on headcount and budget. For example, when United Technologies Corporation began a supplier quality and development initiative, it was necessary to assess the needs of the planned organization as compared to the skills already present in the organization. The budget impact for training, recruiting, and the salaries for the new organization needed to be determined, and then a plan had to be created to gain budget approval.

  According to Intel Corporation's 1998 annual report, the marketplace in 1998 was more cost-competitive than it had been in previous years. Intel responded by setting aggressive new targets in cost management and manufacturing efficiency, tighter controls on discretionary spending, and some headcount reductions. By year end, Intel had reduced headcount by 2 percent (excluding acquisitions) and employed human resources in the areas of maximum return.[7]

- Employment plan — recruiting, development, management succession planning. For example, at Intel Corporation's annual stockholders meeting in May 1998, Craig Barrett was elected chief executive officer, Andy Grove was elected chairman of the board, and Gordon Moore became chairman emeritus. In a letter to stockholders, these changes were described as "the latest phase of a management transition that has been under way for years and reflects our dedication to continuity in the executive office."[8] Another example of employment planning is the need for most manufacturing companies to add technical staff to deal with the complexities of technology — both in the products purchased and in the electronic systems needed to manage the process.

- Capital equipment, facilities, and hardware and software plan. These are the resources other than personnel needed to accomplish the mission.

- System requirements. These are information systems requirements and expenditures, with business cases to justify them.
- Key supplier contracts anticipated. This includes the timing, workload impact, and supply risks associated with each.
- An annual budget covering all planned expenditures. This is time phased and includes any sources of revenue, such as the sale of surplus or chargebacks.

Issues Related to the Establishment of Objectives

The objectives of an individual functional area such as purchasing and supply are not written in a vacuum. They must be aligned and integrated with the goals and objectives of the organization, and the priority given to each objective must be determined by assessing its potential impact on the organization's success.

Priority of Objectives

Not all objectives should receive the same priority. It is necessary to first pursue the objectives that have the greatest impact on the operation of the organization and that will make the greatest contributions to organizational goals and objectives. These priorities should be established and aligned through the three-level planning process and communicated throughout the organization to ensure that the objectives and their assigned priorities are valid.

Integration of Objectives

Purchasing objectives must be aligned with those of the rest of the organization. The integration of objectives assures the success of the overall goal. It is imperative that the purchasing department personnel understand their relationship to the organization they serve. In the Department of Education example, one would expect to see purchasing objectives designed to address expenditures for new textbooks, computers, support services, personnel training, and the creation of the learning centers. Typically, the greater the value of the purchased inputs as a percentage of the outputs, the greater the significance the purchasing objectives will have for the organization.

Goal Alignment

The goals of every function and process of an organization must align with those of the overall organization. This may require several information exchanges between departments and units because most will not achieve alignment on the first pass. It is important to take the time necessary to resolve differences and gain the concurrence needed to advance the plan.

Measurability of Objectives

Objectives also need to be divided into groups (for example, cost savings, product or process improvement, and so on) that allow them to be quantified and measured. First, it is useful to establish a benchmark by measuring or quantifying the existing situation. Then, future measurements can be compared to the internal benchmark, some external benchmark, or other historical data. Performance measurement is discussed in Chapter 8 of this volume.

Planning Timeframes

Generally, short-range strategic plans involve timeframes of three to five years, while long-range strategic plans cover five to 10 years. The timeframes for short- and long-range plans depend on the nature of the industry and the volatility of the market. The village of Kohler, Wisconsin, one of the earliest planned communities, adopted a 50-year Village Master Plan in 1977.[9] Both short- and long-range plans may be developed at all three levels of planning — organization, business unit, and function/department. Operational plans can be instituted over periods of 30, 60, or 90 days, or on a quarterly basis. The timing should be synchronized across functions, operating units, and so on, because timing is critical to planning effectiveness.

Key Points

1. Supply strategy must be aligned with business unit level and corporate level strategy to maximize the supply function's contribution to the achievement of organizational goals and objectives. The more strategic the supply function becomes, the more value

it offers to the organization it serves. All members of the supply function will find this contribution especially rewarding.

2. Supply management is a critical strategic function in an organization because of its ability to affect short- and long-term profitability, its boundary spanning role, and its role in managing external relationships.

3. Planning is an iterative process, and it requires the exchange of great amounts of information. Often the value of the planning is found in resolving differences in expectations, as much as in the plan and its execution.

4. A strategic plan is dynamic. Circumstances will change over time, sometimes in very short periods, which will require changes to keep the plan viable. Regular reviews are critical to success.

Questions for Review

1. How does purchasing contribute to achieving the organization's strategic objectives? Why is it important for supply management leaders to participate in the creation of these objectives?

2. What are the appropriate roles of commodity strategies and supplier strategies in the creation and refinement of higher level corporate and business unit strategies?

3. Why is it important to revisit plans and objectives regularly? What problems might arise if the plans are not updated to address changing circumstances? What areas should be addressed by contingency planning?

4. Who should review and approve supply management strategies before they are finalized? What specific areas of concern might be addressed by various stakeholders, such as engineering, operations, facilities, and finance?

5. How do make-versus-buy and insourcing/outsourcing decisions affect the supply management strategic planning process? What is the appropriate role of supply management in contributing to these decisions?

Endnotes

1. Duffy, R.J. "Trail Blazing," *Purchasing Today®*, April 1999, p. 47.
2. Beall, S.L. "Annual Sourcing Business Plan Followed," *Purchasing Today®*, September 1999, p. 56.
3. Leenders, M.R. and A.E. Flynn. *Value-Driven Purchasing*, 1st ed., Richard D. Irwin, Chicago, 1995, p. 27-28.
4. Stallkamp, T.T. "Beyond Reengineering: Developing the Extended Enterprise," *NAPM Insights*, February 1995, p. 76.
5. All of the information on the U.S. Department of Education's strategic plan was found on www.ed.gov/pubs/StratPln/.
6. Boeing Company, www.boeing.com, "About Us, Vision."
7. *Intel Corporation 1998 Annual Report*, "Letter to the Stockholders," www.intel.com.
8. *Intel Corporation 1998 Annual Report*.
9. Kohler Company and the Village of Kohler, WI, www.kohler-co.com/realestate.html.

CHAPTER 3

BUDGETS AND THE BUDGETING PROCESS

*What resources are needed, and how can purchasing
ensure their availability?*

Chapter Objectives

- To explain the links among the organization's strategic plan, various kinds of budgets, and the budgeting process
- To describe the different types of budgets and the purpose of each
- To describe the typical elements that are subject to budgetary control and selected budgeting techniques
- To illustrate the relationship between the functional responsibilities of purchasing and finance, and to demonstrate ways that purchasers can work with finance to track the value added from the purchasing function

Contribution to the Bottomline

Supply managers are in a position to positively or negatively impact the bottomline of an organization. The contributions of a well-run purchasing function can be realized if supply management and finance personnel understand each other's roles and keep open lines of communication. Purchasing and finance personnel may see themselves as opposing forces in the organization. Purchasers may not fully understand the pressures and demands placed on finance professionals, those who are held responsible for keeping track of the organization's financial resources. Finance professionals may not fully understand the pressures and demands placed on purchasers,

those responsible for making spending decisions. Yet, the two functions need to work together to meet the goals and objectives of the
organization. Supply managers need to understand the purposes and
types of budgets typically used in an organization, and they need to
realize the importance to the organization of managing the flow of
funds. According to Kevin C. Shanahan, senior vice president and
chief financial officer of McHugh Software International:

> Purchasing and supply professionals should understand the
> financial objectives of the whole organization. If someone
> is responsible for purchasing hardware, for example, obvi-
> ously the quality and reliability of the supplier is very
> important. But to put that into perspective in terms of the
> total organization, they need to understand the whole year's
> predictions and issues like financial targets and frameworks.
> If they don't have that broad perspective, if they don't have
> that vision, then they can't contribute.[1]

Purchasing professionals need to talk and listen to the finance
professionals, especially if the finance professionals are able to relate
finance concepts to a current working situation. Supply managers can
increase their ability to contribute to the organization if they can learn
to think like the chief financial officer (CFO).[2] Thinking like a CFO
means:

- Understanding what is important to finance professionals, including the time value of money and the undesirability of terms such
  as C.O.D. and cash-up-front
- Being familiar with finance terminology, the basics of accounting, targets, and budgets
- Bringing a business perspective to all issues
- Examining transactions in relation to organizational objectives,
  not just operational ones
- Asking what decisions maximize value over the long term
- Understanding what and how financial information is reported to
  shareholders

On the other hand, finance managers need to understand the purchaser's role in managing supplier relationships and ensuring that the buying organization lives up to its commitments to suppliers. One area that may be a sticking point between purchasing and finance is meeting payment terms agreed upon by the buyer and supplier. The individuals who set policies and procedures for the buying organization have a responsibility to see that accounts payable lives up to the payment terms specified in contracts. For example, if payment terms are "2/10 net 30," the buying organization should only take the discount if it meets the payment deadline. Supply managers cannot talk meaningfully with suppliers about mutually beneficial relationships when the buying organization doesn't live up to one of the most basic elements of a contract. Something as simple as meeting payment terms may symbolize the level of understanding (or misunderstanding) of the role of suppliers and the potential for supply management's contribution to the organization.

Purposes for a Budget

A budget is a formal written statement that expresses planned future operations in financial or numerical terms. Typically, a budget covers a specified period of time (usually one year), and it identifies financial resources allocated to products/services or the divisions of an organization. Budgets are tools for providing funds to accomplish the objectives of the organization. To be effective, budgets must contain means by which management can determine whether planned operations are being accomplished. As such, two elements are common to all budgets. First, budgets contain a set of specific goals that relate to future operations. Establishing goals is equivalent to defining the standards by which the organization measures its performance. Second, budgets provide a periodic comparison of actual results and established goals. This control feature of the budgeting activity is usually accomplished through the development and use of budget performance reports. According to Lorrie K. Mitchell, relationship manager at BellSouth Telecommunications, Inc., supply chain managers must be able to show internal clients how supply actions affect the clients' capital and expense budgets.[3]

Budgets perform several essential functions including controlling and monitoring expenditures and providing pre-approved funding.

Controlling Expenditures

Budgets control expenditures through the approval and appropriation process and through the analysis of variances.

Providing Pre-approved Funding

Budgets reflect decisions made in conjunction with the strategic and operational planning process regarding activities or purchases approved for the coming year. During the budget year, those responsible for making purchases or expending funds can do so in a timely manner because the monies have already been approved and appropriated.

Monitoring Expenditures

Budgets also provide a monitoring device by which managers can compare actual revenues and expenses against budgeted ones. The areas of greatest variance, favorable or unfavorable, may be targeted for higher-level management attention to determine their causes and cures.

Types of Budgets

Different types of budgets may be used depending on the needs of the organization. The types of budgets include operating budgets, expense budgets, capital budgets, program/project budgets, cash-flow budgets, and sales, production, material, labor, overhead, and profit budgets.

Operating Budget

The organization's operating budget is a total of all the subsidiary budgets, including the sales budget; production budget; material, labor, and overhead budgets; cost budget; expense budget; budgeted income statement; and the financial budget (capital budget, cash budget, budgeted balance sheet, and budgeted statement of changes in financial position).

See the "Purchasing Operating Budget" section later in this chapter for information about the operating budget for the purchasing department. Such an expense budget covers the operating expenses of a particular department, and it should not be confused with the operating budget for the whole organization.

Expense Budget

The term *expense budget* is most often used with respect to planned operating expenses. This key budget category describes the day-to-day operating expenses associated with the functioning of the organization. An expense budget will usually include planned monthly outlays for salaries and benefits, facilities (internal rent), information systems, travel expenses, utilities (power, telephone, and so on), training and education, supplies, and other regularly scheduled, short-term expenditures, along with sources of income, if any. Expenses are typically budgeted for each department or section; then, the expenses are accumulated for the entire operation. Normally, a formal budget review considers the individual departmental budgets, with respect to accomplishment of the organization's objectives, for the next fiscal period. Additions or deletions are made as needed to balance the expected expenses with the expected income and profit objectives, and a final expense budget is approved for the ensuing operating period. The maintenance, repair and operating supplies (MRO) budget addresses the supplies portion of the expense budget. A typical example of an expense budget is shown in Figure 3.1.

Capital Budget

The capital budget is for buildings, equipment, and other long-term assets used for the operation of the organization. The primary purpose of capital expenditures budgeting is to provide a formal summary of future plans for acquiring facilities and/or equipment. This area of budgeting is critical because of the magnitude of funds involved and the length of time required to recover capital investments. Purchasing can use the capital expenditures budget to determine the best possible source in accordance with the funds available.

Capital expenditure budgeting involves both short- and long-range expenditures. Short-range expenditures must be included in a budget for the current year, and they must be evaluated in terms of their economic worth. Long-range expenditures usually will not be implemented during the current budget period; hence, their inclusion in the budget can be in somewhat general terms.

FIGURE 3.1
Sample Expense Budget

Month / Expense Category	January		February		March		April thru		Dec.	Annual	Year to Date	Year to Date
	Plan	Actual	Plan	Actual	Plan	Actual	Plan	Actual	Actual	Plan	Plan	Actual
Salaries & Benefits	25	27	25	24	25					300	50	51
Rent	12.5	12.3	12.5	12.1	12.5					150	25	24.4
Information Systems	15	16.5	15	14.5	15					180	30	31
Travel	7.5	7.3	7.8	7.9	7.2					90	15.3	15.2
Utilities	12.3	12.3	13.1	13.2	11.8					120	25.4	25.5
Training	5	4.8	5.9	5.1	5					60	10	9.9
Supplies	5.8	5.5	5.9	5.3	5.8					70	11.7	10.8
Misc.	2.5	2.2	2.5	2.6	2.5					30	5	4.8
Total	85.6	87.9	86.8	84.7	84.8					1000	172.4	172.6

Note: Budget shown is after 2 months of actual experience.
Variance are tracked by the difference between planned and actual expenses.
Actual expense less than planned is positive variance.
Actual expense greater than plan is a negative variance.

With few exceptions, most budgets are developed in terms of cost. One of the major duties of the purchasing manager is to review and evaluate a seller's actual or anticipated cost data. The evaluation phase requires the purchasing manager to apply experience, knowledge, and judgment to the cost data of the seller. The purpose of this evaluation is to project reasonable estimates of contract costs and, in the case of capital budgeting, the life cycle cost (that is, all costs incurred during the useful life of the equipment). These estimates become the basis for negotiations between buyer and seller, and the estimates are used for arriving at contract prices that are mutually satisfactory to both parties. The costs agreed to in the contract will then be compared to the cost estimates originally made in the budget creation.

Program/Project Budget

Program budgets are also known as Program Planning Budgeting Systems (PPBS). This type of budget is often used by not-for-profit and governmental entities. Program budgets tie the organization's goals and objectives to the programs or sections responsible for meeting those objectives. To further the relationship between goals and funds spent, this type of budget normally uses productivity measurements and cost-benefit analysis. The supply function provides important contributions to program budgets in the setting of realistic target costs and negotiations designed to achieve these targets. Program budgets offer management the ability to evaluate and make decisions based on the need for various programs.

Cash-Flow Budget

A cash-flow budget links expenditures and cash requirements during the budgetary period. In other words, funds are made available as expenditures are required. In this type of budget, cash outlays are forecast over periods of time (such as weeks or months). This type of budget is useful when tight cash controls are necessary.

At Bender Shipbuilding & Repair Company, Inc., the purchasing manager and the cash manager agree that the terms and conditions negotiated by the buyer are critical, given the company's cash-flow budget.[4] Because the company's main receivables come in large, lump sums as payments for completely built or repaired ships, cash flow is inconsistent. Purchasers must consider this fact when making commitments to suppliers. Jon A. Harrison, purchasing manager, and Jack H. Douglas, Jr., cash manager, at Bender agree that communication between purchasing and finance is essential. If purchasing makes commitments to suppliers for the materials and labor for a ship repair job, finance needs to know that substantial bills will be arriving fairly quickly. The company needs to complete the repair quickly so that its customers can be billed. This also pressures purchasing to source materials quickly and get fast delivery.

The time between when cash is spent for supplies and when the job is complete and cash is received from the customer is sometimes called the *cash-to-cash cycle*. In direct-build organizations, such as online computer purchases, the seller may have a negative cash-to-cash cycle. The customer pays by credit card at the time of ordering, so the seller receives its money before assembling and shipping the item, but the seller typically pays its suppliers in net 30 days terms. The net cash-to-cash cycle is thus minus 20 or more days, depending on the order turnaround time.

Sales, Production, Materials, Labor, Overhead, and Profit Budgets

This series of interrelated budgets is essentially the sales forecast for the budget period that is broken down into the manufacturing, purchasing, and support activities that will be required to produce and deliver the goods or services to be sold. The following sections will explore the materials and inventory budgets further, because these budgets are of specific interest to supply managers.

Typical Budget Areas of Concern to Supply Management

Four major areas are subject to budgetary control in a purchasing department: materials/inventory; maintenance, repair, and operating (MRO) supplies; capital; and operating expenses.

Direct Materials/Inventory

The primary purpose of a materials budget is to identify the quantity and cost of the materials necessary to produce the predetermined number of units of finished goods or to provide the designated levels of service. The materials budget typically covers one year or less. The dollar figures in the budget are based on forecasted levels of production or sales and estimated material prices for the coming year. This means that deviations from the budget are likely, which makes a detailed annual materials budget unrealistic in many organizations. Consequently, many organizations use a flexible budget (which is discussed later in this chapter) to adjust for actual production and actual prices.

A properly prepared materials budget provides management with a tool that:

- Permits the purchasing department to set up a purchasing schedule that assures the delivery of materials when they are needed
- Leads to the determination of the minimum and maximum dollar value of levels of raw materials and finished parts that must be on hand
- Establishes a base from which the treasurer or finance department can determine or estimate the financial requirements for purchasing expenditures

Although they are generally based on estimated prices and planned schedules, materials budgets do the following:

- Provide capacity and rate of consumption planning information for suppliers
- Plan for the appropriate pace of production and replenishment
- Reduce transportation costs
- Provide a basis for planning workloads
- Help in forward buying

In addition, the materials budget may improve purchasing negotiations by providing early notice to suppliers about anticipated quantity and schedule requirements.

MRO Supplies

Maintenance, repair, and operating (MRO) supplies are consumed in the operations process, but they do not become part of the product of the operation. Examples of MRO items are office and shop supplies, lubricating oil, machine repair parts, and janitorial supplies.

The number of individual MRO line items is likely to be so large that budgeting each item will not be feasible. An MRO budget is usually determined by the use of past ratios, which are then adjusted for anticipated changes in inventory and general price levels.

Capital Budget

The purchase of capital assets is typically an area of large dollar expenditures. Good purchasing practices and negotiations can save the organization large sums of money. By researching possible sources and building close relationships with key suppliers, a budget can be established that is both responsive to projected needs and limited to only the required amount of spending. Capital equipment purchases often are evaluated not only for initial cost but also for full life cycle cost, including such areas as maintenance, energy consumption, and spare parts. Because of the long-term nature of these expenditures, a net present value calculation is usually applied to their budgeting and approval decisions.

Purchasing Operating Budget

The operating budget for the purchasing function includes all of the expenses incurred in the operation of the purchasing function. Typically, this budget is based on anticipated operating and administrative workloads. Such expenses include salaries and wages, space costs, heat, electricity, telephone, postage, office equipment, office supplies, technology costs, travel and entertainment, educational expenses, and costs for trade publications. The operating budget of the function should reflect the goals and objectives of the organization. For example, if an organizational goal is to reduce overhead expenses, the budgeted amounts for overhead in the operating budget should reflect this. The Center for Advanced Purchasing Studies (CAPS) provides a number of operating expense ratios from a variety of industries that may be useful as possible benchmark information.[5]

Steps in the Budgeting Process

Budgets are often based on past experience, and then they are adjusted to meet predicted future needs. The budgeting process typically includes the following steps:

1. Review organizational goals and objectives, as well as the methods or processes needed to achieve them
2. Estimate the dollar value of needed resources
3. Develop standard material purchase costs
4. Present the budget and obtain the appropriation
5. Analyze variances

Review Goals and Objectives

The first step in the budget process is to review the organizational goals and objectives. This information is used to determine the specific tasks, the personnel, and the support activities that will be required to achieve the desired results. These determinations are important, because the budget will demonstrate in financial terms how the organization's goals and objectives are to be met. The next step is defining the needed resources (for example, personnel, equipment, furnishings, and training). It is necessary to begin with general forecasts in terms of economic trends, sales, purchase prices, and profit. This will provide more realistic figures for revenues and expenditures. While budget targets may be provided by top management, finance, or marketing, it is generally agreed that the budget requests are developed best at the level where implementation takes place, usually at the department level or lower. This approach tends to work best because those responsible for implementation can identify their own needs, and they can be better motivated if they take part in the decision-making process.

Estimate the Dollar Value of Needed Resources

Clearly, the dollar value of needed resources must be estimated accurately for budgets to be valid. There are different approaches to establishing needed resources. One approach is to estimate values by closely analyzing the previous year's expenditures. This information can then be used to extrapolate resource figures for the new budget year.

Another approach is to use zero-base budgeting, which does not use past experience to determine future needs. All budget items are justified in detail, and they are viewed as new requests, as opposed to continuations of current programs. The assumption is that the budget is prepared from scratch, that is, from zero-base. The zero-base budget is helpful in questioning the traditional way things have been done because all programs, including those that have been in effect for years, are justified, prioritized, and subject to scrutiny and approval.

Few organizations use a "pure" zero-base budget. Those that do use the concept generally employ it for selected segments of the operation, and they use the "historical/extension" concept to develop the budget for the rest of the operation.

Develop Standard Material Purchase Costs

Standard costs are established primarily when it is difficult to cost out individual units of a product, for example in a mass production environment. The standard costs are used for materials and inventory budgeting purposes and for analyzing variances between actual costs and the previously established standard costs. Therefore, standard costs provide a convenient means of evaluating cost management performance.

Standard material purchase costs serve as targets to buy against for a forthcoming period. Standard costs are an estimate of the actual cost expected to be paid for a particular line item. The standard costs of all components in a product are added to determine the standard cost for the product. The standard costs of all items in inventory are accumulated to determine the value of the inventory at the end of the period.

Present the Budget and Obtain the Appropriation

This step is handled differently by each organization. It is common for a committee to review and consolidate all budgets and make recommendations, but there are many other approaches. After the budget has been presented and any changes have been made, appropriations are set to cover the approved expenses during the budgetary period.

Analyze Variances

The final step in the budget process is to control expenditures during the budgetary year. The budget is the most widely used tool in organizations to provide financial control. This control occurs through matching appropriations and expenditures, as well as by tracking expenditure trends against budget estimates.

One way to track expenditures is by using purchase price variance (PPV). *Purchase price* variance is the difference between the standard prices and the actual prices paid during a budget period. Figure 3.2 shows a tracking of price variance against the standard cost for a purchased component during a one-year budget period.

FIGURE 3.2

Purchase Price Variance

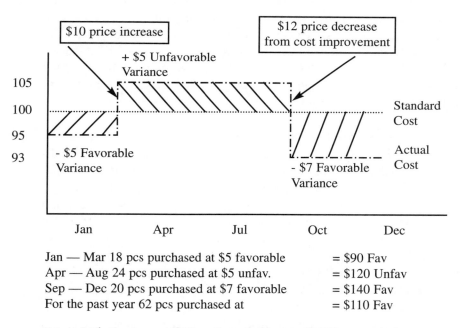

Jan — Mar 18 pcs purchased at $5 favorable   = $90 Fav
Apr — Aug 24 pcs purchased at $5 unfav.   = $120 Unfav
Sep — Dec 20 pcs purchased at $7 favorable   = $140 Fav
For the past year 62 pcs purchased at   = $110 Fav

Special Areas of Budgeting and Financial Management

Because many organizations have turned their focus to cost reduction and cost avoidance strategies, two innovations, target costing and activity-based costing, have been developed. These techniques influence the way purchasing professionals think about activities and costs, both internally and with suppliers. The following section examines these strategies.

Target Pricing and Target Costing

The concept of target costing starts with the selling price of an end product and works backward to establish cost targets for materials, labor, production, sales, and administration. This mindset may affect the manner in which the budgeting process is undertaken, and especially the way that cost estimates for materials budgets are determined.

For example, L. Dean Williams, C.P.M., lives by target pricing.[6] He is the manager of the procurement department for an engineering construction company, The Pritchard Corporation, a Black & Veatch company. Williams sees an even greater emphasis on target pricing as he aligns his organization with key suppliers in strategic alliances. For Williams, the power of effective target pricing is obvious. "We save at least 10 to 12 percent on projects that can cost us anywhere from $80 to $120 million."

Activity-Based Costing

Activity-based costing (ABC) is an approach to allocating indirect costs that is in stark contrast to traditional cost accounting, which bases the allocation of overhead on direct labor. With ABC, indirect costs are turned into direct costs by tracking the cost drivers and assigning the costs to the appropriate activity. According to Mary Lu Harding of Harding & Associates, the biggest impact of activity-based costing on purchasing is in the budgeting process and head-count justification. Prior to activity-based costing, purchasing's budget was determined by a calculation that was based on the volume of materials coming in. Because more materials meant more work, more headcount could be justified. Activity-based costing changes this thinking by focusing on work volume, not materials volume.[7]

At Hewlett-Packard's Boise Surface Mount Center, which manufactures circuit boards, the switch from traditional cost accounting to activity-based costing changed the unit costs of some products.[8] For some products the unit cost went up, and for others it went down. Overall, the increase or decrease in the unit manufacturing cost was between 5 and 20 percent. Activity-based costing can impact decisions made about costing, pricing, and sourcing.

Line-Item Budgets

A line-item budget is formatted to show individual expenses during the budgetary period without tying those expenses into broad programs or goals. A typical line-item budget would include such categories as salaries, office supplies, travel, equipment, telephone expenses, and postage. Each category contains further detail regarding expenses. For example, the travel category would show exactly what travel is scheduled and the estimated cost of each trip. Line-item budgets are generally incremental — to a large extent, they are based on the previous budget period.

Flexible Budgets

Flexible budgets are developed to reflect changing conditions, such as an increase or decrease in output. Often, flexible budgets use a formula to determine the needed budget amount based on the output. The advantage of flexible budgets is that they respond quickly to change. Flexible budgets should be used for materials budgets to reflect changes in planned versus actual volume.

Open-to-Buy[9]

Open-to-buy (OTB), a term used commonly in retail, is similar to the concept of a cash-flow budget in manufacturing circles in that it links available cash to controlled expenditures. OTB deals with the authority to expend dollars, the commitment to a specific category or program, and the management of authority. Available cash and timing are the two key elements in OTB. OTB limits the actions of the purchaser because of the restrictions placed on cash expenditures and the timing of cash outflows. This may, for example, cause a purchaser to miss an opportunity for a price discount. Because OTB is typically expressed in terms of revenue and not purchase dollars, purchasers must explain to suppliers exactly what dollars are available for purchases. Replenishment dollars may be expressed in terms of a product category, such as rings in a jewelry establishment. Dollar expenditures would be capped for the category, in this case rings. Under this arrangement, poor sales in ruby rings would limit what could be reinvested in rings as a category. Therefore, even if diamond rings were selling well, the available replenishment dollars would be determined by the category, not the individual item.

Strategic plans establish the direction the organization is moving and identify its goals and objectives. The organization's budgets allocate resources to achieve these goals and objectives, which should ultimately lead the organization to achieve its mission. Once the plans and budgets are in place, managers and employees at all levels of the organization assume responsibility for carrying out the actions developed through the planning and budgeting processes. Chapter 4 addresses the issue of management.

Key Points

1. The supply management function's potential financial contribution to the organization is arguably the greatest of any functional area. Purchasing should develop a close relationship with finance in order to capitalize on this position.
2. Because monitoring expenditures is a primary purpose of budgets and purchasing is responsible for the management of expenditures, purchasing should play a key role in the budgeting process.
3. The areas of budgetary control that are of greatest interest to supply management are materials and inventory, MRO, capital expenses, and operating expenses.
4. Budgets are vital to the business planning process and, therefore, are subject to both the direction and the approval of top management.
5. In recent years, overhead costs have become a larger portion of the cost structure, and today, they represent an area of significant cost improvement potential. As a result, activity-based costing is now a key tool in purchasing-led cost reductions.

Questions for Review

1. How are budgets related to strategic plans and the business planning process?

2. Why is the supply management organization interested not only in its own departmental expense budget, but also in the budgets of other departments?
3. Why are variances between budgeted and actual expenditures tracked regularly? How should management respond to substantial variances from plan?
4. What are the differences between expense budgets, capital budgets, and direct materials budgets? What role does supply management play in each of these budget processes?
5. How are standard costs used to manage spending in the direct materials budgeting process?

Endnotes

1. Duffy, R.J. "Accounting for Cash," *Purchasing Today®*, August 1998, p. 37.
2. Duffy, 1998, p. 40.
3. Mitchell, L.K. "Show Me the Money — Measuring Supply Chain Management's Financial Contribution to the Corporation," *Proceedings of the 1999 NAPM International Purchasing Conference*, NAPM, Tempe, AZ, 1999, p. 313.
4. Duffy, 1998, p. 37.
5. Center for Advanced Purchasing Studies, Tempe, Ariz., www.capsresearch.org.
6. Newman, R.G. "Target Pricing: A Cost Reduction Strategy," *NAPM Insights*, September 1995, p. 33-34.
7. Harding, M.L. "Effects of Activity-Based Costing on Purchasing," *Proceedings of the 1995 NAPM International Purchasing Conference*, NAPM, Tempe, AZ, 1995, p. 104.
8. Lere, J.C. and J.V. Saraph. "Activity-Based Costing for Purchasing Managers Cost and Pricing Determinations," *International Journal of Purchasing and Materials Management*, Fall 1995, p. 26.
9. Yates, R.A. "Open to Buy: Managing Cash and Inventories," *Purchasing Today®*, July 1998, p. 42.

CHAPTER 4

LEADING, MANAGING, AND SUPERVISING

How can theories of management be applied to the supply function?

Chapter Objectives

- To explain the differences between leaders and managers, and the role of each in an organization
- To describe the various schools of management thought that have influenced organizations
- To describe issues and challenges involved with working in teams
- To describe different approaches to motivating employees to achieve the goals and objectives of the organization

Leaders and Managers

Peter Drucker said, "Management is doing things right; leadership is doing the right things." In a *Harvard Business Review* article titled "What Leaders Really Do," John Kotter, the Konosuke Matsushita Professor of Leadership at the Harvard Business School, identified outcomes as the key distinction between leaders and managers. Leaders produce desirable, effective change, while managers produce order, predictability, and consistency.[1] In an article for *NAPM Insights*, Chris Chen, program manager with the Center for Creative Leadership in San Diego, California, described the management behaviors that keep complex systems in order and leadership behaviors that help create effective change.[2] These behaviors are discussed in the following sections.

Management Behaviors

According to Chen, the following management behaviors keep complex systems in order:

- **Planning and budgeting** – Planning and budgeting behaviors include setting time-phased performance measures, establishing targets and goals, defining detailed steps to accomplish these goals, and allocating resources.
- **Organizing and staffing** – These behaviors ensure that the organization has the capacity to carry out goals. They include creating the organizational structure (who reports to whom, who has decision-making authority, and how information will flow), defining job roles, interviewing and selecting organization members, and monitoring job performance.
- **Providing supervision and problem solving** – These behaviors include monitoring results versus the plan, identifying deviations or exceptions, and solving problems or disputes.

Leadership Behaviors

According to Chen, the following leadership behaviors help create effective change:

- **Setting a direction** – When acting as a leader, purchasing managers must develop a vision of the future and then define strategies for producing the changes needed to accomplish their vision.
- **Aligning people** – This behavior involves communicating to those who will help reach the vision, building teams, and making sure everyone in the organization understands where they are going and that they are acting cohesively — directing their efforts in the same direction.
- **Motivating and inspiring** – These are encouraging, supportive behaviors that keep people energized in the face of resistance to change.

Organizations need both leaders and managers. Sometimes the attributes necessary for leadership and management do not exist to the same degree in the same person. Any individual can assess his or her strengths and weaknesses as a leader and a manager and then focus on improvement. The behaviors a person will be called on to exercise will depend on the needs of the organization. If the organization needs dramatic change, as many purchasing and supply organizations do these days, being able to motivate and inspire may be the most important skills a person can bring to the organization.

John F. "Jack" Welch, chief executive officer of General Electric Corporation, was named CEO of the Decade by *Industry Week* magazine in November 1999. A glance at the credentials that earned Welch this distinction tells a lot about the qualities of today's leaders. Welch has the special ability to identify, nurture, deploy, and stretch leaders, said Ram Charan, a Dallas-based executive consultant. He added that Welch is "the standard against which the rest are compared — not just for the decade, but for the whole century." Noel M. Tichy, a professor at the University of Michigan's Business School in Ann Arbor, said of Welch, "He has really turned the management paradigm that has dominated the latter half of the century upside down." Tichy also said that Welch "is about ideas, about building a gene pool of diverse human capital and leaders, and being able to get synergy. . .through subtle orchestration of ideas and networks of people."[3]

Current Issues in Organizational Management

Managers and leaders in supply management can no longer limit their focus to the operational side of the business. They must also be strategic thinkers with an eye to the strategic plan of the organization. Three major initiatives that have been undertaken in many organizations have broad implications for the way the supply function is managed. These initiatives are:

- A focus on continuous improvement
- The creation of lean organizations
- Use of emerging technologies and knowledge management

Continuous Improvement

As competition increases, enterprises look for sources of competitive advantage. Continuous improvement techniques have helped many companies create such advantages. In the book *Powered by Honda* the authors write, "There is a buffet of continuous improvement programs in industry today. Step up to the bar and make your selection: reengineering, TQM, teams, work flow analysis, MRP, finite scheduling, etc."[4]

Some organizations are turning the continuous improvement focus to the supply base and to the supplier-customer relationship, where improvements shared between customers and suppliers are proving to be valuable to both. *Powered by Honda* describes the approach to continuous improvement taken by Honda of America through Honda's Best Partner/Profit/Productivity/Quality (BP/BQ) program for supply-based excellence. The authors write:

> The test of any philosophy is the degree of commitment that members of an organization demonstrate, not by simple mental or verbal assent, but by real action. BP is Honda's demonstrated commitment to continuous improvement in its suppliers — the Honda Way philosophy in action. BP activities, as Honda calls its toolbox of continuous improvement methods, are simply an extension of Honda's own approach to internal manufacturing excellence. . . The goal — to create a highly productive, cost-effective manufacturing method — draws on the knowledge of production associates. These are "the experts," working in the targeted improvement areas, combined with the findings of the team. Immediate benefits flow to the work site and supplier associates as the team makes the plant more organized for production.[5]

Kaizen and Kaikaku – Masaaki Imai, introduced the word *kaizen* to the world in his book *Kaizen, The Key to Japan's Competitive Success* (1986), and he revisited the concept in *Gemba Kaizen, A Commonsense, Low-Cost Approach to Management* (1997). Kaizen translates roughly as "continuous incremental improvement." The two basic elements of kaizen are improvement and continuity. Kaizen can be applied to one's personal life, home life, social life, and working life, where it involves managers and workers alike.[6] The kaizen approach to management means constantly seeking and implementing methods and processes that lead to continuous incremental improvement, such as lower costs, enhanced service response, and greater contributions to overall profits. Process reengineering flows logically from the kaizen concept.

Kaizen can be applied to any setting. Mount Edgecumbe High School in Sitka, Alaska, has pioneered in using TQM or kaizen methods to dramatically improve schooling. Mount Edgecumbe's simple goal is to produce quality individuals. The results of the application of kaizen have been astounding. Almost 50 percent of all graduates are in college or have graduated from college — much higher than the national average — and few students drop out. The school has four pilot companies that give students hands-on opportunities to apply what they are learning in a business setting. All students learn either Chinese or Japanese, and their curriculum is strong in the history, culture, and languages of the Pacific Rim, as well as in English, social studies, mathematics, science, marine science, computers, business, and physical education. School administrators are confident that all students will continue to grow and learn. The kaizen principles of improvement and continuity are applied at Mount Edgecumbe in the following ways:[7]

1. Teachers and students are regarded as co-managers. They set targets and goals, individually and collectively, and they evaluate themselves regularly against agreed upon standards of excellence. For example, all students set improvement goals, such as receiving all As, avoiding conduct reports, and reducing tardiness.

2. Students continuously improve. Each year one week is set aside for self-esteem building and quality training. This is reinforced by 90 minutes per week of quality-improvement training and schoolwide problem solving.

3. As customers, students participate in defining their needs. For example, the students felt it was inefficient to have seven short study periods a day, so the school switched to four 90-minute classes. These four classes provided time for lab work, hands-on projects, field trips, thorough discussions, varied teaching styles, and in-depth study. The reorganized schedule also allows for an extra three hours of staff development and preparation time each week.

4. Teachers rethink their teaching styles as part of the continuous improvement approach. One science teacher changed from being an 80-percent lecturer to a 95-percent facilitator. Staff training receives top priority, and teachers are encouraged to challenge and justify every learning process.

On the other hand, *kaikaku*, which translates into "radical improvement," is associated with lean production and lean thinking, and it implies more dramatic change in an organization.[8] This concept will be discussed in greater detail later in this chapter.

Process Reengineering – A review of typical cost structures for most manufacturers today would show that overhead costs have become a large portion of the total cost, sometimes 40 to 50 percent. Because indirect labor and support activities usually evolve in support of direct labor over long periods of time, they often are not well documented, and in many cases not well understood. This leads to significant opportunities for reducing cost and cycle time by identifying low-value-adding and non-value-adding activities and then reducing or eliminating them. A proven method used for analyzing processes and identifying such opportunities is the creation of a process flow diagram or process map.

Process flow diagrams and process maps break a process into key activities, transfers, decisions, and approvals. This facilitates analysis and allows people involved in the process to understand where the low- or non-value-added work exists. Process improvements can be planned, and then a new map can be created to document and standardize the improved process. Many organizations today are working with suppliers to map joint processes that provide opportunities to reduce costs and cycle time.

Process reengineering can be applied to the purchasing department to shape and control growth, to improve the function's effectiveness and efficiency, or to give the department a more strategic focus. Process simplification and cycle time reduction will also reduce the cost of the purchasing process. Purchasers must make the benefits of their services tangible by tracking and reporting cost avoidance, reductions and savings and, ultimately, value creation. The identification of low-priority or low-value work allows purchasing to consolidate resources and focus on higher-leveraged activities. Speed and simplicity are pivotal elements.

In the quick-service restaurant industry, one focus of process reengineering is speed of service. Wendy's International, Inc., announced on Jan. 13, 2000, that same-store sales at Wendy's U.S. company restaurants increased nearly 7 percent in December 1999 and about 6.5 percent in the fourth quarter, which ended on Jan. 2, 2000.[9] The company attributed much of this increase to store-level productivity gains. Wendy's service excellence program is one example of how reengineered processes contribute to bottomline performance. Wendy's uses a full-line timer to track cycle time from the menu board through the first window (ordering and payment) and the second window (pick-up). This has resulted in a 33 percent reduction in cycle time, increased throughput during peak hours, and improved order accuracy.[10] Wendy's also reported dramatically improved ratings in the speed of service and pick-up window service compared to their largest competitors.

Quality Improvement – Quality improvement methods are closely related to process improvement activities. Process control and root cause analysis are two of the most popular of quality improvement methods.

Process Control – Whether it is a manufacturing or a service/office work process, the ability of the process to repeat the same results time after time is vital to meeting customer expectations. By observing and documenting the process, a team can identify causes of variation and their effect on the outcomes of the process. Then by applying control mechanisms to limit the variation of these critical factors, the results of the process will be predictable and consistent over extended periods of time.

Root Cause Analysis – In many cases, quality problems have been addressed by noting the easily observed outcome (symptom). Solutions were adopted based only on these observations. For example, consider the case of an incorrect purchase order number being entered on an invoice by the person preparing the invoice. The invoice will not be paid because the purchase order number does not match, and a quality problem has surfaced. A simple observation will determine that the individual who entered the PO number on the invoice made a mistake. The conclusion might be that this was carelessness on the part of this individual, and this person will be asked to be more careful in the future. But if this was not the root cause, the error will likely be repeated.

Studies have shown that such errors are more likely to be caused by something in the system than by simple carelessness. A systematic root cause analysis may show one or more specific conditions that caused this mistake. Possible examples of root causes in this case might include poor task lighting, sources of distraction, number sequences leading to transposition, and lack of proper training in the task.

Root cause analysis typically involves several analytical steps:[11]

1. Identify proximate causes and systems.
2. Review related systems and processes.
3. Identify the underlying/system-related cause(s) of the proximate cause(s), and explain their potential role in the event.
4. Continuously focus on opportunities to improve systems, and if none are apparent, explain why.
5. Outline a plan to address opportunities to improve, or explain why the organization is not addressing those opportunities.
6. Explain, when improvement plans are justified, who will carry out the plan, when that person(s) will carry out the plan, and the methods for measuring results.

To be successful, root cause analysis should:

- Involve people closely associated with all aspects of the systems and processes under review.
- Receive support, authorization, and encouragement from senior leadership.
- Present findings that are consistent and written in clear, direct language. Conclusions should be endorsed by all root cause analysis team members.
- Consider all relevant literature.
- Distribute the root cause analysis to anyone who can benefit from the findings.
- The benefits to searching for and identifying the root cause include the following:

- The individual is not blamed for the error, but he or she is involved in determining what led to the opportunity for the error to occur.
- System elements that may be contributing to this and similar errors are identified.
- Corrective action may be taken to prevent future occurrences.
- Customer satisfaction is improved by providing consistent results at lower costs.

Lean Production and Lean Enterprises

James P. Womack and Daniel T. Jones first wrote about Toyota's lean production process in their 1990 book, *The Machine That Changed the World*.[12] In 1996, they published *Lean Thinking*, which discusses the basic principles of lean thinking and offers examples of companies whose managers are attempting to create lean enterprises. Lean production is simply "doing more and more with less and less."[13] Lean thinking is defined as "a way to specify value, line up value-creating actions in the best sequence, conduct these activities without interruption whenever someone requests them, and perform them more and more effectively."[14]

Womack and Jones distinguish lean thinking from process reengineering in a couple of ways. First, integral to the concept of lean thinking is the idea that new work is created in the process, and jobs are not lost. This is in contrast to the practice, if not the principle, of reengineering. Second, lean thinkers view the value stream not as distinct processes, for example the handling of accounts payable or order processing, but as a flow of value-creating activities for a specific product. In the case of lean thinking, employees and departments are part of the process of rethinking functions, departments, firms, and careers to create value.

For example, Womack and Jones described the value stream for a carton of cola as 319 days, of which only three hours resulted in value being created.[15] Ninety-nine percent of the time was wait time.

The five principles of lean thinking identified by Womack and Jones are the following:[16]

1. Precisely specify value by specific product.
2. Identify the value stream for each product.

3. Make value flow without interruption.
4. Let the customer pull value from the producer.
5. Pursue perfection.

Emerging Technologies and Knowledge Management

As more and more simple tasks are being relegated to automation, it should be apparent that the nature of work is changing from task-related (do as instructed) to knowledge-related (do as circumstances require). In *Industry Week* magazine's survey of CEOs, more than 80 percent of the respondents said that knowledge management, acquiring and spreading information and best practices across the enterprise, was the biggest internal obstacle to company growth in the global marketplace.[17]

The shift to knowledge-related work holds profound implications for management:

- Leaders must clarify the desired direction of the enterprise so that individuals can contribute as appropriate and as they are able.
- Communication must be open to all levels of the organization regarding what needs to be done and what others are doing.
- Individuals must be knowledgeable about their area of contribution, and they must be free to express themselves.
- The members of the workforce must be provided with incentives to join in multifunctional team efforts and to make their maximum contributions.
- Measurements and rewards must be appropriate for individual efforts and for team results, rather than tracking and rewarding functional achievement.

The Structure of Management

There are many different ways to structure the management of an organization. Ultimately, the organization's value-creating activities should drive the management structure. Time and stagnation, organizational politics, complacency, and many other hazards may make a management structure ineffective and inefficient. While many different management structures are in operation, features common to all of the structures include:

- Some means of delegating authority and responsibility
- A chain of command
- Line and staff relationships
- Span of control

These features are covered in the following sections.

Delegation of Authority and Responsibility

In principle, *delegation* involves assigning tasks, granting the authority to make commitments on behalf of these tasks, and assuming responsibility for the results. Figure 4.1 shows how the authority to spend flows from the principals (owners) to the agents (buyers). Ideally, the three elements — tasks, authority, and responsibility — should increase and decrease together. Any change in one element should be accompanied by a corresponding change in the other elements. Effective organization not only requires a recognition of this principle, but also a recognition of the degree to which it should be practiced (that is, the degree to which management should delegate tasks and the authority to perform them). Because delegation and decentralization are often used synonymously, it is useful to expand on the meaning of delegation.

FIGURE 4.1
Authority to Spend

The authority to spend the funds of the enterprise is specifically passed from owners to buyers. Those employees not in the specific chain of authority may not commit the enterprise to payment for goods or services, regardless of their position in the organization's hierarchy.

Task Assignment – In enterprises that employ two or more people, there must be a division of labor or a grouping of activities. Otherwise, a chaotic situation will result. To translate the division or grouping of labor into jobs for people, specific job assignments must be made. Employees need to be told what tasks they are to perform and the goals to which these tasks will contribute. This might be regarded as the initial phase of delegation.

Granting Authority – It would be pointless to assign employees a task, such as purchasing supplies for the office, without giving them authority to complete their task. In this case, they would need the authority to obligate the organization to pay for the office supplies. By the same token, the person with the task of supervising the office must have authority to direct the activities of his or her subordinates (for example, to requisition supplies) and to determine how equipment entrusted to the department will be used. This phase of delegation naturally accompanies the first phase: task assignment.

The Presence of Responsibility – The third phase of delegation is implicit in the preceding two. When tasks are assigned and authority to discharge them is given, the recipients have a moral obligation and a responsibility to fulfill their assignments to the best of their abilities. In a similar manner, the executive who assigns duties and grants authority to subordinates does not absolve himself of all obligation for the tasks' proper fulfillment.

Management literature makes it clear that the concept of delegation refers to the accomplishment of work, not the avoidance of it. Therefore, assigning one's subordinates to do part of one's work does not free managers from responsibility for the work's completion. In short, responsibility has both immediate and ultimate connotations. The subordinate has an immediate responsibility for the performance of his or her assignments. Those who have delegated assignments have the ultimate responsibility to see that subordinates perform the assignments in accordance with the operating standards and objectives of the organization. The nature of responsibility makes it imperative that managers who delegate assignments match the responsibility they have conferred on their subordinates with an equal level of authority. This concept is called the parity of authority and responsibility.

The Parity of Authority and Responsibility – While the principle of equal authority and responsibility does not directly affect how operating groups are arranged within an organization, it does influence the degree of delegation, which in turn influences the way activities are grouped and the need for staff. There can be little delegation of authority by managers who believe their subordinates are incapable of assuming responsibility. Because individuals can be held responsible only for actions over which they have control, the willingness to accept responsibility sets the outside limits on the authority that can be entrusted to them.

The balance between authority and responsibility is especially important for employees who are responsible for price negotiations and decisions regarding warranties, leadtime, order splitting, credit terms, and policy exceptions. The director or manager of a purchasing department may be willing to allow buyers to make some decisions, but not others. Confusion often develops as a result of the responsibilities implied by an individual's title, such as senior buyer, and management's intent that certain buying decisions will be made by a manager, rather than by a senior buyer. An effective solution for this problem is good communication, which can be accomplished through a clear chain of command.

Chain of Command

The responsibility of a subordinate to a superior, whether it is between a senior buyer and a manager or an assistant buyer and a buyer, is essentially a personal relationship. Responsibility carries an obligation to accomplish desired results as well as accountability to a superior for the degree of success achieved in the pursuit of results. It follows that manager-buyer, buyer-assistant buyer, and buyer-expediter relationships can be clearer and communication can be more direct if the purchasing department is designed so that each subordinate has one superior to whom he or she is responsible. This one-on-one, superior-subordinate relationship reveals the structure of delegation and is most evident in the traditional line and staff form of organization. Figure 4.2 shows the chain of command for the supply management function in a typical organization.

FIGURE 4.2

A Typical Organization Chart

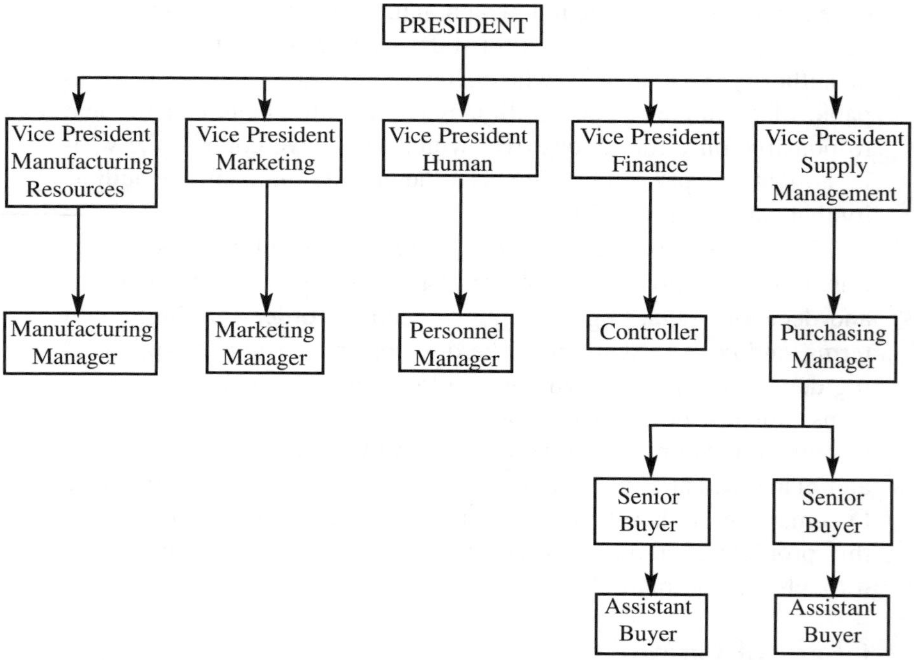

Line and Staff Relationships

On some occasions, such as a departmental reorganization, the addition of new positions or job titles, or a change in a department's mission, it is important to distinguish line positions from staff positions. The most basic distinction is that *line personnel* are responsible for making and executing decisions. They are responsible for deciding what should be done and issuing appropriate instructions down the chain of command. Line managers act based on their responsibility within the limitations that are imposed by their immediate superiors.

The function of *staff personnel*, by contrast, is advisory in nature. There is no connotation of authority, beyond that which one member of a staff may have with respect to another member of the same staff. Staff officers may exercise the line authority over subordinates in their own departments, but they have no other line authority. The recommendation of a staff member goes to his or her superior. Whether or not these recommendations are transformed into action is the prerogative of the superior. In essence, staff personnel do the tasks line executives would do if they possessed the time, expertise, and energy to do them.

The simplified diagram in Figure 4.3 illustrates line and staff positions. It is evident that a number of positions, particularly those at the top of the diagram, have elements of both line and staff positions. The purchasing manager (like other senior-level managers) is in a staff position with respect to the president, but he or she is in a line position with respect to subordinates in his or her department. Depending on the size of the organization, senior buyers might be in a staff position with respect to the purchasing manager.

FIGURE 4.3

Strategic Supply Management Organization

Span of Control

The number of people a manager supervises is his or her *span of control*. For example, if a purchasing department has 25 buyers, all of whom report directly to the department manager or director, the executive has a span of control of 25. This is an exceptionally wide span of control. It is probable that a department with 25 buyers would have two or three assistant managers, each of whom would supervise a group of buyers. In this instance, individuals responsible for other functions, such as price analysis, contract administration, and office management, may also report directly to the department director, giving him or her a span of control of five or six. This is a more reasonable arrangement; however, downsizing continues to influence span of control decisions.

No formal criteria exist for determining a reasonable span of supervision or control for any given manager. How many people a person should supervise is largely a matter of individual capacity and the work environment. Factors such as the complexity of the supervisory situation, the demands on the manager, and the capabilities of subordinates are important to consider.

Flat Organizations – The term *flat organization* indicates that one supervisor has a large number of people reporting to him or her. Flat organizational structures include few middle-ranking personnel. Layers of middle management are removed to provide more direct communication from the top to the bottom of the organization and vice versa. Automation and work teams make it possible to "flatten" the organization without losing control or productivity. Figure 4.4 shows how Porsche's management was flattened or delayered in the early 1990s.

FIGURE 4.4
Delayering Operations at Porsche in 1992

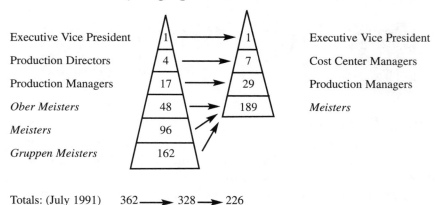

Totals: (July 1991)   362 ⟶ 328 ⟶ 226

Source: Womack and Jones, 1996, p.199.

An *Industry Week* magazine survey of CEOs indicated that 78 percent of the executives felt that a flatter organizational structure was an effective or very effective response to competitive pressures. Dow Chemical Company of Midland, Michigan, used this approach, among several others, in improving its global position. According to the *Industry Week* article, "In reengineering for global processes, the company deployed a global IT (information technology) infrastructure for the required real-time delivery of information, cut $5 billion in costs (over five years), and flattened the organization from 10 to 12 layers down to 4 to 6 from the CEO to the most junior employee."[18]

Matrix Organizations – A matrix organization combines function and product in a dual authority structure. Chrysler Corporation uses a matrix of function, versus platform responsibility, at the executive level. At Pratt & Whitney, efforts to adopt lean thinking led to a number of structural changes, including those shown in Figure 4.5.

FIGURE 4.5
Pratt & Whitney Organization, 1996

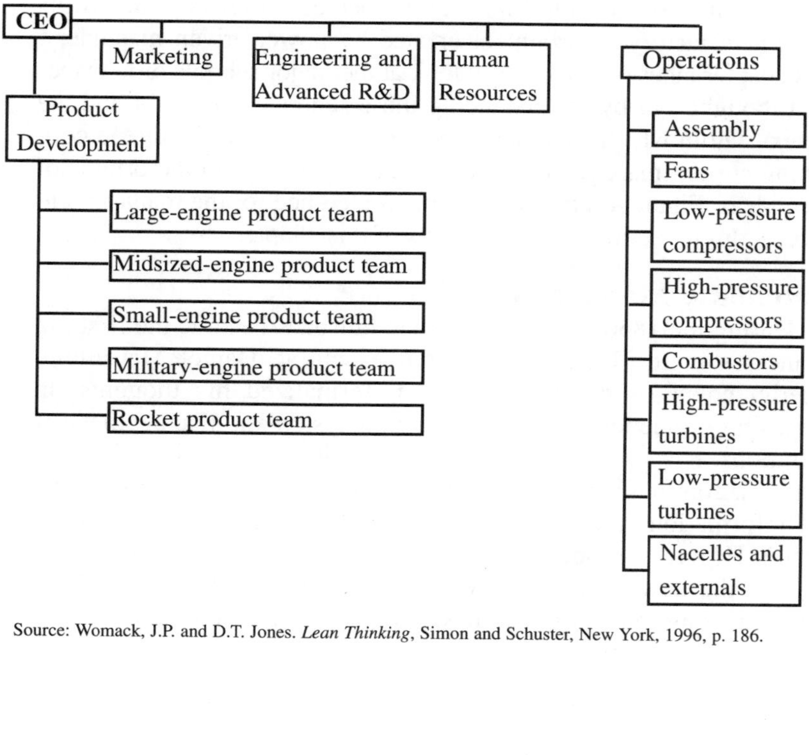

Source: Womack, J.P. and D.T. Jones. *Lean Thinking*, Simon and Schuster, New York, 1996, p. 186.

Theories of Management

In today's Information Age, knowledge and knowledge management are the keys to competitive advantage. In his book *Building Wealth: The New Rules for Individuals*, Companies, and Nations in a Knowledge-Based Economy, Lester Thurow writes that knowledge will replace natural resources as the asset most critical to economic success.[19] This modern concept is driven in large part by the easy accessibility to vast stores of knowledge made available by rapidly advancing technology. Yet, in the late 1800s, in his book *The Twelve Principles of Efficiency*, Harrington Emerson espoused the belief that ideas produced wealth. His first three rules of efficiency dealt with knowledge: a clearly defined ideal, common sense that strives for knowledge and seeks advice, and competent counsel.[20]

The development of management thought and practices can be traced back to early human organizations. The Sumerians started keeping written records in 4000 B.C., and the Egyptians recognized the need for planning, organizing, and controlling as early as 4000 B.C.[21] The Industrial Revolution of the 1800s (the first Industrial Revolution) catalyzed the movement to find ways to increase efficiency and profits in the new factory environment created by power-driven machinery. This chapter takes only a cursory look at the major schools of management thought, but by understanding these schools of thought and the context within which each developed, readers can see the thread connecting current management thought and behavior with the origins of these ideas. Figure 4.6 provides a quick reference for the management theories discussed in the next sections of this chapter.

Systematic Management

During the 1850s and 1860s, when railroads became the first big businesses in the United States, rail executive Daniel McCallum, superintendent of the Erie Railroad, formalized his thoughts on increasing efficiency and profits through systematic management of operations. His six points basically dealt with organization (division of labor), communication (creating a management reporting system), and information (managing information for analysis and improvements). He saw technology as the tool for managing information. In his day, the new technology was the telegraph, and it allowed for faster transmission and wider dissemination of information than anything else imaginable.

FIGURE 4.6
Timeline of Major Theories of Management

Dates	School of Thought	Major Contributors	Major Contributions
1850s-1860s	Systematic Management	Daniel McCallum Henry Poor	• Organization = Division of labor • Communication = Management reporting system • Information = Analysis of reports to improve operations
From the 1880s on	Scientific Management and Operations Research	Frederick W. Taylor Henry L. Gantt Frank Gilbreth Lillian Moller Gilbreth Harrington Emerson	• Application of scientific study • Efficiency studies • Wage systems and motivation • Specialized management knowledge • Use of mathematical models in managerial decision-making.
Late 1880s through early 1900s	Universal Theory or Administrative Theory of Management	Henri Fayol	• Universality of management • Principles of managerial thinking • Elements of management: planning, organizing, command, coordination, and control
1920s and 1930s	Behavioral Theory	Hugo Munsterberg Walter Dill Scott Mary Parker Follett Elton Mayo	• Focused on social needs of employees and motivation • Applied psychology to business • Link physical and mental qualifications with ideal psychological conditions and provide optimal motivational influences • Concept of working with, not under, someone

Dates	School of Thought	Major Contributors	Major Contributions
Early 1900s on	Organization Theory	Max Weber Chester Barnard Herbert Simon	• The central unit of analysis is the total organization • Weber's model of bureaucracy • Organization must be effective and efficient to be successful • Function of management is to keep organization (decision-making structure) running • Limit decisionmaking scope through policies, procedures, hierarchy, and so on
1960s and 1970s	General Systems Theory	Ludwig von Bartalanffy	• Identify parallels among disciplines • Integrate into one theory
1970s on	Contingency Theory	Fred Luthans Todd I. Stewart	• Focus on flexibility and adaptability • No universal management principles, circumstantial

1980s on	Excellent Companies or Best Practices	Thomas J. Peters
		Robert H. Waterman
		Nancy K. Austin
			• Attributes of excellent companies:
			• Bias for action
			• Bias for action
			  • Bias for action
			  • Closeness to the customer
			  • Autonomy and entrepreneurship
			  • Productivity through people
			  • Hands-on, value-driven management
			  • Stick to the knitting
			  • Simple form, lean staff
			  • Simultaneous loose and tight properties

1980s and early 1990s	Management by Objectives	Peter Drucker Douglas McGregor Edward Schleh George Ordiorne	• Integrates planning, participation, communication, managerial development, performance appraisal

Dates	School of Thought	Major Contributors	Major Contributions
1980s on	Lean Organization Theory	James P. Womack Daniel T. Jones	• Precisely specify value by specific product • Identify the value stream for each product • Make value flow without interruption. • Let the customer pull value from the producer • Pursue perfection
1990s on	Learning Organization	Peter M. Senge	• Systems thinking • Personal mastery • Mental models • Building shared vision • Team learning

Scientific Management

Following on the heels of McCallum in the late 1880s came Frederick W. Taylor, Henry L. Gantt, Frank Gilbreth, Lillian Moller Gilbreth, and Harrington Emerson. These individuals were the first to apply scientific methods and objective analysis to study the way work was organized on the factory floor. It is easy to see how scientific management developed from its precursor, systematic management. The battle cry of scientific management was efficiency.

Frederick W. Taylor (1856-1915) was interested in what he called soldiering, or workers restricting their output. His studies led to the conclusion that workers engaged in natural soldiering, the tendency to take it easy on the job, and systematic soldiering, the conscious effort of workers to produce at an output level considered acceptable by the group of workers. Taylor's work resulted in four practical outcomes on the factory floor:

- Scientifically determining the most efficient process for doing a job, such as shoveling
- Matching the most well-suited worker to the task
- Paying workers on a piecework basis to motivate them to produce

- Developing specialized management knowledge (multiple supervision) for different parts of the task

Taylor's work laid the foundation of concern for motivating workers — developing a "we are in this together" mentality among workers and managers — and of process mapping to discover ways to improve processes.

Henry L. Gantt (1861-1919), a protégé of Taylor, is remembered primarily for Gantt charts, planning and scheduling tools that use bar charts. He also expanded on Taylor's work on output and motivation. He suggested using a day-rate-plus-bonus wage system rather than a piecework system. Gantt believed that workers needed the security of a minimum daily rate without the threat of a penalty, plus the potential for a bonus if they exceeded the daily quota. He also built in a bonus system for foremen based on the output of each individual worker and all the workers as a whole.

Frank Gilbreth (1868-1924) and Lillian Moller Gilbreth (1878-1972) are probably remembered most because of the book and movie *Cheaper by the Dozen*, which was co-written by two of their 12 children. This book detailed the application of their time and motion studies to running a large household. Along with producing and raising 12 children, Lillian Gilbreth, the first woman in the United States to receive a doctorate in psychology, collaborated with Frank on studies of motion and fatigue. She continued the work for more than four decades after his death.

Among the lasting contributions of the Gilbreths to the practice of management were the focus on eliminating wasteful and unproductive movement and the concept of the three-position plan of promotion. This plan was designed to attract and retain the best employees by having them prepare for the next higher position and train a successor while performing the job for which they were hired. This plan also allowed for the creation of a master promotion chart for the organization.

Harrington Emerson (1853-1931) continued the study of efficiency and formalized his thoughts in the book *The Twelve Principles of Efficiency*. Emerson's work is most notable for its emphasis on ideas, rather than land, labor, and capital, as the means to wealth. This sounds remarkably similar to the words of today's concept of knowledge management.

Scientific management or operations research has continued to develop through the years with the application of scientific tools and techniques to the practice of management. For example, today managers use mathematical models to aid in decisionmaking. The scientific tools and techniques being used include decision theory, experimental design, game theory, information theory, inventory control, linear programming, probability theory, queuing theory, replacement theory, sampling theory, simulation theory, statistical decision theory, and symbolic logic.

Universal Theory or Administrative Theory

The theory of the universality of management (late 1880s through the early 1900s) claims that management skills are transferable to any industry or business. In practice, this means that a manager possessing excellent managerial skills could be put in charge of any group or any company, regardless of the technical basis of the industry. Management skills, then, are more important than technical skills for those running an organization or department. Henri Fayol (1841-1925), a French mining engineer, was the main advocate of this theory. In 1916, he published the book *General and Industrial Management*, which presented a general theory of management. His theory consisted of three main propositions:

- Management is universal; all managers perform the same basic functions.
- A set of flexible and adaptable principles or guidelines exist that all managers can follow.
- The five elements or functions to management are planning, organizing, command, coordination, and control.

Fayol's book was not translated into English until 1930, and it was not readily available in the United States until 1949. Much like W. Edwards Deming, Fayol received more attention outside his country than within it. His elements of management have stood the test of time, and they are still widely regarded as the cornerstones of management practice.

Behavioral Theory

The behavioral theorists of the 1920s and 1930s argued that people and human relations should be the focus of organizational theory. In some ways, behavioralists were reacting to the impersonality of the time and motion studies and the emphasis on efficiency of the scientific management theorists. The behavioralists thought that meeting the social needs of workers was a key determinant in workers' productivity. These researchers focused on the people side of the organization, and they applied psychology to industrial problems. The key to productivity was thought to be linking physical and mental qualifications with ideal psychological conditions of work, as well as providing optimal motivational influences. Two of the lasting ideas of the early behavioralists and industrial psychologists were the concept of working with, not under, someone, and the influence of the employees' social needs on their on-the-job behavior.

Elton Mayo (1880-1949) conducted the famous Hawthorne studies at the Western Electric Company in Chicago between 1924 and 1932. In the initial design of the experiment, workers were observed and their output was measured when they had worked under differing intensities of light. After getting perplexing results, Mayo and his colleagues ran additional experiments in which variables, such as wage rates, rest breaks, length of workday, and so on, were manipulated. Each time, when they returned to longer workdays and no rest breaks, output increased. Eventually, they concluded that the workers' output was influenced by the special attention they had been given by the researchers and test room observers. These experiments led to the coining of a now commonly used term, the *Hawthorne effect*, which refers to the idea that outside observers bias an experiment through their involvement.

The human relations movement was an outgrowth of these experiments. It represented a dramatic shift in management thinking toward an emphasis on providing for the social needs of workers.

Organization Theory

The German sociologist Max Weber (1864-1920) is the father of organization theory. The central unit of analysis for Weber was the total organization. The negative connotations surrounding the term *bureaucracy* must be set aside to understand Weber's contention that adherence to his model would lead to the ideal organization, the height of efficiency. His model of bureaucracy outlined five key elements for managing large-scale operations:

- A clear division of labor and development of specialization
- An explicit chain of command
- A formally established system of rules and regulations to govern decisions
- Objective decisionmaking, devoid of sentiment by decision makers
- Employee selection on the basis of technical qualifications, advancement through achievement, and/or seniority

Other organizational theorists criticized Weber's model because it ignored the informal side of the organization. In the 1930s, Chester Barnard (1886-1961) argued that an organization must be effective and efficient to be successful and that the function of management is to keep the organization running. He identified three management functions: providing a system of communicating, securing the essential services of individuals, and formulating and defining organizational purpose. Barnard's book, *The Functions of the Executive*, which was published in 1938, expanded on the often conflicting tasks of management to be both efficient and effective.

Herbert Simon (1916 -), another organizational theorist, described an organization as a decision-making structure in which policies, procedures, and hierarchy circumscribe the individual's decision-making scope.

In organization theory, the thoughts of the efficiency experts and the behavioralists become intertwined.

General Systems Theory

General systems theory (GST) became a major school of thought in the 1960s and early 1970s. Ludwig von Bartalanffy (1901-1972), the founder of GST and a biologist, believed a theoretical framework could be established and applied to all disciplines. He sought to identify parallels among disciplines and to integrate the parallels into one general systems theory. According to this school of thought, each discipline is a system within an environment. Inputs into the system are processed and provide outputs to the environment. Feedback loops provide a means of control, adjustment, and correction. Systems are either open or closed to varying degrees.

While the concept appears to be somewhat abstract, systems thinking is the basis for many modern innovations, including supply chain management, management information systems, matrix organization design, and the planning-programming-budgeting system.

Contingency Theory

The contingency theorists of the 1970s argued that there are no universal prescriptions in management. Rather, each specific situation should be assessed and the optimal principle applied. This approach focuses on the flexibility and adaptability of the manager to apply the correct management principle depending on the circumstances. Recent researchers have focused on trying to identify which principles work best in which circumstances.

Excellent Companies or Best Practices

Two books published in the 1980s, *In Search of Excellence*[22] and *A Passion for Excellence*,[23] attempted to identify commonalities among successful companies that might explain their success. Successful U.S. companies were identified from financial returns and a record of innovation over a 20-year period. Attributes of excellent companies were identified as:

- A bias for action, or the ability to take effective action due, in part, to a successful informal communication system
- Closeness to the customer, or an ability to listen to and learn from customers and respond with quality, service, and reliability
- Autonomy and entrepreneurship, or an organizational tolerance of failure and a system that designates individuals as champions of products and ideas
- Productivity through people, or the belief that people are an organization's best resources
- Hands-on, value-driven management, or managers who talk to those in functional areas
- Stick to the knitting, or staying focused on central skills or core competencies

- Simple organizational form and lean staff
- Simultaneous loose and tight properties, or strong central direction with maximum individual autonomy

Thomas J. Peters and Robert H. Waterman's research method described in *In Search of Excellence* is similar to that of best practices benchmarking in that both approaches concentrate on identifying attributes of excellence. For example, Shell Oil participated in a benchmarking study conducted by A.T. Kearney that identified three best practices that Shell used as the basis for their Total Procurement Process initiative. These were:

- Strategic procurement
- Rationalizing the supply base
- Measuring supplier performance[24]

The development of these three initiatives resulted in many savings, such as total cost improvements of more than $3 million through the efforts of a cross-functional team for control valves and reduced total travel costs of more than $2 million through competitive agreements with two airlines, leveraged hotel business, and a more competitive supplier for rental cars.[25]

The Center for Advanced Purchasing Studies (CAPS) conducts industry- and government-wide benchmarking studies of the purchasing function. From these studies, efforts are being made to identify best practices for specific purchasing processes.[26]

Management by Objectives

In many organizations, Management by Objectives (MBO) has become an operating management philosophy. MBO seeks to link activities, performance metrics, and rewards to the strategic goals and objectives of the organization. Chapter 2 of this volume deals with strategic planning and the links between the levels of planning in the organization. Although the term has occasionally been misused, the basic concept embodied in the MBO literature of recent years can be used effectively in evaluating and improving the performance of individuals. When properly implemented, the MBO concept can:

- Produce specific realistic objectives toward which each individual works. This typically results in more effective job performance and more extensive professional development for each individual.
- Require extensive involvement of each individual in the establishment of his or her objectives. When properly done, this results in the development of more meaningful objectives for each individual. At the same time, it produces a stronger commitment by the individual to attempt to achieve the objectives.

The basic steps for conducting an MBO program as the basis for performance planning and evaluation activities are:

1. **Define responsibilities and prepare the job description** – Each individual reviews, modifies, and updates his or her job description. After the initial effort, this procedure typically involves give-and-take discussions with the supervisor until a mutually acceptable decision is achieved.
2. **Establish individual objectives** – After the individual and the supervisor agree on the details of the job description, the individual is asked to plan how he or she will accomplish the results necessary to fulfill the job responsibilities. This requires the establishment of specific objectives within a specific time schedule. The planning typically addresses a period of six months or one year.
3. **Agree on objectives** – After the preliminary preparation of the objectives has been accomplished, the individual discusses the tentative plan with his or her supervisor. During the discussions, the role of the supervisor is that of questioner, developer, and counselor. During the process, it is important for the individual to feel that the resulting objectives are his or hers, and at the same time, agreement is needed between the supervisor and the individual concerning the objectives established.
4. **Establish evaluation criteria** – It is important that the individual and supervisor jointly determine in precise, quantifiable terms what checkpoints and criteria will be used in evaluating progress toward achievement of the objectives. Typical criteria include project due dates and formats, cost/profit figures, and the com-

parison of performance with historical trends or other performance levels within the organization.

5. **Compare performance to the plan** – The individual and his or her supervisor review the performance and compare it with the plan (or standard). Performance must be evaluated as objectively as possible in light of objectives and expectations established in the prior planning process. From the results of this planning and evaluation process, subsequent plans can be developed to move toward further achievements in terms of both departmental and individual progress.

Motivational Theories

The extent to which a manager is successful in motivating and developing employees depends largely on his or her skill in creating an operating environment that elicits voluntary dedication and the desire to excel among departmental employees. An effective human resources manager involves employees in decision-making processes in an attempt to create a harmonious blending of individual and departmental objectives.

As a basis for creating such an environment, it is important for a manager to understand the basic factors that motivate individuals, as well as the relationship between motivation and ensuing behavioral patterns. The three major schools of thought that emerged to explain motivation and its relationship to performance are the following:

- Content theory, which focuses on the needs of the individual
- Process theory, which focuses on the variables that influence and motivate behavior
- Reinforcement theory, which focuses on the influence of consequences on behavior

Maslow's Hierarchy of Needs

One of the most well known and widely accepted theories, content theory, was developed by Abraham Maslow (1908-1970). His theory, Maslow's Hierarchy of Needs shown in Figure 4.7, holds that the satisfaction of basic human needs, in varying degrees, produces certain, somewhat predictable, behavior patterns. Physiological and security needs are more basic and concrete than the other needs. On the other hand, social, esteem, and growth needs are abstract and more difficult to recognize. Maslow suggests that each lower-order need must be at least partially fulfilled before the next higher-level need becomes dominant in terms of an individual's motivation.

FIGURE 4.7
Maslow's Hierarchy of Needs

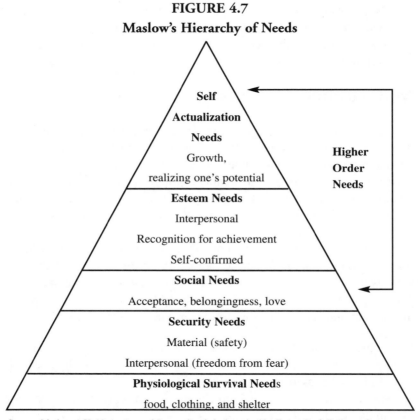

Source: Maslow, A.H. *Motivation and Personality*, 3rd ed., revised by Frager, R., J. Fadiman, C. McReynolds, and R. Cox, Harper Collins, New York, 1987. Reprinted by permission of Harper Collins Publishers, Inc.

In practice, assuming that concrete needs are reasonably fulfilled, purchasing managers should attempt sequentially to provide satisfaction first for each employee's social needs, then his or her esteem needs, and finally his or her growth needs. Progressive satisfaction of each of these types of needs tends to produce a higher and more positive level of motivation.

Herzberg's Hygiene-Motivation Theory

A related and somewhat more application-oriented theory of motivation was developed by Frederick Herzberg (b. 1923) and his associates during the 1950s. Herzberg's Hygiene-Motivation theory (sometimes called the *two factor theory*) separates motivational factors into two categories: those intrinsic to the job and those extrinsic to the job.

According to this theory, for most people the major sources of job satisfaction — and hence motivation — stem largely from the work itself in the form of intrinsic job-related rewards. These rewards include achievement, recognition, responsibility, personal growth, and advancement. An individual gains these rewards (typically in a developmental sequence) by good job performance.

Extrinsic factors that exist outside the job are not thought to be motivators in a positive sense. Factors such as working conditions, pay, relations with co-workers, supervisory style, and organizational policies tend to be "dissatisfiers" if they do not exist at an acceptable level. Most people expect a minimum level of satisfaction with respect to these peripheral elements of their working environment. However, beyond this threshold, enhancement of these extrinsic factors does not turn them into "satisfiers," which produce a stronger positive motivation. Hence, Herzberg calls them *hygiene* factors. Figure 4.8 shows Herzberg's two-factor theory.

FIGURE 4.8
Herzberg's Two Factor Theory of Motivation

Satisfiers	Dissatisfiers
Achievement	Job Security
Recognition	Status
The work itself	Company policies
Responsibility	Working conditions
Advancement	Supervision
Personal growth	Personal life
	Interpersonal relationships
	Salary

Source: Killen, K.H. and J.W. Kamauff, *Managing Purchasing: Making the Supply Team Work*, Irwin Professional Publishing, Chicago, IL, 1995, p. 209-210.

McClelland's Achievement Motivation Theory

David C. McClelland (1917-1998) also focused on the needs of the individual. He identified three needs that motivate human behavior, the needs for power, affiliation, and achievement. Individuals exhibit some degree of need for each of these, but in varying degrees. For example, a person with a high need for achievement would be driven by the need to reach his or her goals. A person with a high need for affiliation would be driven by the desire to form social or interpersonal relationships. And a person with a high need for power would derive satisfaction from being in charge and in control.

From a managerial perspective, an assessment of employees along these lines may help a manager determine the types of activities that individual employees might perform best, the work environments that might be most conducive for success, and the rewards that might motivate each employee.

Expectancy Theory

Another approach to understanding employee motivation, the expectancy theory, has more recently been suggested by Victor H. Vroom, Michael E. Porter, and Edward E. Lawler. Expectancy theory is a process theory that finds that an individual's course of action will be guided by two factors:

- The importance or value attached to a successful outcome of the action
- The individual's assessment of his or her ability to achieve a successful outcome of the action

Hence, this common sense concept holds that people will select alternatives that they believe to be both attainable and highly rewarding.

Equity Theory

Another process theory of motivation is equity theory. Equity theorists argue that the motivation level of employees is determined by how fairly or equitably they believe their work is judged in comparison to others. Each employee will make this assessment, and the outcome (positive or negative) will impact job motivation and performance. The original equity theory focused on pay, but other variables have been included in recent research.

Reinforcement Approach

The reinforcement approach to motivation is based on B.F. Skinner's work on operant conditioning. The basic concept is that individuals will be motivated to continue behavior if the consequences are favorable, and they will be motivated to stop or alter behavior if the consequences are unfavorable.

Measurement and reward/incentive programs are applications of the reinforcement approach to motivation. Incentive programs are means of sharing the benefits of cost reduction and other financial improvements with those who helped to achieve them. For the supply management function, incentive programs may be designed to reward and motivate employees of the function and/or suppliers to the organization. Performance measurement is discussed in greater detail in Chapter 5.

Management Styles

The views that managers hold about the theories of motivation, and about people in general, influence the management styles they develop and employ. The application of certain theories of motivation produces a related management style.

Frederick Taylor, discussed earlier in this chapter for his soldiering concepts, is generally accorded the distinction of being the father of scientific management. In studying the elements of work and job design at the turn of the century, Taylor observed that the output of individual workers increased as their jobs became more specialized. Removal of the elements of planning and control, as well as some peripheral operational elements, permitted the individual to become more proficient at the core job activities and, hence, to become more productive. Subsequently, the concepts of functional job specialization and detailed job supervision became accepted as a basic management technique. When carried beyond a certain point, however, functional specialization can produce repetitive, monotonous, and at times, "demotivating" jobs.

In recent years, this traditional approach has been tempered or supplemented with a variety of human-centered (as opposed to job-centered) approaches. Among these are Douglas McGregor's Theory X and Theory Y, William Ouchi's Theory Z, and the team concept. The following sections discuss these theories.

Theory X and Theory Y

In the 1960s, Douglas McGregor (1906-1964) developed his widely known "Theory X-Theory Y" approach to management. McGregor found that many managers who employed the traditional approach treated their subordinates as though they were lazy, uncreative, undisciplined, and generally not interested in doing a good job. He called these characteristics Theory X assumptions about the nature of people. In the work environment, Theory X assumptions tended to lead to an autocratic, close-supervision style of management.

In contrast to Theory X, McGregor proposed another set of assumptions — Theory Y — that he believed to be more consistent with the underlying nature of most people. Theory Y assumes that:

- Work is a natural activity, just like recreation and rest.
- Under appropriate conditions, most people tend to accept and to seek responsibility.
- Creativity and imagination are possessed to a reasonable extent by a large number of people, but these skills are not fully utilized in most jobs.
- Most people naturally take pride in what they do, and consequently they want to do a good job if they think the job is worthwhile.

McGregor holds that managers who believe Theory Y assumptions will employ a participatory management style that is designed to involve subordinates actively in the planning/operating/controlling process. The result should be greater development of individuals' capabilities and greater fulfillment of individuals' personal goals for self-actualization, according to McGregor.

Theory Z

In the early 1980s, William Ouchi conducted an intensive study of major Japanese companies to identify the management characteristics that contribute significantly to their success. He found one common thread running throughout the fabric of Japanese management. Virtually all Japanese firms employ a companywide managerial philosophy that is built around an overriding concern for individual employees and managers. The extensive use of quality circles and other techniques of participatory management may appear to the Western observer to represent an extension of the Theory Y concept. However, Ouchi calls the Japanese approach Theory Z, because it successfully integrates the achievement of personal goals of employees with the collective goals of the organization. Four key elements characterize this type of management:

- Long-term employment
- Slow but steady advancement to higher-level positions
- Shared decisionmaking at all levels of the organization
- Intense individual loyalty to the organization

As noted earlier in this chapter, one's management style can assume two broad orientations: an employee (human) orientation or a job (production) orientation. Few managers use a style that focuses completely on one orientation or the other. In daily operations, most managers employ a mix of the two orientations, depending on their commitments concerning the nature and motivation of their subordinates. Additionally, as the type of job and working environment change, a perceptive manager will vary the management mix to suit the circumstances at hand. One management style that attempts to meld the human orientation with the job orientation is the use of teams.

Teams

The focus on teamwork has received such widespread attention in the past 20 years that it may be hard for some to comprehend that as early as 1945 Elton Mayo (famous for the Hawthorne studies) wrote about the importance of groups in *The Social Problems of an Industrial Civilization.* Mayo was interested in methods of understanding the behavior of groups, whether the groups were formally organized and recognized by management or self-constituted, informal organizations.[27]

Today, many organizations use teams to accomplish organizational objectives. The supply management function is no exception. New product design teams, process improvement teams, source selection teams, and system implementation teams, to name a few, may include team members or team leaders from the supply function. Some purchasing teams include only purchasing department staff members, while others may include personnel from other functions in the organization (cross-functional teams) and/or suppliers. For example, at Shell Oil a cross-functional team reduced the total cost of ownership of personal computers by more than 25 percent by consolidating purchases with two major suppliers, decentralizing buying decisions to the department level, implementing electronic ordering, and establishing a dedicated PC support group.[28]

Regardless of its composition, a team is made up of a collection of people who work or function together in varying degrees to achieve a common goal. Variations on the team concept range from informal teams to highly structured teams to self-directed teams. The team concept is also discussed in Chapter 5.

Informal Work Groups

Within every formal organization, one or more informal groups will exist. Typically, these groups are fairly small and structured informally around the specific interests of their members. They may be social groups, special-interest groups, or sometimes pressure groups pushing for change. Whatever the case, informal groups are an integral part of the organization, and their attitudes and actions can either assist or hinder the attainment of objectives.

A wise manager uses the potential influence of informal groups in a constructive manner. To do this, the manager must first recognize the existence of such a group and identify its leader or leaders. Then, by practicing the concepts of open communication and group involvement in the decisionmaking process, the manager should attempt to align the objectives of the informal group with the objectives of the department. This represents an extension of the participatory management strategy employed in dealing with individuals and formal work groups within the department and organization. Specific approaches that can be used include:

- Solicit appropriate input on decisions that affect individuals and the informal group through individual, committee, and brainstorming techniques. Use this input to arrive at group-oriented decisions whenever possible.
- Create and develop a work climate and a reward system that encourage teamwork and cooperation.
- Develop informal group cohesiveness that produces a positive influence on the activities of the formal work group.

The manager's goal in using this integrative approach is to promote cooperation among the various groups, formal and informal, in the daily activities that contribute to attaining the department's overall objectives.

Formal Teams

Formal teams are made up of individuals who are designated as members. The following sections examine various aspects of formal teams.

Cross-Functional Teams – Organization's assemble cross-functional teams for many reasons, including product quality improvement; process improvements; sourcing; evaluating and selecting suppliers; or new product development.

Self-Directed Teams – Using self-directed teams is a concept in which groups supervise themselves, rather than relying solely on traditional supervisory management.

Team Building Process – The team building process begins when the need or reason for creating a team is identified. Then clear, compelling, and worthwhile goals or objectives that can only be accomplished by a team need to be established. Team bonding, or the identification of and commitment to individual roles and responsibilities, is essential. The team must have effective leadership in order to succeed, and there must be interdependence among team members to accomplish goals. The team must be supported and empowered by management and receive prompt, effective feedback on both individual and team performance. Chapter 5 discusses some of the approaches to evaluating and rewarding team performance.

Many team initiatives have been implemented in purchasing departments over the past few years. They often are designed around projects to reduce costs, conduct value analysis, acquire capital equipment, or generally, improve the operation. Such processes involve looking at new problem-solving techniques as well as becoming aware of the personality profiles of team members, because each team member must accomplish work through the other members of the team.

Team Characteristics – Diversifying team membership by including persons of different backgrounds, races, and both genders may enhance team performance by broadening the scope of ideas and providing opportunities to historically under-represented groups. This topic is discussed in Chapter 5.

Benefits of Cross-Functional Sourcing Teams – In 1993, the Center for Advanced Purchasing Studies published a study of cross-functional sourcing teams conducted by Robert Monczka and Robert Trent at the Eli Broad Graduate School of Management at Michigan State University. The researchers collected data from 107 cross-functional sourcing teams at 18 U.S.-based companies. Results from the study included benefits and limitations of cross-functional sourcing teams. The greatest benefit of sourcing teams was found to be the ability to bring greater knowledge and skill together.[29] Figure 4.9 shows the primary benefits of cross-functional sourcing teams as reported by survey respondents.

FIGURE 4.9

Cross-Functional Sourcing Team Interaction Benefits

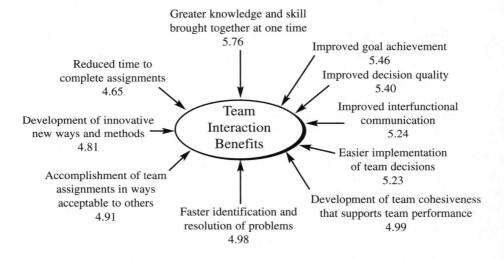

N=621 team members   Scale: 1=Not a benefit
                                                  4=Marginal benefit
                                                  7=Major benefit

Source: Monczka, R.M. and R.J. Trent, *Cross-Functional Sourcing Team Effectiveness*, Center for Advanced Purchasing Studies, Tempe, AZ, 1993, 21.

Limitations of Teams – The CAPS study on cross-functional sourcing teams also identified the following potential limitations to cross-functional team effectiveness:[30]

- The team has no real power or authority to make major decisions.
- The team has little insight into how well it is performing over time.
- Managers outside the team attempt to control activities or influence decisions.

- Certain members dominate team meetings or control team activities.
- Commitment of resources does not meet performance requirements.

These limitations can be minimized or eliminated if teams are set up correctly, with attention paid to team composition, team training, and the culture of the organization supports team activities.

Group or Team Leadership

Leading a group or a team of any size requires the skills and attributes described by Chris Chen at the beginning of this chapter, namely the ability set direction, align people, and motivate and inspire them. Leaders empower others to work together to achieve the vision of the organization.

Empowerment includes being empowered (creating power for oneself), giving empowerment (helping others grow toward a state of empowerment), and working toward an empowering environment (giving power to other groups to benefit the organization). For empowerment to work, there must be a vision of where the organization needs to go as well as a strategy for getting it there. Managers need to delegate more, and employees must have more control over daily and future work. Implementing empowerment requires background work, preparation of all of the people involved, careful training, and the development of interpersonal skills, incentives, resources, and action plans.

The CAPS study, *Cross-Functional Sourcing Team Effectiveness*, identified five factors that critically impact team performance:[31]

- The availability of organizational resources
- The participation and involvement of suppliers, when required
- Higher levels of internal and external decisionmaking authority
- Effective team leadership
- Greater emphasis on team assignments

Key Points

1. Three major changes in the way the supply function is managed include a focus on continuous improvement, the creation of lean organizations, and the application of emerging technologies and knowledge management.
2. There are distinct differences between being a leader and being a manager. Attributes of leaders include setting a direction, aligning people, and motivating and inspiring them. The attributes of a manager include planning and budgeting, organizing and staffing, providing supervision, and problem solving.
3. The concept of "parity of authority and responsibility" calls for managers to match the responsibility they confer on subordinates with an equal granting of authority to carry out the responsibilities.
4. Advances in information technology have created an Information Age in which knowledge and knowledge management are keys to competitive advantage. Empowered employees with access to key information are able to respond quickly and effectively to changing customer requirements.
5. Scientific management or operations research has developed through the years by applying scientific tools and techniques to the practice of management.
6. The views managers hold about theories of motivation, and about people in general, influence the management styles they develop and employ. The application of a certain theory of motivation produces a related management style.
7. Teams are a collection of people from diverse backgrounds with different areas of expertise who work together to achieve a common goal. Teamwork is vital to the achievement of many purchasing objectives, such as new product design, process improvement, source selection, and system implementation.

Questions for Review

1. Under what circumstances is a managerial response required? When are leadership skills more appropriate?
2. Why are lean management behaviors becoming necessary to meet competitive pressures? What characteristics of lean behaviors distinguish them from other types of behaviors?
3. What essential elements are needed to create employee empowerment? How does empowerment demonstrate the principal of parity of authority and responsibility?
4. What is the meaning of the term knowledge-related work? How has information technology created the need and the opportunity to replace task-related work with knowledge work?
5. Can managers motivate individuals and teams in the same way? What methods of motivation would be most appropriate for individuals? What methods would be most appropriate for teams?
6. How could Maslow's Hierarchy of Needs be used to determine appropriate incentives for team performance?
7. What are the differences among management theories X, Y and Z? Under what circumstances is each appropriate to guide the behavior of a groups?

Endnotes

1. Kotter, J. "What Leaders Really Do," *Harvard Business Review*, May-June 1990 (found in C. Chen."Managing and Leading," *NAPM Insights*, April 1, 1995, p. 5).
2. Chen, C. "Managing and Leading," *NAPM Insights*, April 1995, p. 5.
3. McClenahen, J.S. "CEO of the Decade," *Industry Week*, November 1999, www.industryweek.com.
4. Nelson, D., R. Mayo, and P.E. Moody. *Powered by Honda: Developing Excellence in the Global Enterprise*, John Wiley and Sons, New York, 1998, p. 145.
5. Nelson, Mayo, and Moody, 1998, p. 145-146.
6. Kaizen Institute, "What is Kaizen," www.kaizen-institute.com.
7. Vos, J. and G. Dryden. *The Learning Revolution*, Jalmar Press and Innerchoice Publishing, Carson, CA,1999.
8. Womack, J.P. and D.T. Jones. *Lean Thinking*, Simon and Schuster, New York, 1996, p. 23.

9. Wendy's International, Inc., "Wendy's Announces Strong December and Fourth Quarter Sales," www.wendys.com.
10. Wendy's International, Inc., *1998 Annual Report*, "Domestic Operations," p. 9.
11. "Briefings on Adverse and Sentinel Events," Medical Risk Management Associates, Opus Communications, Marblehead, MA, July 1999, www.sentinelevent.com.
12. Womack, J.P. and D.T. Jones. *The Machine That Changed the World*, Simon and Schuster, New York, 1990.
13. Womack and Jones, 1996, p. 15.
14. Womack and Jones, 1996, p. 15.
15. Womack and Jones, 1996, p. 43.
16. Womack and Jones, 1996, p. 10.
17. Stevens, T. "Winning the World Over," *Industry Week*, Nov. 15, 1999, www.industryweek.com.
18. Stevens, 1999.
19. Thurow, L.C. Building Wealth: *The New Rules for Individuals, Companies, and Nations in a Knowledge-Based Economy*, HarperCollins, New York, 1999, p. xv.
20. George, C.S. *The History of Management Thought*, 2nd edition, Prentice-Hall, Englewood Cliffs, NJ, 1972, p. 108.
21. George, 1972, p. vii.
22. Peters, T.J. and R.H. Waterman, Jr.. *In Search of Excellence*, Warner Books, New York, 1982.
23. Peters, T.J. and N. Austin. *A Passion for Excellence*, Random House, New York, 1985.
24. "Total Procurement Process – An Overview," Supply Chain Management, Shell Services Company, p. 7.
25. Shell Oil, p. 7-8.
26. Center for Advanced Purchasing Studies (CAPS), www.capsresearch.org.
27. Mayo, E. *The Social Problems of an Industrial Civilization*, The Andover Press, Andover, MA, 1945, p. viii.
28. Shell Oil, p. 6.
29. Monczka, R.M. and R.J. Trent, *Cross-Functional Sourcing Team Effectiveness*, Center for Advanced Purchasing Studies, Tempe, AZ, 1993, p. 21.
30. Monczka and Trent, 1993, p. 23.
31. Monczka and Trent, 1993, p. 7.

CHAPTER 5

SELECTING, RECRUITING, AND RETAINING PERSONNEL

How can managers find and keep good people?

Chapter Objectives

- To describe the process of determining position requirements and writing effective job descriptions to attract highly qualified individuals
- To discuss the skills and attributes most desirable in candidates for supply management positions given the changing role of the function
- To identify the types of professional development opportunities available to supply personnel
- To review legal issues that should be considered when hiring and firing employees

Creating a Learning Organization

Peter Senge, author of *The Fifth Discipline: The Art and Practice of the Learning Organization*, defined a learning organization as one "where people continually expand their capacity to create the results they truly desire, where new and expansive patterns of thinking are nurtured, where collective aspiration is set free, and where people are continually learning how to learn together."[1] According to Arie De Geus, head of planning for Royal Dutch/Shell, "The ability to learn faster than your competitors may be the only sustainable competitive advantage."[2] What does this mean for an organization when it comes to developing hiring policies, interviewing job candidates, or making promotion decisions? If an organization is only as good as the people who work for it, then identifying the skills and abilities required for each position in the organization, as well as determining the type of person who will fit into the organization's culture, can be a daunting task. The changing nature of the purchasing and supply function, and the increasing role and demands placed on the people in the function, has altered the skill sets required for rapid learning and, hence, for success.

Issues in Selection and Recruitment

This chapter addresses the process for determining the requirements for personnel in different areas of supply management, and it discusses the specific skill sets that most progressive purchasing/supply organizations are seeking. This chapter will provide valuable insights for purchasing and supply professionals to use in planning and managing their careers.

Position Requirements

A departmental organization plan should serve as the blueprint from which all employee selection activities are developed. Careful consideration must be given to the goals and objectives of the organization when determining individual roles and responsibilities. From these individual roles and responsibilities, job descriptions can be created. It is important to look not only at today's needs but also at future requirements. This will help to pinpoint the specific duties and responsibilities each job entails, any unusual working conditions involved, and any specific qualifications and characteristics required of the person holding the job. The latter determination focuses on the skills, abilities, knowledge, training, experience, and personal qualities necessary to perform the job satisfactorily. While practices differ from organization to organization, most organizations condense all of these characteristics and qualifications and include them in a written job description for each job.

While numerous job titles and positions exist in purchasing and supply management, one approach to categorizing these jobs is to establish a hierarchy of positions. This hierarchy may be based on the duties and responsibilities, the level of decisionmaking authority, and the scope of the position in terms of supervisory or managerial oversight. Job descriptions should reflect the different levels of the hierarchy. For example, the chief purchasing/supply officer may hold one of the following titles: vice president of purchasing, or strategic sourcing, or supplier management, or procurement. In the appendix at the end of this chapter are sample job descriptions of a vice president of purchasing position, a director of purchasing a global commodity manager, a sourcing manager, and a senior buyer position.

A review of these sample job descriptions indicates the differing levels of responsibility and focus (strategic versus operational) and the corresponding qualifications (education and experience) for each position.

Knowledge, Skills, and Attributes of Applicants

In A *Skills-Based Analysis of the World-Class Purchaser*, published in 1999 by the Center for Advanced Purchasing Studies (CAPS), a world-class purchaser is defined as:

> an individual who visualizes and approaches his or her job from a strategic perspective in dealing with the supplier firm-purchaser firm-customer linkage. This individual continually embraces and leverages his or her skills and knowledge of critical supply chain activities to provide value in meeting organizational and customer objectives.[3]

Along with this definition, the author identified eight broad skills common to world-class purchasing and supply professionals:

- Interpersonal communication
- Team skills and facilitation
- Analytical problem solving
- Technical competence
- Computer literacy
- Negotiation aptitude
- Education and professionalism
- Continual learning[4]

These eight skills are covered in the following sections.

Interpersonal Communication

Interpersonal communication appears at the top of many lists of desired attributes for employees in general and supply management professionals in particular. Job Outlook '99, a national forecast of employers' hiring intentions published by the National Association of Colleges and Employers (NACE), found that good communication skills are the top personal quality sought by employers evaluating job candidates. "Employers must look beyond good grades and the right technical skills to judge the potential success and effectiveness of a job candidate within their organizations," said Camille Luckenbaugh, NACE manager of employment information.[5]

The interest in the interpersonal communication skills of job candidates has been addressed in three CAPS publications. The 1993 CAPS *Training Report* identified communication as one of the top 10 skills for purchasing and supply professionals. The 1998 CAPS study *The Future of Purchasing and Supply: A Five- and Ten-Year Forecast* identified relationship management skills as vital. The 2000 CAPS study *A Skills-Based Analysis of the World-Class Purchaser* ranked interpersonal communications as the number one skill required of world class purchasers.[6]

The emphasis on interpersonal communication represents a shift from transaction-oriented communication to communication that optimizes relationships with others (suppliers and customers).

The American Express worldwide procurement group conducts two-day visits at various locations around the world to focus on its internal customers and suppliers. On the first day, the supply group meets with 20 to 30 internal customers to present its global strategic initiatives. Then, the internal customers are asked to critique the strategy to identify how the supply group is (or is not) creating value. The supply group must have well-developed listening skills and an ability to take criticism. Following the critiques, the supply group works as a team to incorporate the internal customers' wants into its strategy. On the second day, the supply group visits local suppliers to communicate changes in strategy and negotiate expectations and desires. Within 24 hours of meeting with suppliers, the supply group presents the results of those meetings to the internal customers. "At this point, we're really putting it all together, combining the customer wants with the suppliers' abilities and making sure all parties are informed and satisfied," said Joseph Yacura, former senior vice president of worldwide procurement at American Express. "We won't accomplish this if we can't communicate well with those groups."[7]

Team Skills and Facilitation

Teams are a way of life in many organizations. According to the CAPS 1999 study on the skills of world-class purchasers, learning to serve as a team leader, team member, or team facilitator is critical to the success of a purchasing and supply professional. Well-developed presentation skills are also essential to working in teams, because presenting one's ideas to others is part of the team process. In the previous example, the supply group at American Express needed strong team skills to be able to work quickly and effectively at integrating internal customers' needs and wants into the procurement strategy.

An organization's managers must decide how teams will be used and how they will be structured. Figure 5.1 shows a continuum of control for teams, from hierarchically driven to self-directed. If team members are going to work in a self-directed team, they must receive appropriate training from the organization before embarking on a self-led project.

FIGURE 5.1
Structure Control Continuum

Hierarchically Driven Teams				Self-Directed Teams
1	2	3	4	5
Specific tasks and methodology defined by management; team membership based on balance of power.		Some ability to define tasks and methodology, but structure is permission-driven. Team members are interested in preserving the position of the functions they represent.		Vision and desired outcome provided by management; strategy and tasks decided by team. Members' primary concern is achievement; accountability is to the team.

Source: Aranda, E.K. and L. Aranda with K. Conlon. *Teams: Structure, Process, Culture, and Politics*, Prentice-Hall, Upper Saddle River, NJ, 1999, p. 5. Reprinted by permission.

According to Roger M. Schwarz, author of *The Skilled Facilitator*, group facilitation is a process in which an outside person intervenes to help a group improve the way it handles and solves problems and makes decisions, thus increasing the group's effectiveness.[8] An outside facilitator must be acceptable to all members of the group, be substantively neutral, and have no decisionmaking authority. According to Schwarz, a team member can adopt the skills of a facilitator to act as a *facilitative leader* who focuses attention on the group processes used to solve problems and make decisions. Figure 5.2 shows the differences in the role of a facilitator and a facilitative leader. Developing facilitative leaders who possess the skills of a facilitator, and creating the core principles and values necessary for open, free communication, is a challenge for team-based organizations.

FIGURE 5.2

Differences between Facilitators and Facilitative Leaders

Characteristic	Facilitator	Facilitative Leader
Group membership	Third party	Leader of group
Involvement in substantive issues	Substantively neutral	Deeply involved in substantive issues
Use of expertise	Process expert	Content and process expert
Decisionmaking authority	No	Yes

Source: Schwarz, R.M. *The Skilled Facilitator*, Jossey-Bass Publishers, San Francisco, 1994, p. 252. Reprinted by permission.

Analytical Problem Solving

Analytical problem solving refers to an individual's ability to apply basic problem-solving techniques to analyze any type of problem, reach a decision, and act on that decision. The basic steps in problem solving are to identify the problem, determine its importance and urgency, analyze the problem quantitatively and qualitatively, generate alternatives, compare alternatives to a set of decision criteria, make a decision, and develop and carry out an action and implementation plan.

Being *analytical* refers to the ability to identify and gather relevant information; to synthesize, compare, and interpret such data in light of the problem; and to recognize relationships, issues, obstacles, and opportunities in the process of generating alternative courses of action. A problem solver is one who can take this analysis (whether self-generated or provided by someone else) and select an appropriate course of action. Decisions are rarely made in an atmosphere of complete information or complete certainty. Being decisive means being able to recognize when enough information is available and enough analysis has been done to make a decision. The ability to act on the decision rounds out the process. It is difficult to find individuals who can conduct the analysis, make the decision, and implement or oversee the implementation of the decision.

Technical Competence

For the supply professional, technical competency refers to the ability to understand and use technical information. Possessing the knowledge relevant to a process, organization, commodity, or position enables the individual to communicate with technical specialists.

At Glaxo Wellcome, a research-based pharmaceutical company, acquiring technical competency is part of the training process for purchasing professionals. For example, Glaxo Wellcome has outsourced reprographics. The employees who manage the supplier relationship "have become experts in photocopiers, including market dynamics, cost, and technical issues. But even more, they're being trained on [the] development and manufacture of paper. They know what types of trees are being planted and harvested for production; they've been to the paper mills."[9]

Computer Literacy

Computer literacy refers to the level of facility an individual has with different types of hardware, software, and systems. Supply chain management is largely driven by the ability to manage information within and among organizations. Information technology is an essential tool in the growth of the supply chain management concept. According to David L. Oppenheim, manager of supply chain processes at the Cessna Aircraft Company, "Best practices equal information; information equals technology; and technology equals computer literacy."[10]

While many organizations seek individuals who already know how to use their systems, in the long-run it is more important for individuals to be able to quickly become proficient with any hardware, software, or system. The computer is merely the tool. The supply professional's talent lies in possessing the ability to identify relevant information in a format that will facilitate decisionmaking.

Negotiation Aptitude

The skills of expert negotiators have become more important as the management philosophy of compliance and control gives way in many organizations to a philosophy of empowerment, shared control, and commitment on the part of individuals and teams. In the supply arena, managing relationships with key suppliers is an ongoing process of influencing, persuading, and resolving conflicts. An important area in negotiation training for supply professionals is cost-based negotiations.

"There is a misconception about win-win," said Bradley J. Holcomb, vice president of supply chain management and chief procurement officer for American Precision Industries, Inc. "People mistakenly believe that there is a softness to it — that you have to play to the other person. It's actually more like tough love. The bottomline is being truly competitive, and it doesn't do either party justice to be soft on anything."[11]

Education and Professionalism

The CAPS study, *A Skills-Based Analysis of the World-Class Purchaser*, identified education and professionalism as hallmarks of a world-class purchasing professional. The form that these attributes will take for an individual depends on the nature of the industry and requirements of the company in which he or she works. Some organizations may require formal education at the bachelor's or master's level. Many large technical manufacturers seek individuals with a master of business administration (MBA) degree, an undergraduate degree in engineering or business (supply chain management is a plus), and four to eight years of experience. Others may be satisfied with a professional certification, such as NAPM's Certified

Purchasing Manager (C.P.M.) or Accredited Purchasing Practitioner (A.P.P.) designation as evidence of educational attainment in the field. Other organizations may require specific training in engineering, marketing, chemistry, and so on, depending on the nature of their industry. A technical degree may be required if a company is engineering-driven, if everyone in top management has an engineering degree, and if the routes to higher levels of management require technical proficiency. At American Express, the training budget for each individual is increasingly used to develop the consultation and analysis skills needed by purchasing personnel.[12]

Continual Learning

An individual's commitment to continual learning reflects a perspective that focuses beyond merely acquiring skills on an as-needed basis. It reflects a desire and drive for continuous personal improvement. Chapter 4 covers theories of motivation, such as Maslow's Hierarchy of Needs, and management styles that may contribute to the development of employees who are committed to continual learning. Identifying, hiring, and retaining individuals who are committed to continual learning is critical for organizational success in a rapidly changing business world. Identifying these individuals can, however, be a difficult process.

The Recruiting Process

The process an organization uses to recruit new hires can take several forms, depending on the level of the positions to be filled and the speed with which it must fill these positions. Campus recruiting, search firms, and internal and external job postings can be used to solicit résumés from potential hires.

For entry-level positions in purchasing and supply management, many organizations require a bachelor's degree, often in purchasing and supply chain management or another area of business. Building a strong campus presence through on-campus recruiting, participation in career fairs, and involvement with faculty and student professional associations can result in a steady flow of newly educated talent in entry-level positions. Developing a summer internship program or a six-month co-op program for continuing students can allow an organization to check out potential hires and take advantage of hard-working, talented temporary help.

Mid-level and higher-level positions, or positions requiring a more strategic sourcing orientation, may lead a hiring manager to campuses to look at MBA candidates who have several years of work experience. Also, hiring managers may work through a search firm to find working professionals interested in changing positions. The demand for highly qualified supply professionals is so great that many hiring managers are finding that it is takes months of diligent searching and very competitive packages to attract the best candidates.

References, Experience, and Training

Reviewing the references, experience, and training of job candidates is essential in creating a short list of people for personal interviews. The résumé is usually the first step in the process. Today many organizations, including college and university career services offices, manage Web résumé books. For example, at Arizona State University, Tempe, all on-campus recruiting is coordinated online. Students post résumés, view the recruiting calendar, and submit résumés to employers, all online. Employers can view résumé submissions and select interview candidates online, view résumés that students have included in the Web résumé book, and post job opportunities on an online job board that is accessible to all registered students.

Desired skills, attributes, and education and experience levels should be established for each position at the time the job posting is written. For example, Appendix 5-A includes a job description for a senior buyer position, and identifies the skills and education required for the position.

Questions in the Interview Process

Recruiters may take a number of different approaches when interviewing a potential new hire. These approaches include behavioral interviewing, case study responses and discussions, team interviews, and problem-solving exercises. The type of questions asked and the way in which they are posed should be driven by a clear purpose. The interviewer should be aware of the types of questions that are inappropriate, and possibly illegal, to ask job candidates. For example, interviewers should never ask about an individual's marital status, number of children, or plans to have children. Questions must be relevant to the job. For example, if a job requires extensive travel, this information should be provided in the job description. An interviewer should not assume that a working mother would be unable to meet the travel demands of the job. It would be inappropriate to pursue a line of questioning regarding children and child-care arrangements. However, an interviewer could ask the candidate about his or her interest and willingness to travel and about past jobs that involved traveling. Interviewers should check with their human resources professionals regarding the legality of specific questions.

The following section[13] provides sample questions that might be asked in an attempt to determine a candidate's skill level for each of the eight areas identified by the 2000 CAPS skills analysis study. These questions are not intended to be all-inclusive.

Interpersonal Communication

- What writing achievements are you most proud of?
- What are some of the most difficult writing assignments that you have been given or taken on? Explain.
- Describe how you go about preparing for written or oral presentations.
- Do you prefer to communicate verbally or in writing? Why?
- Tell me about a situation when you weren't clicking with a person on your team and what you did about it.
- Give an example of a time when you were able to successfully communicate with another person who may not have liked you.
- Tell me about a time when you had to use your oral communication skills to get a point across that was important to you.

Team Skills and Facilitation

- Give an example of a time when you felt you were able to build motivation in your co-workers or teammates at work.
- What did you do in your last job to contribute to a teamwork environment?
- Tell me about a time when there was a conflict in your team and how the team handled it. Explain your role in the situation.

- Have you ever led a team of people who did not report to you? How did you gain their commitment? How did you motivate them?

Analytical Problem Solving

- Describe a situation in which you had to do a great deal of analysis to make a decision.
- Describe the courses or training programs you have taken that deal with research and data analysis.
- How do you determine when you have gathered enough data to make a decision?
- Tell me about a time when you had to be relatively quick in coming to a decision.
- Provide an example of a time when you had to use your fact-finding skills to gain information to solve a problem. How did you analyze the information to come to a decision?

Technical Competence

- Describe your level of involvement in budget preparation or financial analysis.
- Tell me about your approach to cost analysis when making a purchasing decision.
- Tell me about courses or training programs you have taken that increased your technical knowledge and/or skills in any area.
- Tell me about a time when you didn't understand something technical that related to your job and what you did about it.
- Describe the process you usually go through to get up to speed technically with a new supplier, commodity, or process.

Computer Literacy

- Describe your level of computer literacy.
- Tell me about the computer courses or training that you have attended.
- Tell me how you use computers on a regular basis.
- Describe a time when you have used computers to help you analyze and solve a problem or to analyze and present data.
- How do you go about using a new software package?

Negotiation Aptitude

- Give an example of a situation in which you had to negotiate an agreement. Did you reach a win-win agreement?
- What steps do you go through when you find you are in a situation involving conflicting interests and you must get something done or make a decision?
- How do you know if an issue or item is negotiable?
- What steps do you take to persuade someone?
- What was the best idea you ever sold to your boss? Why did he or she buy into it?

Education and Professionalism

- Why did you/didn't you attain a professional certification in your field?
- What have you done most recently to increase your knowledge or ability in a job-related area?
- What is your plan for the next six to 12 months as far as your personal training and development?

Continual Learning

- Are you satisfied with your current level of training and education? Why or why not?
- To what extent do you think training and professional development is driven by the organization and not the individual?
- What magazines, newspapers, trade journals, or online sources do you read regularly? How does this help you on the job?

Organizational Hiring and Human Resources Policies

Most organizations establish policies for hiring and for managing human resources. The organization's mission and strategic plan should drive these policies, like all organizational policies. Policies provide parameters. A broadly defined policy gives the decision maker greater latitude than a narrowly defined policy. For example, if an organization's hiring policy is to diversify the work force, human resources managers and hiring managers will be expected to take actions that will lead to a larger pool of applicants from diverse populations and a larger number of new hires from diverse backgrounds. If, on the other hand, the hiring policy restricts a hiring manager to promoting from within the organization, the hiring manager has fewer options at his or her disposal.

For example, the following is General Mills' statement about its commitment to diversity:

> General Mills is committed to establishing and growing an increasingly diverse employee and supplier base. Fulfilling this commitment is important to our shareholders, our increasingly diverse consumer base, the communities in which we operate, and ultimately, the success of our company.... We will hire and develop the best people — people who are winners; who meet every challenge with flexibility and fast decisionmaking, ever-striving to exceed past accomplishments.... At General Mills, "diversity" involves recognizing, understanding, and respecting all the ways we differ. Diversity encompasses human differences, such as gender, race, nationality, education, style, functional expertise — just about anything and everything that can make a person unique. At General Mills, we not only accept individual differences, but we actively leverage the unique capabilities and perspectives of individuals for competitive advantage. General Mills fosters diversity internally, through our Employee Networks for people of color, women, and gays/lesbians; with our Mentoring Program for people of color; and through various training and development workshops for employees and managers.[14]

Issues in Employee Promotion

It is important for the management of an organization to have some means of identifying employees with promotion potential, as well as a plan for grooming those individuals for greater levels of responsibility or for higher positions in the organization. In many organizations the number of layers of management has been reduced, and there are fewer rungs on the ladder. As a result, fewer slots are available for employees with managerial capability. This creates a dilemma for an organization whose management wants to retain its best people. Developing lateral moves with increasing responsibilities, challenges, and rewards is essential to retaining the best and the brightest. Management may also have to accept that certain individuals or categories of individuals may not be long-term employees. For example, hiring someone with an MBA degree may be desirable, but it may be realistic to expect that employee to stay for only four or five years before he or she will have peaked in the organization's hierarchy.

Developing solid promotion practices and communicating those practices to all employees can eliminate much of the confusion and anger that the promotion process can generate in an organization. For instance, an organization may require the attainment of a professional certification as the first step in career advancement. Linking the organization's training program and training requirements to specific jobs and job levels can make it clear to everyone what the basic body of knowledge is for the different levels of authority in the organization. In some organizations, promotions always come from within the ranks of the company, thereby signifying to current employees that career advancement is possible. Other organizations take the opposite approach; they fill management slots from the outside in an effort to cross-fertilize from other companies and industries. The behavior of employees will be driven by the approach that an organization takes.

Standards and Professional Certification

The National Association of Purchasing Management (NAPM) has been offering a certification program for supply management professionals for more than 25 years. The Certified Purchasing Manager (C.P.M.) certification consists of a four-module exam (along with other requirements). Two of the modules also apply to the Accredited Purchasing Practitioner (A.P.P.) program, which was designed for those in non-management-level positions in supply management. The exam requirements for these certifications will change on Jan. 1, 2001. Contact NAPM for the current requirements.[15]

Attaining a certification level (either A.P.P. or C.P.M.) requires commitment and a dedication to professional development. The payoff makes it worth the effort. Figure 5.3 gives a profile of people who are currently certified.

FIGURE 5.3
Profile of Certified Purchasing Managers

CATEGORY	
Annual salary range	$25,001 to 85,000
Average for men	$69,300
Average for women	$52,800
Title	Manager of Purchasing/Supply
Purchasing authority	$500,000 to $10 million
Education	32% bachelor's degree 28% graduate degree
Average number of employees at the organization	More than 200 (Total employing organization >900)
Years in purchasing	16 to 24 years
Gender	Male: 56% Female: 44%
Age	36 to 55

Source: National Association of Purchasing Management, 1998, www.napm.org.

Figure 5.4 provides more data on salaries for men and women with and without the C.P.M. certification. As more women attain advanced degrees in supply chain management and their tenure in the work force increases, it is hoped that the salary gap will close.

FIGURE 5.4
Salary versus Certification

	Average Salary (thousand $)	Average Salary (thousand $)	Highest Salary (thousand $)
Certification	**All**	**Men/Women**	**Men/Women**
C.P.M.	$65.5	$69.3/$52.8	$360/$180
Not certified	$52.2	$57.8/$41.1	$530/$214

Source: National Association of Purchasing Management, 1998.

Certification denotes professionalism and a standard of respectability. For individuals, certification can assure peer recognition, better job opportunities, enhanced value to the employer, and quicker professional advancement. For employers, certification provides evidence that purchasers have met professional standards and that they have the tools needed to do a good job. Using certification as a criterion for promotion may help employers establish sound requirements for knowledge acquisition and application, instead of loose, haphazard, or arbitrary promotion practices.

Career Advancement

Most purchasing departments are relatively small. In addition, low purchasing employee turnover can slow the advancement of personnel through the procurement ranks. Every purchasing department strives to hire and develop ambitious, promotable personnel to build a creative, management-oriented organization. However, not all entry-level and buyer jobs should be filled with individuals who will become readily promotable. Usually, there are not enough vacancies into which all employees can be promoted. When a person's job no longer offers a challenge, he or she may either become discontented and leave the organization or perform less effectively. For these reasons, it is essential that personnel be selected with care. During the hiring process, most managers attempt to match an individual's qualifications to the current and anticipated job requirements of the department. It is easier and less costly to address such issues before, rather than after, hiring has occurred. A properly trained purchaser is invaluable; a poor one is a liability.

Promoting from Within

Purchasing personnel at all levels are available either from within the organization or from external sources. When vacancies occur, the common practice in many organizations is to promote personnel from within the department or organization. Some organizations are committed to promoting from within the ranks of existing employees. The advantages and disadvantages of this policy are discussed in the following sections.

Advantages – Promotion from within produces several distinct benefits. First, the practice tends to keep morale high because employees know that they are not "trapped" in dead-end jobs. It stimulates individual performance by offering an avenue of advancement. Second, promotion from within reduces training costs. It entails a minimum of training because the individual's experience in the organization is generally pertinent to his or her new job.

Disadvantages – Promotion from within also can produce problems. One promotion may result in a chain of lower-level promotions that simultaneously move several people one step up the organizational ladder. If chain promotions occur frequently, the organization tends to lose stability because a large number of individuals are continuously learning new jobs. When a company is growing rapidly, this policy sometimes results in the promotion of people who are not ready to be promoted. The mediocre performance resulting from such actions compounds the problem of instability. Finally, promotion from within produces "inbreeding." If carried to extremes, it may stymie the flow of new ideas into the organization.

Recruiting and Hiring Outside Employees

A wise manager promotes from within when it is practical. When such actions tend to generate problems, however, personnel should be drawn from external sources.

Advantages – When a purchasing manager must go outside the department to find personnel, such personnel may be acquired from other departments within the organization or from outside the organization. Transfers from other departments within the same organization usually occur at lower levels and may produce significant advantages for the purchasing department. For example, the person transferred is familiar with the organization's operations and can usually assume full job responsibilities more quickly than a new employee. In addition, such a transfer brings experience in a related functional area into the purchasing department. A person coming from an important related area in the organization will have experience that may be useful in buying activities and may provide a liaison with user departments.

Hiring people from other organizations has considerable merit, particularly in the case of special staff and managerial jobs, because it brings new ideas into the organization. It also prevents the substituting of seniority for management ability.

Disadvantages – Hiring from outside the department or from outside the organization can also have a negative effect on morale and productivity within the department. If high-performing members of the department perceive new hires as a comment on their promotability, they may look elsewhere for advancement. Also, the ability of an outside person to implement change, and the speed at which change can occur, may be hindered if existing employees resist the outside person.

Succession Planning

Management succession planning refers to plans that organizations make for the replacement of their key executive personnel. Some organizations develop a management replacement chart. The chart lists, for each position in an organizational chart, the name of the current holder of the position and the names of one or two replacements for each position. Another method is to predict each individual's expected job in five years and at the end of his or her career.

Measuring an individual's ability to set and meet goals is one indication of his or her management potential. One way to measure goal attainment is to match opportunities provided to people with their record for accomplishing them. Chapter 4 of this volume discussed Management by Objectives (MBO), which focuses on goal attainment.

Determining Training and Development Needs

Organizations can take a number of different approaches to determine their training and development needs. The basic process should compare job requirements to the skills needed to achieve desired performance levels in each position.

Skills Assessment

To address its training and development needs, Deere & Company started by developing a mission statement for supply management and identifying the underlying assumptions about the supply function (see Figure 5-5).

FIGURE 5.5
Deere & Company Supply Management Function

Supply Management's Mission:

...to effectively and knowledgeably manage the business relationships and procurement practices of the company when interacting with the supplier base and those in the company having an interest in the procurement function.

Major Assumptions Representative of the Supply Management Function:

1. *Quality* must be a strategic priority for satisfying customer demand in the face of world competition.
2. Personnel with *diverse professional backgrounds*, many of whom will not have basic materials management understanding, will continue to fill staff assignments. Technical resources will continue to be utilized in supply management to lead Deere personnel in the areas of quality improvement, supplier selection, and new product development.
3. *Ethical* purchasing practices will continue to be a must in understanding and practice by everyone involved in the procurement function.
4. *Cost management* will play an integral role in all phases of the procurement activities. Supply management must establish an effective understanding of a supplier's costs and work to reduce these costs for our mutual benefit.
5. Cooperative *problem solving* relationships will continue to develop with both suppliers and multifunctional disciplines within Deere.
6. *Decentralization* of procurement will continue within the Deere organization. The Coordinated Supply Management program will continue with a greater emphasis by corporate in strategic input versus tactical support.
7. *CPS* will be the primary Deere purchasing system, and expanded use of *EDI* will be implemented by Deere factories to support our movement toward paperless systems.
8. *Analytical skills* will play a significant role in dealing effectively with commodities, markets, and individual suppliers.
9. The *global marketplace* will require further knowledge, flexibility, and sensitivity in our procurement activities.
10. Supply management will play an increasing role in the company's *strategic decisions*.

The team then developed a supply management skills requirement list to reflect the competencies needed to function within the three levels of responsibility in supply, as an employee, as a supervisor, and as a training coordinator. The skill requirements identified represent four key areas: administration, interpersonal, analytical, and commercial.

From this skills requirement list, profiles were developed for supervisors, analysts, buyers, and expediters/schedulers to assist the purchasing department in personnel selection, assessment, development, and career planning. Figure 5.6 lists the skills requirements for supply personnel at Deere & Company.

FIGURE 5.6
Deere & Company Supply Management Skills Model and Recommended Education and Training Curriculum

I.   ADMINISTRATIVE SKILLS

- Planning and Strategic Development
- Project Management
- Supply Base Management and Development
- Contract Development and Administration
- Time Management

II.   INTERPERSONAL SKILLS

- Effective Communication
- Negotiating Skills
- Business Ethics
- Professional Development
- Leadership Skills/Team Building
- Problem-solving Skills

III.   ANALYTICAL SKILLS

- Accounting/Microeconomics/Financial Aspects
- Business Math/Statistics
- Material Management
- Cost and Price Analysis

IV.   COMMERCIAL SKILLS

- Macroeconomics
- Business Law
- Risk Management
- Industrial Processes
- Transportation Basics
- Quality
- International Supply Management
- Supply Management Methods and Practices
- Legislative and Social Responsibility
- Supplier Certification

Job Analysis and Diagnostic Evaluation

Some organizations develop a diagnostic tool to target the specific training and development needs for their purchasing personnel. The diagnostic program typically begins with a job analysis that identifies the important tasks of the organization's purchasing department. Next, each participant is given a diagnostic test that measures his or her comprehension of the basic tasks surveyed in the job analysis. Then participants are compared to norms to determine their strengths and weaknesses in the various purchasing tasks. Finally, the results of the job analysis and the diagnostic evaluation are combined to create a customized training program that targets the areas that are important to the organization but have yet to be mastered by individual staff members. In this way, training programs are designed to maximize the performance of the personnel in the most efficient way possible.

Gap Analysis

Gap analysis refers to measuring the difference (and distance) between the actual skill level of an employee and the desired skill level for the employee's job position. The Deere & Company example uses the width of gaps and the importance rating of the skill to determine training priorities. Figure 5.7 shows a sample gap analysis profile for a supervisor at Deere & Company. The information in the profile is displayed as follows:

Weight =   Average degree of importance to the job. (1 = least, 5 = most)
x   =   Average response for recommended competency to perform the job
o   =   Average response for perceived skill level of today's
            supply management staff
Priority = Difference between o (perceived skill level) and x
            (recommended competency), multiplied by the average
            weight assigned to skill

This profile can be used by an employee and his or her supervisor, in conjunction with performance appraisals or coaching and counseling sessions. The profile allows the employee to conduct a self-assessment of current skill levels. Next, the employee and his or her supervisor establish an action plan providing opportunities, both in training and on-the-job experiences, to enhance the skills consistent with the employee's current position. The profiles also can serve as a discussion tool for supervisors in explaining how skill requirements differ for other job assignments.

FIGURE 5.7
Deere & Company Supply Management Skill Requirements Profile

Supply Management Skill Requirements Profile
perceived skill level vs. recommended competencies
company average - survey 1993

_____Supervisor   Date_____

Supply Management Skills	* Basic 1 2 3	* Intermediate 4 5 6	* Advanced 7 8 9

WEIGHT	ADMINISTRATION		PRIORITY
4.6__	Strategic Development	. . O---------------------------X . .	11.35
3.9__	Project Management	. . . O-------X . . .	7.03
4.3__	Supplier Development	. . . O-----------------X . .	8.96
3.5__	Contract Administration	. . O--------------------------X . .	9.09
4.2__	Time Management	. . O-------------------------------X .	7.83

	INTERPERSONAL		
4.6__	Effective Communication	. . . . O----------X .	10.11
4.1__	Negotiating Skills	. . . . O---------------X .	7.19
4.3__	Business Ethics	. . . . . OX .	8.03
3.9__	Professional Development	. . . . O----X . .	7.16
4.4__	Leadership Skills	. . . O---------------X . .	10.26
4.3__	Problem-solving Skills	. . . O-------------------X . .	8.04

	ANALYTICAL		
3.2__	Accounting/Microeconomics	. . O----------------------X .	5.51
3.1__	Business Math/Statistics	. . O----------------X . .	5.50
3.4__	Materials Management Systems	. . . O-------------X . .	5.63
4.2__	Cost and Price Analysis	. . . O----------------X . .	8.06

	COMMERCIAL		
3.0__	Macroeconomics	. . O---------------X . .	6.32
2.9__	Business Law	. . O--------------------X. .	4.29
__ __	Risk Management		
3.4__	Industrial Processes	. . O--------------------X . .	6.06
3.3__	Transportation	. O---------------------X . .	6.57
4.2__	Quality	. . . O-------X . .	6.62
3.3__	International Purchasing	. O------------------------ X . .	6.50
3.9__	Purchasing Practices	. . O----------------X . .	7.16
3.0__	Legislative/Social Responsibility	. O----------------------X . .	5.75
2.0__	Supplier Certification	. . O-----X . .	2.47

STEP 1
* Weight = Degree of importance 1 to 5 (1=least to 5=most)
STEP 2
* Basic = Understanding of key principles and functions in repetitive situations.
* Inter = Having a depth of knowledge and skills and being able to function in a broad range of moderately difficult situations.
* Adv = Having a broad and deep understanding and skills and being able to function in complex, varied situations. A model of subject matter mastery and skills.

Designing and Planning Training Programs

Once the training needs have been determined, the organization must decide how to provide the training that will achieve the desired results. For example, if a new purchasing procedure has been implemented, the purpose of the training may be simply to teach the new procedure. If the procedure is carried out on a computer, it makes sense to provide the training on a computer to ensure that trainees can, in fact, accomplish the procedure.

Competency-based training is driven by the idea that training should result in trainees knowing how to do something specific. For managers and developers, the key training issues involve the following:

- To The specific skills trainees should acquire
- To How the skills should be taught
- To How results can be measured

Documenting Training and Development Expectations and Resources

The documentation of expected competencies and the resources available to train personnel in the skills needed to achieve the competencies are the responsibility of every purchasing department. New or untrained personnel may be overwhelmed with purchasing job requirements. Policy and procedure manuals provide them with information during and after their orientation and initial training. Procedure guides are especially useful where extensive details regarding routine operations are needed. These manuals, which are often maintained online for ease of access and revision, make supervision easier, define standard practices, ensure consistency of results, and aid in training.

Training, Cost Efficiency, and Measurement of Outcomes

The outcomes of training should be measured in behavioral and operational terms to determine the effectiveness of the training effort (including how trainees behave back on their jobs) and the relevance of the training to the organization's objectives. In this way, supervisors can assess the value of the training. Questions usually addressed when evaluating training programs are:

- Was there a change in knowledge, skills, and/or abilities related to purchasing effectiveness in the various participants?
- Were these changes due to the training?
- Are the new skills positively related to the organization's goals?
- Will similar changes occur for new participants in the training program?
- Was the training cost effective? Was it worth the expense to the organization? Could the same effect have been achieved with another less-expensive training mode?

To determine the answers to these questions, the techniques of educational research — tests, questionnaires, interviews, and experimental design — need to be employed by trained researchers. The evaluators should answer the preceding questions using objective, quantitative, and qualitative research methods that provide data for deciding whether to continue, discontinue, or modify a training program. Only in this way can supervisors make an objective, informed assessment of a training mode.

Initial Job Training or Functional Orientation

Employee orientation involves the introduction of the new person to the job and the organization. The applicant will receive some information about his or her new job during the hiring process, but this is usually a superficial introduction. The new employee will need a more formal and complete orientation. An employee will want to know what is expected of him or her on the job. This will help eliminate possible future problems. An orientation program should be designed to relieve the employee's feelings of insecurity in a new environment. The employee should be told about the organization's history, products, services, and operations. Such orientations often include formal instruction and use personnel manuals, employee handbooks, and tours. Usually, the human resources department runs orientation programs, but the new employee's supervisor will also play a major role. Today many organizations provide orientation materials via an internal Web site.

Because a new employee is expected to achieve a desired level of productivity in a reasonable period of time, a certain amount of job training is inevitably required. There are four major approaches to initial job orientation: sponsor or mentor, functional rotation, learning-by-doing, and classroom training.

Sponsor or Mentor System

A commonly used practice involves the assignment of a sponsor (or a "buddy") to the newly hired person. After the supervisor has provided adequate initial orientation, the new employee is assigned a specific job in which he or she typically receives a certain amount of basic job instruction from the same supervisor. The bulk of the training load, however, rests with the individual's sponsor, who is an experienced employee who does similar work. The sponsor acts as an informal trainer during the period when the new person is learning the job. A sponsor should be chosen for his or her experience and, more importantly, teaching ability. The sponsor may require training as well to perform this role effectively.

This approach can be effective if the sponsor is a good teacher. It has the disadvantage, however, of restricting the new person's initial training to a single job. Some time may elapse before he or she realizes the implications of the activities of the job and how they relate to departments outside purchasing. Also, the time devoted to such training activities may significantly reduce the sponsor's productive output.

Functional Rotation

Many organizations modify the "buddy system" by adding an element of functional rotation training. Before a new employee is assigned to a specific job, he or she is considered a trainee for a period varying from several weeks to several months. Much of this initial training period can be spent in departments other than purchasing, such as operations, materials management, strategic planning, and finance. The idea is to expose the individual to a number of functional activities, both within and outside the purchasing area. This exposure will facilitate his or her understanding of the needs of various stakeholders in the organization and the relationship of purchasing to other operating functions. A typical program may include assignments in such areas as receiving and stores, purchasing records, expediting, assistant buying activities, inventory control, and selected line-production departments. Specific assignments vary depending on the person's background and on his or her first permanent job assignment. The program's objective is to develop a general understanding of the key processes in the organization. Upon completion of rotational training, the new employee is assigned to a specific job where he or she may receive further job training from a sponsor or from the supervisor.

Learning-by-Doing

The most basic method of training new employees is to give them general guidelines about what needs to be done and then to have the employees teach themselves the nature of the job. Many new employees learn their jobs through this process. Of course, this method cannot be employed in all instances, and it should be used with caution. A likely scenario for employing learning-by-doing is when the employee is already well trained or experienced in the work he or she has been hired to perform, and when no peer, supervisor, or training facilities are available as resources. In such a case, the new employee is left to his or her own devices and will have to rely on intuition and experience to understand how the job should be performed.

Classroom Training

In some organizations, initial job training consists of a series of brief classroom courses that cover the theoretical principles underlying the purchasing role and related tools and standard practices. Such programs prepare the new purchasing employee to do a better job, and they also aid him or her in establishing a rapport with personnel in related departments.

Continuous Professional Development

If a manager expects to use employees effectively over the long term, he or she must assume the responsibility for assisting and guiding them in the continued development of their capabilities. The determination of an individual's development needs is a product of observation and periodic counseling between the manager and the individual employee. These needs should be jointly determined, and plans for training should also be determined jointly for the ensuing six- to 12-month period.

Each employee can continue his or her professional development in two places, either on-site or off-site. On-site development can take the form of job rotation, on-the-job training, peer-to-peer training, and self-training. Off-site training can be in the form of classroom training, either for-credit or non-credit courses, site visits to other organizations, including suppliers, and self-training.

On-Site Professional Development Training

The following sections examine the common forms of on-site professional development training.

In-House Training Programs – Many organizations have in-house training programs that are provided by professional training departments, or they use outside groups, including NAPM and its affiliated local associations, colleges and universities, and the American Management Association (AMA). Organizations often combine on-site instruction, filmed lectures, case study work, and programmed instruction.

Job Rotation – Job rotation training can take several forms. As the name implies, it involves rotating the purchasing employee from one job assignment to another until the employee develops a reasonable competence in each of the jobs. The objective is to give the employee a wide base of skills that are useful to the purchasing function.

For example, a supply management professional might spend some time serving as a financial analyst, a materials planner, and a researcher or systems developer, before assuming full buying responsibilities. Buying assignments are often structured to provide an increasing scope and complexity of responsibility to build the individual's skills and confidence. If conducted wisely, this technique not only fosters the professional development of personnel, but it also provides buying flexibility within the department. Care, however, must be taken not to dilute technical buying competence by rotating buyers too frequently.

A second form of job rotation is functional rotation, discussed earlier in this chapter. It involves moving among different functions or departments (for example, purchasing, logistics, and operations) to ensure that the employee has a systems view of the supply management function. For example, the employee may spend time as a buyer, then rotate to logistics services to serve as a transportation analyst, and then move on to operations to serve as a production planner. Besides developing a more integrated understanding about the supply chain, the employee and manager may develop a better sense of where in the supply management process the employee could maximize his or her potential.

On-the-Job Training – Most on-the-job (OJT) training is conducted informally. It can be initiated by various members of the purchasing department in response to the manager's observation of needs among departmental personnel. Such training may simply consist of supervisory coaching for selected individuals. In other cases, it may take the form of periodic discussions among management and selected groups of personnel. Each session is conducted in seminar fashion and focuses on the exchange of ideas about relevant purchasing topics. On-the-job training may also include periodic lectures and demonstrations.

Another form of OJT practiced today is process analysis and improvement. After determining the need to improve a process and establishing the scope of the activity, a team is drawn from the individuals who are involved in the process. The process is mapped, and areas of potential improvement are identified. By participating in this improvement activity, employees create better methods that they can adopt and pass on to others. This can be an effective learning experience. Some firms periodically hire consultants to conduct workshops on such topics as value analysis, cost estimation, negotiations, and similar practical purchasing skills and techniques.

Apprenticeship training is a detailed form of on-the-job training that typically involves rotation between an employer and schooling. This is also called a co-op program by many organizations and schools.

Peer-to-Peer – Purchasing professionals can learn an enormous amount from their peers who have more training and experience in different areas. An atmosphere of cooperation and harmony (not competition) is necessary for such interactions to take place. This type of training may be formal or informal. As discussed earlier in this chapter, in a formal program, each new hire is assigned to a seasoned employee — a sponsor or mentor — who will guide and oversee the new hire's first few months on the job. In an informal environment, new hires and seasoned employees may operate with the understanding that they are there to help each other understand policies, processes, and procedures.

Experiential Learning – Experiential learning is based on performing hands-on activities while reflecting on what has been gained and what could be done differently next time. It is necessary to evaluate the experience not only from the standpoint of whether the results were as good as expected, but also from the standpoint of how the outcome differed from what was predicted and why it was different. As a result, regardless of the degree of success, there is an opportunity to learn from the experience.

Self-Training – As noted previously, responsibility for the recognition of specific training needs lies with the individuals and their supervisors. For this reason, much of a buyer's professional development is acquired through carefully directed self-training. Self-training takes many forms, but it commonly involves the following:

- Conducting purchasing and market research on the Internet
- Learning about a specific topic by watching or listening to CD-ROMs, videotapes, and audiotapes
- Studying purchasing periodicals, books, and research reports
- Studying selected business publications
- Studying trade magazines and special resource books on materials
- Attending purchasing association meetings and special commodity group meetings

Computer-Based Training – Computer-based training can take many forms, including one-way and interactive forms. The World Wide Web offers many opportunities for self-paced learning. Because so much information is available from so many sources, individuals must establish a clear scope and focus for their computer-based learning to be effective. Each individual must structure his or her own learning, because the learning process will not be led by a live instructor. Consequently, computer-based training is not effective for all learners. During the course of an individual's self-training, one of his or her manager's responsibilities is to help the individual balance the development of business skills with technical knowledge about materials. Both the manager and the employee are responsible for identifying skills needed for future performance and determining where and how the individual might acquire these skills.

Off-Site Professional Development Training

Often managers decide that the available on-site training does not meet the training needs of their employees. The organization may lack the resources to develop and conduct the appropriate level of training, to develop highly technical training, or to provide a diversity of ideas in a class filled with people from the same organization. Whatever the reason, many organizations send their employees to outside training programs. These include for-credit courses and non-credit courses taught in a variety of media.

For-Credit Courses – A growing number of colleges and universities offer degree programs in purchasing and supply management at the bachelor's, master's, and doctoral levels. The National Association of Purchasing Management Web site (www.napm.org) links to a current list of schools that offer degrees and certification programs in purchasing and supply management. Individuals often have the option of enrolling in university courses through evening programs, correspondence courses, or Internet-based courses. Many organizations now require at least an undergraduate degree for professional positions in supply management. The 1998 NAPM Membership Demographics report indicated that 69.3 percent of NAPM members had some type of college degree, up from 66 percent in 1995. Of the NAPM members with college degrees in 1998, 21.3 percent had graduate degrees.[16]

Non-Credit, Continuing Education Programs – Smaller organizations that lack the funds needed for formal, internally developed training programs often turn to outside agencies and programs, such as the Harvard Seminar Case Study Program and non-credit seminars offered by the National Association of Purchasing Management (NAPM) and the American Management Association

(AMA). Larger organizations may also turn to outside providers of training to expose their employees to colleagues from a variety of organizations. The content of these programs tends to be general in order to meet the needs of a broad scope of purchasing and supply participants.

NAPM offers numerous one- to three-day seminars around the country, as well as week-long programs in conjunction with a number of universities. For example, Arizona State University has been running a week-long purchasing management program in conjunction with NAPM for more than 30 years.

A growing number of seminars, workshops, and training programs are being offered through distance learning. *Distance learning* means that the learner accesses the class via the Internet rather than traveling to a classroom setting. The advantage to distance learning is that employees can structure the courses to fit their schedule, while interacting with participants from other organizations without the high cost of travel and time away from the job.

Site Visits to Organizations or Suppliers – Training for purchasing personnel should include visits to suppliers and leading organizations. These visits should be carefully planned to maximize the opportunity for learning. Before visiting a supplier, personnel should research the supplier's strengths and potential weaknesses. During the visit, data is collected by observation and interviews to corroborate earlier information or to provide added insights. From such visits, personnel learn about the suppliers' capabilities as well as the industry. With such knowledge, the individual can evaluate each supplier for potential business. A similar form of learning comes from gathering benchmark data and visiting the benchmark leading organizations to determine what best practices these organizations are using to achieve the benchmark results.

Professional Association Involvement – Another means of improving professionally is through active involvement in a professional association, such as a local affiliate of NAPM.

Management Development Training

In addition to developing their professional purchasing competency, individuals who show potential for future management positions must also develop general administrative and managerial skills. To move to a management position, an individual needs to develop an understanding of key stakeholders along with firsthand knowledge of products, key processes, and the employer's business in general.

With appropriate management guidance, an individual can develop such administrative and managerial skills through expanded self-training activities and practice. This often needs to be supplemented by formal training. Procurement management programs sponsored jointly by NAPM and leading universities are a significant management development opportunity. These programs are typically designed for experienced purchasers, and they involve one week of intensive study on a university campus. Program content typically focuses on management and decisionmaking concepts outside of, but related to, the materials and supply function.

Equal Employment Opportunity Laws and Regulations

During the 1960s and 1970s, legal and social changes influenced organizations' policies and practices in administering personnel functions. In effect, the federal government created an umbrella of regulations that apply to all of the personnel programs and practices discussed to this point. The major thrust has been directed at preventing discrimination. Key regulatory actions are the federal Civil Rights Act of 1964 (specifically Title VII), Executive Order 11246 in 1965, the Age Discrimination Act of 1967, and the Equal Employment Opportunity Act of 1972. Appendix A at the end of this book provides information on equal employment legislation.

Issues in the Termination of Employees

Consistent documentation and evaluation is the key to the ethical and above-board termination of employees. Employees should never be terminated on a "whim" or for vague, personal reasons. Generally, employees should be terminated for consistently poor performance, insubordination, serious violations such as theft, or chronic substance abuse. Employees should be given a reasonable amount of time to improve the poor performance or change their behavior (except, per-haps, in the case of theft). The reasons for termination should be doc-umented, and the employee should be notified that he or she is on probation prior to any termination action. Otherwise, the manager may leave the organization open for legal action by the employee.

Adherence to Established Processes

Most organizations have established procedures and documenta-tion requirements for ensuring that the termination of employees is handled as objectively as possible. These may include personnel poli-cies and procedures, union requirements, and due process. Due process refers to the rights of the individual regarding the adminis-tration of the law through courts of justice in accordance with estab-lished and sanctioned legal principles and procedures, and with safe-guards for the protection of individual rights. In the case of union employees and layoffs, union contracts usually specify that a work-er's right to be recalled after a layoff are based on seniority.

Outplacement

Many organizations offer some form of outplacement services, especially for employees whose positions have been eliminated by downsizing. Often an outside agency is hired to counsel former employees and assist them in moving on to other positions. In areas of the country where similar jobs are unavailable, outplacement serv-ices may focus on helping individuals identify transferable skills and find different types of positions that require those skills.

Exit Interviews

Exit interviews with employees who are leaving the organization can be a useful tool for gathering feedback about the organization's climate and culture. People leave organizations for many reasons. If employees resign because they perceive that there are better opportu-nities elsewhere, perhaps with a competitor, then an exit interview might provide useful information for the human resources planning process.

Key Points

1. Many believe that a learning organization will provide a significant competitive advantage.
2. Careful documentation of job requirements; individual knowledge, skills, and abilities; and training requirements will ensure effective organizational performance and minimize disputes.
3. The first step in training is to determine and clearly state the scope and the focus of the required learning. Training is then designed to meet these needs.
4. Standards are important to establish the abilities required for effective work performance and to establish the knowledge, skills, and abilities of the individual.
5. Three elements used to achieve the best training results are job analysis, diagnostic testing, and gap analysis.
6. Technology and other business changes are causing a dramatic increase in the need for general management and interpersonal skills in purchasing.
7. Managers must be cognizant of numerous legal boundaries affecting the proper handling of personnel matters.

Questions for Review

1. Why is it important to align functional tasks with organizational goals?
2. How do team facilitation skills enable greater supply management performance?
3. How have the required skills for purchasing professionals changed in the past decade? How are they likely to change in the next decade?
4. How does individual training and development contribute to retaining employees who make the greatest contributions to business results?
5. What role do standards play in defining organizational expectations and individual abilities? How is the documentation of job requirements and individual abilities important in assuring that employees meet expected performance standards?
6. Why has it been necessary to enact laws to guarantee fair and equitable treatment of employees?

Endnotes

1. Senge, P.M. *The Fifth Discipline: The Art and Practice of the Learning Organization*, Doubleday/Currency, , New York, 1990, p. 3.
2. Senge, 1990, p. 4.
3. Guinipero, L.C. "A Skills-Based Analysis of the World Class Purchaser," Center for Advanced Purchasing Studies, Tempe, AZ, 2000, p. 5.
4. Guinipero, 2000, p. 5-6.
5. "Employers Rate Communication Skills Number One," *Purchasing Today®*, March 1999, p 4.
6. Guinipero, 2000, p. 46
7. Duffy, R.J. "The Steps You Take, The Moves You Make," *Purchasing Today®*, July 1999, p. 39-40.
8. Schwarz, Roger M., *The Skilled Facilitator*, Jossey-Bass Publishers, San Francisco,1994, p. 4.
9. Duffy, 1999, p. 43.
10. Duffy, 1999, p. 44.
11. Duffy, 1999, p. 44.
12. Duffy, 1999, p. 44.
13 The sample interview questions were drawn from the following sources: Employee Career Enrichment Program, Department of Human Resources, Arizona State University; Arizona State University Career Services/Career Development Center; and *Performance Skills Dictionary*, Rocky Mountain Placement Conference, July 27, 1995.
14. General Mills, Inc., www.generalmills.com.
15. National Association of Purchasing Management, Certification, www.napm.org.
16. "NAPM Members and Education," *Purchasing Today®*, March 1999, p. 4.

APPENDIX 5-A

EXAMPLE JOB DESCRIPTIONS

Job Description, Vice President of Purchasing

Position Profile

The vice president of purchasing is responsible for the development and execution of a global sourcing strategy that supports the aggressive growth plans and efficiency objectives of the company. The position assumes responsibility for the director of purchasing and six senior buyers, as well as the director of sourcing and two source development managers. The company currently procures approximately $100 million per annum, across 150,000 bulk stock keeping units (SKU).

The vice president of purchasing reports directly to the chief operating officer and is a key member of the "operations steering team," which is comprised of other operations-related vice presidents and directors. This team meets quarterly to determine and manage the operational direction of the corporation. In addition, the vice president of purchasing is a member of a corporationwide, cross-functional team that meets regularly with the executive committee, as well as on their own, to offer input into corporate strategic planning and to perform budget and goal reviews. This position is based at the company's corporate center. Estimated amount of travel is approximately 30 percent.

Responsibilities

The responsibilities of the vice president of purchasing include the following:

- Develop and execute a global procurement strategy that supports corporate objectives.
- Create a unified purchasing group focused on reducing the "total cost of procurement," including on-time performance, quality,

ease of receiving, and reductions in supply chain inadequacies overall.

- Develop tools/reports to enable measuring/quantifying "total cost" as well as supplier performance.
- Improve relationships with suppliers by creating more alliances.
- Work as a key member of the cross-functional "operations steering team," and participate in the strategic direction as well as day-to-day execution of the organization's goals.
- Maintain a work environment that facilitates trust, creativity, teamwork, open communication, and employee participation. Motivate and encourage individuals to contribute to their full potential. Attract, select, develop, motivate, and retain high-caliber employees.
- Advance the skills and abilities of the purchasing group to enable team members to contribute more effectively within their individual product teams and overall.
- Assure that all local, state, federal, and international regulations are adhered to.
- Lead and manage by example.

Required Skills and Attributes

The required skills and attributes of the vice president of purchasing include the following:

- A four-year college degree in a related field, MBA a plus
- A minimum of 10 years of progressive management experience in global procurement, including developing and managing an aggressive global procurement strategy
- Experience with SKU-intensive purchasing
- Solid understanding of MRP, DRP, and ERP fundamentals
- Excellent communication skills – written, verbal, and interpersonal
- A progressive, proactive mentality, eager to embrace technology and modern management principles
- Strong analytical skills with great attention to detail
- Solid overall organizational and managerial skills
- A desire to achieve and assume more responsibility
- Ability to thrive in a team-based corporate culture

Job Description, Director of Purchasing

Position Profile

The director of purchasing focuses on the strategic direction of the purchasing department and the development and implementation of corporate policies and procedures. Specifically, this position partners with marketing (including industrial sales), sales, and manufacturing in understanding and implementing major programs and initiatives. The position focuses on cost reductions, supplier base consolidation, and improved supplier service.

The primary objectives of this position include competitive sourcing, supplier certification and management, contract negotiation, the legal aspects of purchasing, and system administration. The director reports to the vice president of purchasing and assumes responsibility for six senior buyers.

Responsibilities

The responsibilities of the director of purchasing include the following:

- Develop a strategic direction for purchasing in line with the company's strategic plan.
- Set and monitor favorable material price variance goals and activities.
- Develop, implement, and monitor appropriate purchasing policies and procedures.
- Oversee the training and career development of all purchasing employees.
- Develop, implement, and monitor a supplier selection and certification process.
- Provide data as needed for budget preparation, updates, and reporting.
- Maximize cash flow related to purchasing activities.
- Monitor data integrity in all systems.
- Negotiate key long-term contracts.
- Oversee domestic sourcing activities.

Required Skills and Attributes

The required skills and attributes of the director of purchasing include the following:

- A four-year college degree in a related field, MBA preferred
- A minimum of five years of progressive purchasing experience
- Experience with high SKU count
- APICS, CIRM, and/or CPIM or NAPM, C.P.M. certification
- Proven track record of inventory reduction and cash flow improvements
- Proven ability to work in cross-functional teams to exceed corporate goals and objectives
- Proven ability to work with third parties to develop, implement, and ensure the success of corporate and purchasing initiatives
- Forward-thinker with the ability to develop, implement, and monitor programs and initiatives for a customer-centered, growth-oriented company
- Strong analytical and problem-solving skills

Job Description, Global Commodity Manager

Position Profile

The global commodity manager crafts, coordinates, and implements the worldwide supply base strategies for a commodity category with $1 billion or more in annual spending. The manager works with the materials division senior leadership to ensure a shared vision and alignment with the overall business objectives. The manager is responsible for ensuring that the strategy for the category is specific, fact-based, comprehensive, consistent, well-communicated, and delivers superior financial returns and a competitive advantage to the business. In addition, the manager ensures that the strategy developed is dynamic and responds to market, customer, supplier, and company needs. This individual serves as the primary owner for the supplier relationship and drives supplier selection, development, and overall supplier management.

Responsibilities

The responsibilities of the global commodity manager include the following:

- Translate strategies and initiatives into measurable results with an impact on the bottomline.
- Develop team members' ability to contribute to bottomline performance.
- Develop tactical implementation plans and initiatives based on broad business strategies (markets, competition, customers).
- Provide linkages among the senior executive team, the operations steering team, and front-line employees.
- Attract, develop, and retain high-caliber people with growth potential.

Required Skills and Attributes

The required skills and attributes of the global commodity manager include the following:

- A bachelor's degree is required, and an advanced degree is preferred.
- Minimum of 10 years of increasingly responsible global supply chain management experience with industry background
- Sourcing experience in the commodity preferred
- Demonstrated success in change management and organization transformation within performance-oriented organizations
- Exceptional strategic planning and implementation skills
- Strong leadership and interpersonal skills
- A proven track record as an innovator and non-traditional problem solver

Job Description, Sourcing Manager

Position Profile

The sourcing manager works with business unit leaders to develop and implement regional strategic sourcing strategies for international requirements. The manager leads complex, international contractual negotiations, oversees supplier relationships, and serves as the primary liaison between the internal customer and the supplier senior management team for European, Asian, and South American strategic sources. The manager also participates in global best practice teams to align sourcing practices and build procurement competencies.

Responsibilities

The responsibilities of the sourcing manager include the following:

- Develop regional strategic sourcing plans for international requirements consistent with best practice supply chain objectives for Europe, Asia, and South America.
- Integrate with the existing RRD sourcing structure to deliver strategic sourcing plans.
- Develop recognition as global industry expert; maintain and communicate an understanding of competitive conditions in key markets.
- Dotted line responsibility for three to six people.

Required Skills and Attributes

The required skills and attributes of the sourcing manager include the following:

- Bachelor's degree or equivalent, MBA preferred
- A minimum of 10 or more years experience in supply chain optimization, international business management, supplier sourcing, price negotiation, quality improvement programs, and imports and exports
- Demonstrated sourcing experience in developing and maintaining best practice supply chains
- Experience working in at least one international market (Europe, Asia, or South America)
- Demonstrated excellence in negotiating complex contracts
- Strong communication and interpersonal skills
- Proven success leading cross-functional work teams and interacting with senior business leaders
- Excellent planning and organizational skills
- Global mindset. Willingness to travel globally up to 50 percent initially
- Foreign language skills, especially Spanish

Job Description, Senior Buyer

Position Profile

The senior buyer works in conjunction with suppliers and internal customers to assure a continuous supply of defect-free materials at the lowest total cost of ownership. The senior buyer performs analysis of current suppliers and potential new suppliers to ensure that company requirements are met. The senior buyer is responsible for assuring the cost-effectiveness of the operation and represents the purchasing perspective in meetings with other company departments. Related responsibilities include helping to manage inventories and maintaining market and technological awareness.

Responsibilities

The responsibilities of the senior buyer include the following:

- Develop requests for proposals, specifications, long-term agreements, and blanket orders for corporate products and services.
- Negotiate best overall terms and conditions under competitive and single-source conditions, while maintaining good supplier relations.
- Negotiate and coordinate the procurement of materials and services necessary to support the manufacturing schedule, taking into consideration the objectives of pricing, quality, leadtime, and inventory control.
- Manage activities between internal departments and the suppliers that produce the goods and services necessary to support the manufacturing schedule.
- Issue and approve purchase orders as required to procure production-related material as well as items required for maintenance, repair, and facility operations.
- Negotiate material pricing levels to support budget and standard cost goals.
- Communicate production planning and capacity planning to suppliers.
- Ensure material delivery requirements to support production.

- Monitor the quality of products purchased and communicate with suppliers.
- Coordinate supplier returns and the replacement of non-conforming material.
- Coordinate new model introductions with suppliers, including requests for quote, supplier selection, product approval, and product on-time delivery.
- Confirm material requisitions for correct bill of material information.
- Coordinate with production and inventory control to manage raw material inventory levels.

Required Skills and Attributes

The required skills and attributes of the senior buyer include the following:

- Bachelor's degree
- Three to five years experience, with a minimum of one year purchasing experience
- Ability to communicate effectively with internal clients and suppliers
- Good writing skills for documenting procurement transactions
- Ability to work independently, prioritize, and handle multiple tasks concurrently
- C.P.M. certification a plus
- Working knowledge of the SAP purchasing system a plus
- Ability to work well with others in a team environment
- Proficiency in Microsoft Office programs (Excel, Word) in order to provide professional communications to upper management as required

CHAPTER 6

OPERATING POLICIES, GUIDELINES, AND PROCEDURES

How can work flow be organized for maximum efficiency and effectiveness?

Chapter Objectives

- To identify the types of management controls used to monitor the progress of the supply function
- To demonstrate how policies and procedures are used to routinize tasks and ensure efficient and effective work flow
- To identify the skill sets required by purchasing personnel to achieve the operational and strategic goals of the organization
- To describe process reengineering and explain key areas of interest in reengineering purchasing and supply processes

Nature of Management Control

Management must control the activities of the organization. Most controls are financial in nature, and they form the basis by which progress is monitored. The planning process hierarchy starts with the overall objectives that the organization wants to achieve. These objectives are communicated to the functional units whose leadership must develop corresponding objectives for the unit to achieve. The next step is to create the policies that will guide all actions toward achievement of the objectives. Procedures — or the step-by-step actions and activities that move the operation toward fulfilling its objectives — follow from the policies. Finally, desk routines and forms or documentation are used to implement the procedures to accomplish the work. Figure 6.1 illustrates the flow of management control.

FIGURE 6.1
Flow of Management Control

Organizational Objectives

Departmental Objectives

Policies

Procedures

Desk Routines

Forms or Documentation

Activity

Three types of control mechanisms are considered: before-the-fact controls, during-the-fact controls, and after-the-fact controls.

Before-the-Fact Controls

Before-the-fact controls are measurable controls that are based on the budget, business plan, forecast, or established procedures that represent the formulation of plans for a specified future period of time. They establish a benchmark against which performance can be measured. Before-the-fact controls include budgets, plans (strategic, operational, and disaster), forecasts, policies, and procedure manuals, which are discussed in the following paragraphs.

Budgets – One of the more obvious ways to establish management control is through the organization's budgets. Funds are allocated to high-priority projects. Chapter 3 describes the different types of budgets used by organizations and the role each of these budgets plays in management control.

Plans – Business plans combine the budget process with the assessments of other areas, such as organizational mission, market penetration, market share, competitive analysis, staffing, and other managerial concerns, that affect the strength of the organization. The strategic and operational planning process is discussed in Chapter 1 of this volume.

Disaster Plans – Disaster planning is a contingency plan that is being developed more and more today. These plans serve the organization's needs in the event of earthquakes, hurricanes, major fires, and so forth. From a supply perspective, a disaster plan may include back-up suppliers to replace a usual supplier that is incapacitated in some way.

Forecasts – Forecasts generally relate to the demand for finished goods or services, but they also describe concerns for internal capacity and external availability of materials and services.

Policies – The management of an organization or of a department typically establishes policies to cover normal operating conditions. These policies guide the behavior of employees and standardize their responses to typical events. In this way, employees can rely on routine behaviors for most activities and develop customized ways of dealing with ad hoc situations.

Purchasing personnel must be sensitive to overall organizational policies as well as departmental policies, including policies from functional areas, such as safety, operations, quality assurance, and human resources, that may not be listed in the purchasing manual.

For example, General Mills, Inc., has the following corporate policy on diversity: "General Mills is committed to establishing and growing an increasingly diverse employee and supplier base. Fulfilling this commitment is important to our shareholders, our increasingly diverse consumer base, the communities in which we operate, and ultimately, the success of our company." [1] This corporate policy is carried out at the functional level by the Corporate Diversity Department, which has a full-time manager of supplier diversity.

Procedures Manual – A procedures manual details the specific actions to be taken to accomplish a given task. The manual establishes guidelines for achieving an organization's objectives and contains an organization's major procedures for easy reference by users.

For example, at General Mills the procedures for minority and women business owners to qualify for the supplier diversity program include the following steps:

- Completing a Supplier Profile Form
- Including a letter describing business capabilities
- Providing brochures and other marketing material
- Including a copy of certification by one of three designated bodies (a National Minority Supplier Development Council [NMSDC] regional council, a Women's Business Development Council, or a recognized governmental organization)

During-the-Fact Controls

During-the-fact controls relate to quality. Monitoring and measuring the task while it is occurring or before it is finalized allows the process to be adjusted to stay within the designated parameters. Industry standards are one way that during-the-fact quality controls can be exerted. International Organization for Standardization (ISO) 9000 standards and military specifications are two types of standards that relate to quality.

After-the-Fact Controls

After-the-fact controls measure performance so that it can be compared with planned benchmarks. This type of gap analysis provides information that can lead to improvements in processes, products, and services.

Audits – Audits are conducted to determine if the work performed mirrors the original intent. Generally, the auditor takes a sample of transactions and compares them to established benchmarks. The auditor usually reports his or her findings and leaves the development of conclusions to management.

Audits are performed to prevent problems, gauge system and process efficiency and effectiveness, and meet regulatory requirements.[2] Policies and procedures are critical, and auditing mechanisms determine if there are shortcomings within the policies and procedures. If the policies and procedures are sound, an audit may reveal whether personnel are adhering to them. For example, one company had a procedure requiring all software purchases to be coordinated with information resources. After a buyer purchased $12,000 worth of software that was incompatible with the network, it was revealed that the procedure was routinely ignored.[3] An audit may have uncovered this lapse in procedures before it cost the company money and the purchasing department credibility.

The following steps outline the auditing process using an example of an audit of a newly acquired operating unit or field office:

1. Determine the scope of the audit. The scope may be one procedure, such as adherence to proper dollar limits, or the entire process, such as an ISO 9000 system audit. A comprehensive audit of the acquired operating unit would probably be called for in order to determine the extent to which all procedures conform to those of the acquiring organization.

2. Determine how the results will be used. Before the audit begins there should be a clear understanding of who will see the results and how they will be used. Will the results be used to improve a process, to guide training, or to supplement employee reviews? How the results will be used will also determine who should be involved in the opening and closing audit meetings and who should receive the final report. In the case of the newly acquired operating unit, the audit results would be used to determine the changes needed, if any, to bring the operation into conformity with the acquiring organization.

3. Determine the standard. Because an audit measures performance against a standard, the standard must be established prior to the audit. A standard may be a procedure, a policy, a regulatory requirement, or an ISO requirement. In the example, the acquiring company's policies and procedures would be a suitable standard.

4. Determine what type of audit is appropriate. The three basic types of audits are the following:

   - An *internal audit* is performed by a person or a team of people from inside the organization who have no vested interest in the outcome of the audit.
   - An *external audit* is performed by an outside party. Before hiring an auditor, check their credentials or consider hiring an

American Society for Quality (ASQ) Certified Quality
Auditor or a RAB ISO 9000 auditor.

- *Self-inspection* is performed by members of the department
  who have a vested interest in the outcome of the audit.

In the example, an internal audit would probably be chosen. The
scope of the audit and the available leadtime will factor into the decision about what type of audit to use (see Figure 6.2).

FIGURE 6.2
Guideline for Determining Audit Type

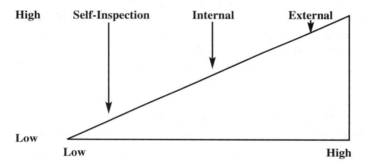

Source: Lloyd, R.L. "Why and How You Ought to Audit," *Purchasing Today* ®, May 1999, p. 56.

5. Establish the format of the audit. Typically, a preliminary list of
   staff members to be interviewed and any escort requirements (for
   external audits) will be provided prior to the audit. The lead auditor will conduct an opening meeting with key stakeholders to discuss the scope of the audit. After the audit, the lead auditor will
   present the draft audit report to the same people who attended the
   opening meeting. In the example, the staff of the acquired operation would provide access to their current procedures, and these
   would be matched with the acquiring organization's requirements.
6. Prepare and distribute the final audit report. The final report presents the factual data, gathered by the auditor during interviews and
   from observations of performance, as compared to the standard. In
   the example, key differences would be reported to the local staff.

7. Establish a corrective action plan. The key stakeholders will develop a plan of action and a timeline for dealing with the findings of the audit. Typically, the auditor or management and the affected managers negotiate an acceptable corrective action plan. A timeline and specific actions to bring the new unit's procedures into compliance would be an appropriate response in the example case.

Periodic Reports – The periodic report is another means of review that can be used to compare performance with the organization's plan. The timeframe for periodic reviews should be established during the planning stage, and the quantitative information should be summarized at intervals that will facilitate the review process.

Procedure Reviews – Procedure reviews are initiated to ascertain if those charged with following established procedures are indeed doing so.

Workload Distribution

The assignment of purchase requests to purchasing personnel varies from organization to organization based on its particular needs and the size and capability of the purchasing function. This can be accomplished in any of the following ways, singly or in combination: commodity or class segmentation, department, special project, volume, in rotation, type of contract, staff expertise, supplier, and purchasing councils and lead buying.

Commodity or Class Segmentation

Assignments can be made to buyers based on the commodities that the organization requires. The term *commodity* is used to define all goods and services purchased by an organization. Each buyer can specialize in a group of similar commodities or, in the case of large organizations, in a single commodity that is a significant enough part of product cost to justify the purchaser's position. The purchaser for a single commodity must have a strong product orientation.

Purchases can also be categorized in a number of ways, including monetary delineations, critical versus standard commodities, or individual units. Pareto analysis (also known as ABC analysis or the 80:20 Rule) can be used to categorize purchases according to dollar value. By conducting this analysis, a manager can identify the 10 to 20 percent of purchased goods and services that account for 80 to 90 percent of the total annual expenditures. These A items and the suppliers of these items would be the commodities that receive the greatest resources (time, people, and attention). For example, Walter Quade, the purchasing director for a food distribution company, describes the monetary delineation his company uses:[4]

> We break down our spending into three major commodity groups using the ABC method. We set plateaus for dollar spends. The high-value A items (above $5 million) are our critical mass items. These include raw materials, such as grains. We spend approximately $12 million annually on grains. B items ($1 million to $5 million) might include a specific packaging item. The C purchases (under $1 million) would include small MRO items. In each commodity grouping you need different levels of skills and different levels of personnel. Commodity teams with strategic skills handle the over $5 million items. The B items require less team emphasis, and the C items fall into the transactional category.

Portfolio analysis is another approach that is used in conjunction with Pareto analysis. Portfolio analysis assigns risk levels to value levels to further refine the categories. Figure 6.3 is an example of this approach. This analysis recognizes the importance of risk levels when determining resource allocation for management of a specific commodity.

FIGURE 6.3
Sample Portfolio Matrix

RISK / VALUE	Low	High
High	Leverage	Strategic
Low	Acquistion	Critical

Department

When purchase requisitions are assigned by department, a buyer will handle all the requests from certain assigned departments. This type of buyer is oriented toward serving a department and handling all of its needs, as opposed to the commodity buyers who focus on what is being purchased, rather than for whom it is being purchased.

Special Project

Requisitions may be assigned to a purchaser according to a special project or a new product line. The buyer will provide the materials and services needed to support the assigned project. This type of assignment is often applied to research laboratories or construction projects. For example, Arizona's Department of Transportation (ADOT) uses "partnering," after a competitive source selection process, in every construction contract. The project team, consisting of ADOT project representatives and the contractor's representatives, meet to identify shared objectives and establish a decision-making process that will apply to every issue that comes up on the job. The contracts contain cost incentives that encourage contractors to propose innovations to reduce costs during the contract term. ADOT and the contractors share the benefits of the reductions. The results of this project management approach have included sharply reduced claims and projects completed ahead of schedule and under budget.[5]

Volume

So that the buyers will have similar levels of responsibility, some departments make assignments based on the dollar volume or the number of requisitions handled annually. Care must be exercised to ensure that the workload is reasonably distributed. Consider the difference between an MRO buyer handling hundreds of low-value transactions versus the capital equipment buyer who spends the same amount on a single machine tool.

In Rotation

Some organizations rotate buyers through different buying groups to develop expertise and tap as wide a range of skills as possible. Attention is paid to the individual's training, rather than to the purchasing activities. Rotational programs are often used to train new hires before placing them in a permanent position. This allows new employees to understand the various jobs and functions within the purchasing department, to forge relationships with co-workers, and to help the employee and the manager decide where the employee's skills can be used best.

The rotational method can also be used for routine purchases, such as replenishing crib items. Buyers are rotated regularly to broaden their experience and to keep their work from becoming too repetitive.

Type of Contract

Assigning the workload according to the type of contract is especially useful if specific types of contracting involve a large learning curve. One approach to delineating contracts is to apply portfolio analysis to develop a matrix of contract alternatives (see Figure 6.4). According to Gary L. Hopper, northwest purchasing manager for Intel Corporation, this matrix should take "into consideration the goal to mitigate reasonable business risk and optimize purchasing resources . . . . Per the matrix, the 'Strategic Alliance' segment equates to the greatest risk, increased resource commitment, and more complex terms and conditions. . . . Better supplier segmentation and contract selection will result in reduced cycle time of contract negotiations, more informed understanding of risk, and increased optimization of the purchaser's time to achieve cost savings."[6]

Staff Expertise

The workload can also be distributed according to the skills and capabilities of the individuals in the purchasing group. This approach can be used in conjunction with other methods of workload distribution. For example, a manager may conduct portfolio analysis and identify critical suppliers for each of the quadrants, acquisition, critical, leverage, and strategic (see Figure 6.3). The skills required of the buyers assigned to each category would be tailored to achieve the goals of the category. Figure 6.5 gives an example of possible categories, the key goal for each, and the associated skill sets required of personnel.

FIGURE 6.4
Sample Portfolio of Contract Alternatives

Segment	Buyer's Time	Contract Type	Drivers	Attributes
Strategic Alliance	Extensive	Custom	Sole source High risk Revenue impact	Executive involvement Technology sharing Software development Intellectual property Requires legal review
Key Supplier	Ongoing	Boilerplate plus pricing and detailed specifications	Single source Medium risk Moderate to high dollar value	Negotiated pricing Statement of work Performance indicators Supplier management tools
Repetitive Purchases (plug and play)	Exception basis	Boilerplate Autofax Pricing agreement only	Low risk Multiple sources Moderate to high dollar	High cost savings potential Standard product UCC prevails
Standard Rebuys (Below the Line)	Negligible	Procurement Card Oral agreement	Very low dollar Nominal risk	Delegated authorization to internal customer Cash and carry Catalog item

Adapted from Hopper, G.L. "A Portfolio of Contract Alternatives," *Purchasing Today®*, November 1998, p. 10.

FIGURE 6.5
Required Skill Sets by Quadrant in Portfolio Matrix

Category	Key Goal	Required Skill Set
1. Acquisition	Minimize effort	Organized, procedural, steady worker, detail-oriented
2. Critical	Reduce risk	Tenacious, committed, innovative
3. Leverage	Maximize profit	Committed, tough-minded, good negotiator
4. Strategic	Competitive advantage	Analytical, relationship, builder, good negotiator

Adapted from William L. Michels, chief executive of ADR North America, as reported in Whyte, C.K. "The Great Divide," *Purchasing Today®*, November 1998, p. 36.

Supplier

The workload can also be distributed according to suppliers or groups of suppliers. This is often the genesis of the supplier manager or manager of supplier relationships concept.

Purchasing Councils and Lead Buying

Decentralization of buying, particularly in large organizations, has given rise to purchasing councils or lead buying groups. With councils, all the buyers of an item get together and decide how volume can be used to maximize value. In lead buying situations, the site or group that has expertise regarding certain purchases will buy for others in that organization. For example, the buying personnel serving the information systems department, who have expertise in computer systems, would be the lead buyer of computing equipment for all departments.

Sara Lee Corporation, a global manufacturer and marketer, is divided into five lines of business: Sara Lee Foods, coffee and tea, household and body care, food service, and branded apparel. The company, which is committed to the principle of decentralized management, has a large number of discrete profit centers, each led by an operating executive. Even in this decentralized environment, Sara Lee management initiated a cost reduction program that includes an effort to benefit from the leverage of the company's purchasing power.[7]

Procedures for Controlling Purchase Requests

To maintain traceability, some departments keep a register of the purchase requests they receive. A manual or electronic log may include the requisition number, date, number of line items, description, and assigned buyer. When the purchasing system is computerized, the same data can be captured as the transactions are entered and then quickly summarized for management review. When an organization employs several buyers, a *log* will help locate a particular requisition in the files. Some systems are designed to provide requisition status. Depending on organizational requirements, this may include whether requisitions are in the quote, proposal, purchase order, or contract stage. Electronic purchasing systems capture the transactions as they are generated on the system and provide automated logging, tracking, and status reports on demand. Requirements may be channeled to particular buyers because of their expertise in dealing with specific types of contracts.

Alternative Release Systems

An alternative release system is a method of ordering that involves minimum resources for obtaining repetitive materials. These systems may use either written or verbal means of communication, and they often rely on electronic transmission.

Systems Contract

The systems contract is a release system in which off-the-shelf items are identified and priced in anticipation of usage. Usually, the supplier will carry sufficient inventory to minimize the buyer's inventory. Designated users make delivery releases against existing orders placed by purchasing. In the public sector, this type of contract is often called an *indefinite-delivery* type or *term* contract. Systems contracts are being used less frequently as more supply management organizations establish long-term agreements with a single supplier for a range of similar items. The organization can call on the single supplier to track consumption and provide automatic replenishment.

For example, at the Corning Martinsburg plant in West Virginia, 19 local and corporate systems contracts have been implemented. In 1996, as a result of commodity team efforts, 64 percent of total MRO purchase order line items were processed from these systems contract suppliers. Of storeroom items (totaling more than 5,000), 71 percent were ordered through system contract suppliers. The teams continue to work to increase these numbers.[8]

Kanban or Pull Systems

Kanban is a demand system developed in Japan to expedite ordering and delivery of production materials and minimize inventories. From a review of historic consumption patterns, the buyer and seller jointly develop plans to provide automatic replenishment. Once in place, these programs depend on a pull signal from the station consuming the goods to trigger the replenishment activity from upstream. This trigger mechanism, called a kanban, is usually a card calling for another delivery of a specific quantity or an empty bin returned to the supplier for immediate refilling.

Direct Release Arrangements

Direct release arrangements are used to allow the end user to control the scheduling of incoming shipments. The release is placed against a pre-existing order that was originally handled by the purchasing department.

Supplier- and Vendor-Managed Inventories

As in the case of a kanban system, the buying organization first studies consumption patterns for a group of similar items. Then, a single supplier is selected to fulfill all requirements for that group of items. Once an agreement and plan are established, the supplier monitors the organization's use and demand for an item and automatically replenishes stocks as needed. The materials are usually kept in the supplier's inventory until they are drawn for use by the customer.

Priority Sequences for Handling Purchase Requests

As one of the first steps in time and task management, the managers of a purchasing department must establish some means of prioritizing requests from internal customers. The different approaches to prioritization include first-come, first-served, arrangement by need date, rush orders and emergencies, order of importance, and seasonal.

First Come, First Served

This is the standard means of processing. The priority is to place and complete commitments as the buyer receives them.

Arrangement by Need Date

In this system, purchases that are needed sooner than others are identified and given first priority for processing.

Rush Orders and Emergencies

First priority is assigned to rush and emergency commitments when they are identified by the requester. After completion, the buyer will revert to one of the routine systems. While this approach is necessary at times, if rush orders are allowed to become commonplace, daily activities will be seriously disrupted. Following the satisfaction of the emergency requirement, the root cause of the situation must be determined, and corrective action must be taken to prevent the situation from recurring.

Order of Importance

First priority is based on how important a commodity is in the schedule, to the customer, or other criteria. These criteria often conflict. The organization needs to determine a proper balance concerning the best overall order of importance.

Seasonal

The importance of orders will increase or decrease according to the seasonal need for goods. Similar to arrangement by need date, seasonal prioritization is common in the retail trade where certain styles or goods are in demand only at certain times. For example, purchasing skis will be top priority in the fall, but there is little point in buying them in the spring.

Organizational Structure of the Purchasing Function

Each organization must determine the best way to structure the purchasing function to maximize its value and contribution to the overall strategy and goals of the organization. The structure will, in part, determine the extent to which the organization can control annual expenditures.

Centralization vs. Decentralization

The possible organizational structures of the purchasing function fall along a continuum from totally decentralized to totally centralized, with numerous combinations in between (see Figure 6.6).

FIGURE 6.6
Continuum of Purchasing Organizational Structures

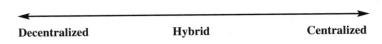

| Decentralized | Hybrid | Centralized |

Centralization is often used for one or all of the following reasons:

- Centralized purchases account for a high percentage of the product cost or the budget.
- Centralized items are used by most of the operating units.
- Management feels the need for tight control over purchases, and it chooses to place the authority and responsibility into one central group that can also assume the responsibility for developing purchasing policy and control measures.

A multiplant or multisite organization must decide to what extent purchasing activities should be centralized at the corporate level. In practice, every organization treats this problem differently. Some centralize the activity so that buying for all sites is done at a central office. Others decentralize the function by giving each site full authority to conduct all of its purchasing activities. The majority of organizations operate somewhere between these two extremes. Each approach offers significant benefits, which are discussed in the following sections.

Advantages of Centralization

Six advantages of centralization are communication with suppliers, buying clout, greater knowledge, job satisfaction, more time to manage, and lower operating costs. These advantages are discussed in the following paragraphs.

Communication with Suppliers – When a central buying group represents the organization, it is easier for both the buyers and the suppliers to explain their objectives and work together efficiently. The suppliers' representatives do not have to spend time and resources selling to, and managing relationships with, people from departments throughout the buying organization. The buying group can identify the organization's key suppliers, focus on building lasting relationships with these key suppliers, and work with the suppliers on continuous improvements, cost avoidance, and cost reduction programs.

Buying Clout – Centralized purchasing permits the organization to consolidate the requirements of all of its operating units. With this buying clout, purchasing is usually able to obtain improved prices and services. Suppliers generally offer more cost-effective terms when they can sell to one department or buyer and know they are reaching the entire organization.

Greater Knowledge – Centralization generally affords more specialization among the purchasing staff. This focus permits buyers to be more effective in obtaining value because they better understand what they buy. The consolidation of purchases through a centralized buying group also allows for better tracking and auditing of expenditures.

Job Satisfaction – The centralized purchasing department gives rise to increased job satisfaction because buyers are able to make a more significant and measurable contribution to the organization.

More Time to Manage – Planning, organization, professional development, and personnel issues require time, and it is easier to allocate resources to these areas if the centralized department is adequately staffed.

Lower Operating Costs – This point may be arguable because the cost of a decentralized organization is difficult to assess. Nonetheless, centralized organizations consolidate their efforts in terms of purchase orders, requisitions, telephone and written communications, sales interviews, and the coordination and scheduling of meetings. These consolidated efforts usually lead to lower operating costs.

Advantages of Decentralization

Five advantages of decentralization include communication with internal customers, broader responsibilities, more authority, better purchase timing, and fast track organizations and project management. These advantages are discussed in the following paragraphs.

Communication with Internal Customers – The closer buyers are to their internal customers, the better they will understand customer needs and respond accordingly. If, for example, the buyer is familiar with the requirements of an internal customer, he or she will be able to evaluate the merits of any alternatives suggested by suppliers.

Broader Responsibilities – The buyer working in a decentralized environment usually is given a wider range of purchasing responsibilities as well as other responsibilities that are not typically considered within the purchasing function, such as financial analysis or oversight of inventory.

More Authority – The buyer working in a decentralized environment often has greater decision-making authority because of the broader areas of responsibility and because of the lack of a purchasing department reporting structure. For example, if a person is assigned purchasing authority within a department (other than a purchasing department), he or she may be given greater spending authority or he or she may have quicker and easier access to the department manager who can authorize expenditures.

Better Purchase Timing – In many circumstances, the timing of requirements will conflict with the organizational objective of maximizing leverage from spending volume. In such instances, the decentralized buyer will be more cognizant of the balance sought by local management. This is particularly true in multiplant manufacturing or organizations with many dispersed sites. The local buyer will be more familiar than a centralized buyer will with local priorities.

Fast Track Organizations and Project Management – Research and development (R&D), construction, new products, and high-tech organizations often decentralize buying at the functional level. Those charged with the ultimate success of a product or project are given complete control over all critical resources, including those overseen by purchasing.

Combining Advantages

Many organizations have attempted to capture the advantages of both centralized and decentralized structures by creating hybrid versions. One common approach is to create a small staff at the headquarters to manage the purchasing of common and high-impact requirements, and then each individual site is responsible for its own requirements for all other goods or services. For example, a school district might purchase or lease furniture, computers, and buses from the central office, and individual school sites might control the purchases of supplies and textbooks.

So far, this chapter has dealt with ways to organize the purchasing function so that it contributes to the attainment of the organization's goals and objectives. Because supply management is now seen as a vital function in most organizations, a detailed and critical analysis of the activities involved is almost inevitable. Many organizations are looking beyond historical and traditional ways of operating the supply function. Process reengineering is a powerful tool used for conducting such analyses and for designing improved procurement processes.

Reengineering Processes

Reengineering became popular during the 1990s as organizations sought ways to reduce costs, become more responsive in the marketplace, and enhance overall competitiveness. Reengineering is described in the book *Reengineering the Corporation*[9] as "starting all over, starting from scratch" to rethink, redesign, and implement completely new processes.

Efforts to reengineer purchasing typically focus on the following key activity areas: the order cycle, direct user releases, inventories, invoice payment, stores, and other areas offering potential cost and time savings. Essentially, all activities required to fulfill the supply needs of the organization are open to reengineering. When IBM won the 1999 *Purchasing Magazine* Medal of Excellence, the changes in IBM's supply management were described as "turning what had become an obsolete approach to supply management on its head." IBM Vice President Gene Richter was credited with:

- Changing away from a decentralized structure
- Increasing outsourcing of work formerly done in-house
- Meeting regularly with suppliers to explore new technology
- Using the Internet to communicate with suppliers
- Selling the IBM supply management capabilities to other companies[10]

As part of a corporationwide reengineering effort, Corning Incorporated changed a number of purchasing processes, including standardizing MRO corporationwide through an integrated supply process, moving its $300 million MRO expenditures to national or regional systems contracts, and outsourcing 21 manufacturing MRO storerooms.[11] The initial projections were for $10 million in profit-and-loss statement savings and a reduction of $10.5 million in inventory corporationwide through reduced labor costs, reduced material costs (10 to 15 percent), and inventory reductions (30 percent). The initial results included:

- An average cost reduction of 19 percent through product substitutions by seeking increased volume with each supplier and improving "fit for function" for products used
- A decrease of 30 percent ($1 million or more) through leadtime reduction (from two weeks to three days), return or buy back of excess inventory ($142,000), and the stocking of critical parts by suppliers with two-hour delivery, seven days per week
- A supply base reduction of 57 percent (1,606 to 698 suppliers)
- An administrative workload reduction through EDI with system contract suppliers for 60 to 70 percent of the 6,136 MRO purchase orders and 10,250 invoices
- Customer service support improvements, including easier access to technical product support, direct access to suppliers for estimated material cost information, streamlined purchase request and receipt procedures, improved material return procedures, supplier availability for emergency support 24 hours per day, and average on-time delivery at 89 percent versus 72 percent for all other suppliers

Order Cycle

The order cycle covers the time from the creation of the order until the supplier begins to respond to the order placement. The process normally involves reaching agreement on terms and conditions, contract creation and distribution, and supplier acknowledgment. Each of these subprocesses offers an opportunity for reengineering. For example, the buyer might create a standard contract template, in electronic form, containing an online acknowledgment that, if the contract is acceptable to the supplier, can be acknowledged immediately upon receipt. In the reengineered scenario, the contract is created by inserting appropriate data into data fields in the standard contract language. The contract is then transmitted to the supplier electronically and the acknowledgment is immediately and automatically returned electronically. In reengineering efforts, old paradigms, such as the need for a handwritten signature in this example, would be challenged.

Direct User Releases

In this form of process streamlining, the user who requires the material to be purchased is authorized to release the goods for shipment without involving the buyer. Direct user release is possible after the buyer has:

1. Established the contract covering all the terms of purchase except the quantity and required delivery date
2. Authorized the user to complete the transaction by adding this information
3. Set appropriate limits for the user with respect to quantities or total value

The buyer is freed from the repetitive release activity to do greater value-adding work.

Inventory

In a classic example of reengineering, information can be substituted for inventory. Inventory is treated as an asset in accounting terms because it has monetary value. In terms of the efficiency of the operation, however, inventory can hide many sources of inefficiency and waste. There are financial costs to carrying inventory and the potential for obsolescence if a better item becomes available. Less obvious is the negative impact inventory can have on quality and cycle time.

Dell Computer is keenly aware of these issues and operates with a "direct-to-customer business mode." The process uses rapid information exchange among customers, Dell, and suppliers to substitute for the need to carry inventory. Five or six years ago, Dell carried 30 to 40 days of inventory. Today, the company operates with about six days of inventory, or less than one-tenth the inventory of the balance of the PC industry, freeing millions of dollars for better use.[12]

Invoice Payment

Most payables systems require a three-way match of purchase order, receiver, and invoice. To authorize payment, the quantity and price (extended value) of what was ordered, received, and billed must be the same. This process has been reengineered at many organizations through the use of *evaluated receipts*. The principle is that if what was ordered (the purchase order) matches what was received (the receiver), the invoice is redundant and unnecessary. Many companies are moving to a two-way match of PO and receiver, eliminating the invoice process. The invoice is never created, mailed, received, handled, or filed, thereby eliminating non-value-adding costs for both the supplier and the customer.

Supplier-Managed Stores

The principle of supplier-managed stores is that the consumption by the customer is varied and the supplier needs to follow the usage pattern closely to satisfy demand without holding excess inventory. If the supplier maintains its inventory at the customer's location, or in the immediate vicinity, the supplier is able to constantly track usage and replenish what is used. Frequently used for low-value items such as fasteners and hardware, this approach removes from the customer the dilemma of balancing quantity on hand against the possibility of being out of stock. The customer does not take ownership until the item is removed from stock, so the customer's inventory carrying cost is close to nil. Because the supplier is better able to match the flow of goods into stock with the actual rate of consumption, carrying costs are minimized for the supplier as well.

Purchasing Cards

Analyses of the spending patterns at most organizations show that a large percentage of the purchasing transactions are for small dollar amounts. (Seventy-five to 80 percent of transactions are for $500 or less.) Many organizations have dramatically improved these transactions by issuing credit cards (procurement or purchasing cards) to key users who require much of this small-value transaction volume. The user's card authorization is limited to certain kinds of items and a maximum dollar amount per transaction and per billing cycle. The user is able to get exactly what he or she wants; the buyer does not spend valuable time on low-value transactions; and if the source selection is inefficient, it is limited to a small portion of the dollars spent. The benefits of purchasing cards include:

- The organization is able to move the buyer from handling a high volume of low-value transactions to concentrating on value-added source evaluation, selection, and negotiation.
- The periodic summary reports from the card issuer provide information about these low-value, but voluminous, transactions. The reports can be used for consolidation or blanket order procurement in the future.
- Controls are applied after-the-fact rather than before-the-fact, which speeds the fulfillment process.

For example, Ray Mazzoleni, purchasing manager at Thomson Financial and Professional Publishing Group (TFPPG) in Boston, Massachusetts, established a procurement card program in which 35 to 40 TFPPG users are authorized to purchase products and services based on a spending limit approved by each cardholder's manager. Reported benefits include quicker ordering of everyday purchases due to a streamlined approval process, more time for purchasing personnel to concentrate on supplier management and procurement-card project improvements, and the elimination of a large percentage of purchase orders.[13]

Beyond Reengineering — The Extended Enterprise

Thomas T. Stallkamp, former vice president of procurement and supplier operations and general manager of large-car operations for Daimler-Chrysler Corporation, said Chrysler has gone beyond reengineering internally to focus on building and developing each supplier into Chrysler's extended enterprise. This enterprise encompasses "all tiers within the supply base and encourages non-competing suppliers to share practices, such as continuous improvement and lean production, that can help all organizations better compete in the global marketplace."[14] In the first five years the effort resulted in 10,000 ideas from suppliers that generated more than $1 billion in permanent annualized savings.

According to Stallkamp, the process of managing the total supply chain has the following essential requirements:

- Open and free communication between and among all tiers in the supply chain
- Mutual trust
- Empowerment to think and act as a full member of the team
- Responsibility

Suppliers must be committed to ongoing research and development leading to technical innovation and continuous cost reduction. Chrysler will work with the suppliers in a long-term relationship based on shared goals.

Internet, Intranet, and Extranet

Communication is an important tool in reengineering efforts because many reengineering improvements are the result of stream-lining of processes and the more rapid exchange of information across organizational boundaries. The Internet, intranets (the internal counterpart to the Internet), and extranets (which link intranets between trading partners) are high-speed communication tools. By using these electronic media to link the computing networks of suppliers, customers, and internal departments, organizations can make vital information available within seconds of its creation. Communication tools and information reporting are discussed in greater detail in Chapter 9.

An example of such communication is the transmission of customer purchase information from a retailer to its suppliers. An intranet may be used to collect sales information from many sales terminals and compile the information into a single data file. Then, this file is segregated by supplier and transmitted within the retailer's extranet to all participating suppliers to trigger their replenishment activities. All of this can take place within seconds of the retail sale, if necessary. In the past, such information was collected over a period of time, often several days, then compiled and mailed or faxed to the supplier, and the full cycle could have taken days or weeks to accomplish.

Key Points

1. The effectiveness of the supply management function is largely dictated by how the organization is structured. The degree of centralization is critical in aligning the supply function with the organization's strategic objectives.
2. Key processes must be well defined, clearly documented, and consistently executed. The processes must be evaluated frequently for opportunities for improvement or reengineering.
3. Controls are necessary to assure conformance with plans and authorized activities. Measurement must be made against an accepted standard or clearly defined expectations.
4. Responsibilities in the supply function must be logically distributed in order to maintain reasonable workloads and to maximize individual contributions.
5. Communication of information is essential to many tasks in supply management, and the speed with which information is transmitted can be a critical success factor for the organization. The advent of the Internet and related electronic communications have provided opportunities for improving the work of supply management.

Questions for Review

1. How do before-the-fact controls differ from during-the-fact and after-the-fact controls? How can an organization minimize the risks of unrealistic before-the-fact controls?
2. How can a manager balance the degree of difficulty and volume of work in distributing departmental workloads? What other factors are vital to equitable work assignments?
3. How do expertise and depth of knowledge affect the ability of an individual to take on greater responsibility in a commodity management role? What is the danger of the individual becoming familiar and comfortable with the assigned commodity?
4. How is work flow logically prioritized? What factors can change the established priorities?

5. What key organizational attributes determine the appropriate degree of centralization for the purchasing function? Are these attributes fixed for extended periods of time?
6. How is process reengineering different from process improvement? Which holds greater potential for gain? Which holds greater risk of failure? How can an organization approach process reengineering to minimize the risks?

Endnotes

1. General Mills, Inc., "Exploring General Mills Diversity," www.generalmills.com.
2. Lloyd, R.L. "Why and How You Ought to Audit," *Purchasing Today®*, May 1999, p. 54-58.
3. Lloyd, 1999, p. 54-58.
4. Whyte, C.K. "The Great Divide," *Purchasing Today®*, November 1998, p. 34-38.
5. Cushman, C. "Transcending Traditional Boundaries: Sharing Best Practices in a World of Change," Proceedings of the 1996 NAPM International Purchasing Conference, NAPM, Tempe, AZ, 1996, pp. 458-459.
6. Hopper, G.L. "A Portfolio of Contract Alternatives," *Purchasing Today®*, November 1998, p. 10.
7. Sara Lee Corporation, "1999 Annual Report, President's Letter," www.saralee.com.
8. Haynes, M.G. "The Value of Integration: Systems Contracts and Integrated Supply," *Purchasing Today®*, August 1997, p. 34.
9. Hammer, M. and J. Champy, *Reengineering the Corporation*, HarperBusiness, New York,1993.
10. Carbone, J. "Medal of Excellence, 'Reinventing Purchasing Wins the Medal for Big Blue,'" *Purchasing Magazine*, Sept. 16, 1999, p. 19.
11. Haynes, 1997, p. 34.
12. Dell, M. "Building the Infrastructure for 21st Century Commerce," 1999 Networld+Interop, Web site: dell.com, May 12, 1999.
13. Rusk, J.A. "Designed for Efficiency: Online Ordering and Procurement Cards," *Purchasing Today®*, August 1997, p. 33.
14. Stallkamp, T.T. "Beyond Reengineering: Developing the Extended Enterprise," *NAPM Insights*, February 1995, p. 76.

CHAPTER 7

TOOLS TO MANAGE WORK FLOW

What information management tools are needed to manage work flow?

Chapter Objectives

- To demonstrate the communication process in the acquisition cycle from need recognition and description to relationship management
- To show the different types of documentation that may be used in the acquisition cycle
- To discuss the role of documentation in managing process flow and in creating and maintaining effective relationships with internal customers and suppliers

Reasons for Operational Documents

In many ways the purchasing and supply management function is an information and relationship management function. As such, communication tools and techniques, both verbal and written, may distinguish the highly effective supply manager and supply organization from the less effective. Besides verbal communication, purchasers rely on numerous written communications (both paper and electronic documents) to facilitate the communication process with internal customers and external suppliers. Operational forms or documents and their use in managing this communication process are the topic of this chapter.

Forms as a Component of Process Flow

In *Reengineering the Corporation*, authors Michael Hammer and James Champy define a process as "a series of activities that delivers value to a customer."[1] They discuss the failure of organizations to identify business processes that cross departmental lines, because organizations focus on individual department activities. Managers are put in charge of departments and not processes, so it is easy for them to lose sight of the complete process and focus only on the piece of the process performed by their staff. If supply managers think of the acquisition process rather than the purchasing department, they will be more inclined to link the activities performed by purchasing with activities that are also part of the process but which are performed by personnel in other departments. The ability to see the system and the integration of activities across departmental or even organizational boundaries will make it easier to identify ways to improve operational and strategic activities.

Effective management of operational documents fulfills the organization's need for a number of things, including:

- **Communication** – As discussed previously, the communication of information in the form of words and data is the primary reason that operational documents are used.
- **Operational Control** – Operational control of transactions, funds, and schedules is another important reason for using documentation.
- **Records** – Documentation provides a record of activities. These records are needed to research information, prove that actions did or did not occur, provide audit trails, and meet legal conditions and requirements.
- **Consistency of Approach** – Standardized documents allow tasks to be accomplished in a consistent way. This is useful for a number of reasons. First, it ensures that all pertinent information is included. Second, it allows for greater efficiency (when compared to preparing needed information from scratch) because the same sequence and placement of information takes place every time the document is used. Third, the individuals receiving or reviewing standard documents are able to glean information easier than if the documents were transmitted in many different formats and styles.
- **Legal Requirements** – Certain types of information are legally required to be in writing. For example, a contact for the sale of goods valued at $500 or more must be in writing to be legally enforceable. Other types of information may not be legally

required to be in writing. However, good judgment would dictate that having information in writing may prevent the need for legal action or assist in the successful resolution of a matter if it required legal action.

Types of Communication Formats

The organizational structure and required documents, or communication vehicles, needed to support a business process should flow from the process itself. Therefore, the operational documents supporting the acquisition process should be created with the understanding that these tools will either help or hinder the effective and efficient achievement of operational goals and objectives and, consequently, the achievement of organizational goals and objectives.

While no standard operational documents fit the purchasing process of every organization, there are some basic communication processes and formats that typically occur in the acquisition cycle to provide relevant information to the appropriate person(s).

Step 1: Internal User Recognizes and Communicates Need to Purchasing

The first step in the acquisition process is identifying and describing the need. Depending on the structure of the purchasing function in an organization and the relationships established with internal customers and suppliers, the buyer may or may not be directly involved in describing the need. The level of involvement has implications for the purchaser's ability to affect value. Approximately 70 percent of the opportunity to affect value occurs in the need recognition and description stages of the acquisition process.[2] Therefore, the skill and ability of the buyer to communicate effectively internally (with internal customers and/or stakeholders) is equally as important as the ability to communicate effectively externally (with suppliers). Early purchasing involvement and early supplier involvement in the initial stages of the process ensure that the information that appears in a standard document truly represents the needs of the organization.

Federal Express Corporation restructured its purchasing and supply organization around the common supply markets that account for its annual expenditures. This allowed the company to become more closely aligned with internal customers and suppliers. According to Edith Kelly-Green, vice president of strategic sourcing and supply,

"An internal customer or supplier no longer needs to go to one of several functional areas within FedEx to make a decision, they now go directly to one category management group that handles all aspects of a particular item being acquired."[3]

The most common method for an internal user to communicate a need to purchasing is through a purchase requisition. Several types of requisitions may be used. A purchase requisition may be a single-use, standard purchase requisition form, a repetitive use or traveling requisition form, or specialized forms, such as a bill of materials or a capital equipment justification form.

Standard Purchase Requisition – The standard, single-use purchase requisition authorizes purchasing to buy goods or services (see Figure 7.1). The internal customers forward this written or computerized form to purchasing to indicate the items they need, where and when they want the items delivered, and necessary accounting and approval information.

FIGURE 7.1
Purchase Requisition

Purchase Requisition

Department requisitioning _____   Number _____
    Budget account _____   Date _____

Quantity required	Unit	Description

Required date _____
Notify in event of problems _____
Special delivery instructions _____

_____
Requisitioning authority

Instructions: Complete in duplicate. Send original to Purchasing Department, requisitioner keep file copy.

Traveling (Purchase) Requisition – Traveling requisitions are similar to standard purchase requisitions except that the same form is used many times for repetitive purchases (for example, inventory items). Often printed on card stock (or appearing in electronic format), traveling forms contain preprinted standard part or item information that does not change from buy to buy. The preprinted information may include stock-level data, potential suppliers, leadtimes, prices and predetermined order quantities, as well as other data needed for ordering.

This form gives requisitioners the advantage of reducing preparation time, because they normally have to enter only the information that changes (for example, quantity). Another advantage of this form is that it may include the history of previous purchases for the item available. When this reusable purchase requisition is sent to the purchasing department, a purchase order is prepared directly from the requisition.

The concept of the traveling requisition is adaptable to electronic purchasing systems. In a computerized system, requests for goods and services and acknowledgments are transmitted electronically, thereby eliminating the paper-based system, reducing clerical processing time, and possibly enhancing decision making and record keeping.

Kanban Card – A kanban (discussed in Chapter 6) is a special variety of traveling requisition. In the case of a traveling requisition, the requirement is derived from the consumption of a specific quantity of the item and the need to replenish that same quantity. In a kanban system, the kanban, which may be a card or a container designed for the exact quantity needed, is sent from the consuming location back to the supplier to trigger an order for replenishment. In both cases, the use of a simple card eliminates waste and inefficiency by reducing cycle time and reducing the number of people involved in the process.

Bill of Materials – The bill of materials (B/M or BOM) is another form that can be used as a purchase requisition. Each BOM is developed by the design engineer for use in manufacturing and production planning. The bill of materials lists the quantity and description of all materials required to manufacture a single unit of a component, product, or facility. After being informed of the total amount of the product to be produced, purchasing determines how many of each of the individual parts to buy. A bill of materials is an essential element in a material requirements planning (MRP) system.

Capital Equipment Justification – Two types of capital assets are usually covered in the financial budget:

- Assets with dollar values that are small enough so that their purchase does not require the special attention of the finance committee or controller
- Assets with dollar values and possibly strategic values to the organization that warrant special financial consideration and authorization

For the latter type of capital acquisition, a formal appropriation request and justification often must accompany the requisition for capital equipment. This justification would include a detailed description of the requested item, cost estimates, anticipated savings resulting from the purchase, the impact of the purchase on the organization, and any other pertinent information.

Step 2: Purchasing Communicates Its Need to Prospective Suppliers

Purchasing plays a critical role in ensuring that the right material or service is requested from the supplier. The process of communicating the needs of the internal user to potential suppliers is critical to the acquisition process. Purchasing can communicate need and intention-to-buy information to suppliers in a number of ways. The form of the communication and the transmittal method used should be driven by the need itself. If the good is a standard re-buy or a standard item, a simple request may suffice. If, however, the buyer wants the supplier to assume some degree of responsibility for finding and proposing a solution to a problem, the supplier will need a more detailed account or description of the need. If the buyer wishes to place the burden of performance on the seller rather than defining performance by specifications, the initial information needed by the seller may be more involved.

The typical tools used to communicate a need to the supplier are the request for information (RFI), request for quotation (RFQ), request for proposal (RFP), and invitation for bid (IFB). As with requisitions, no standard forms are used by every organization. In fact, the meaning and use of an RFP or RFQ in one organization may not be the same as in another organization.

Request for Information – At times, a buyer may want to gather information from suppliers without asking them for quotes. The easiest and most commonly used method for obtaining information from a supplier is to place a telephone call. A formal method is to issue a request for information (RFI) for the sole purpose of obtaining planning information. In some organizations, however, the RFI is actually an invitation to do business, and the term is used interchangeably with request for quotation (RFQ), request for proposal (RFP), or invitation for bid (IFB).

For example, when preparing to purchase paper for printer and copier use, the buyer would prepare a request for information from a cross-section of potential suppliers. The buyer will want to get answers to his or her specific questions, and he or she will not want to receive sales pitches from the suppliers. The buyer would describe the following information to the potential suppliers:

- Scope of requirements — grades, sizes, and types of paper to be included; quantity and type anticipated for each delivery location; the expected term of the purchase agreement; and any special requirements, such as point-of-use delivery of paper direct to copy centers.
- Issues to be addressed by suppliers — how prices will be determined and presented; how quality of delivered paper will be managed; how distribution and delivery will be handled; and how the point-of-use delivery will be addressed.
- When and where the response from the supplier must be delivered.
- Acceptable forms of presenting information, such as written documents via mail, spreadsheet completed and returned on diskette, or response via e-mail.

Request for Quotation – When the buyer is ready to issue an invitation to do business, the question becomes how much information do potential suppliers need, and in what format, to facilitate the response process. The buyer may include specifications or descriptions in the form of engineering drawings, blueprints, brand names, and so on in the solicitation document. The solicitation document may be called an RFQ, an RFP, or an IFB depending on the terminology of the buying organization. Figure 7.2 is an example of a typical request for quotation.

FIGURE 7.2
Quotation Form

QUOTATION TO

ITEM NO.	DESCRIPTION	QUANTITY	UNIT PRICE	TOTAL PRICE	DELIVERY DATE FROM "GO AHEAD"

DATE

F.O.B.

REQUESTED BY

REFER INQUIRIES TO

QUOTED PRICES AND CONDITIONS FIRM FOR 30 DAYS

AUTHORIZED SIGNATURE   TITLE

In the private sector, the RFQ usually is considered to be the same as the RFP. In some organizations, however, an RFQ is used to obtain approximate information for planning purposes. In such cases, this fact should be clearly stated in the request. In federal government purchasing, the RFQ is used only for the purpose of obtaining planning information.

No matter what title is given to the form, the simplest request is a request for quotation. In this case, the specifications are clearly defined and the price quoted will be one of the significant factors affecting supplier choice.

Request for Proposal – An RFP is a solicitation document used to obtain offers to be used either in a firm-bid purchasing process or in a negotiated purchasing process, as stipulated in the request. Often the buyer wants to leave room in the solicitation for the supplier to offer innovative and creative solutions or alternatives to the original specifications that may represent better value. RFPs, or similarly designed solicitations, are best used when the supplier has the capabilities to assess and recommend alternatives, sufficient leadtime exists, and the buyer has flexibility in determining how a need will be filled. A sample table of contents for an RFP for a large, complex purchase is shown in Figure 7.3.[4]

Invitation for Bid – An IFB is the request made to potential suppliers for a bid on goods or services to be purchased. The term IFB is also used in government purchasing to refer to the solicitation document used in sealed bidding and in the second step of two-step bidding. From a forms design and management standpoint, sealed bidding presents a special challenge to the writer(s) of the bid solicitation package. Clearly defined, well-supported specifications along with clear instructions for completing and submitting the bid are required for a successful sealed bid process. Confusion over requirements or the process may lead to an aborted bid process or a poor supplier selection that may negatively impact attaining short- and long-term goals and objectives.

Statement of Work – A statement of work (SOW) outlines the specific services a contractor is expected to perform, generally indicating type, level, and quality of service, as well as the schedule required.

FIGURE 7.3
Typical Request for Proposal Format

Instructions to Offerors

Section 1: Enclosures

A full list of all documents applicable to the RFP.
Order of precedence: cover letter, instructions to offerors, listed enclosures.

Section 2: General Requirements

General information regarding the proposal: number of copies, where proposal is to be sent and when, its experation date, order of precedence of RFP documents, subcontract terms and conditions, and special provisions that are applicable.

Section 3: Technical Proposal Organization and Content

This is the table of contents for the technical volume.

Section 4: Schedule Proposal

Instructions on what is to be included in the schedule volume.

Section 5: Cost Proposal Requirements

Costing instructions, including proposed contract type.

Section 6: Management Proposal Requirements

A section concerning the management requirements for the proposal.

Section 7: Certifications and Acknowledgments

This section includes prime contract flowdown requirements, if applicable. (These are requirements that the buying organization's customer imposes, requirements that "flow down" to all subcontractors.)

Step 3: Suppliers Communicate Ability and Willingness to Meet Need

After receiving a solicitation from the buyer, a supplier typically prepares a quotation, bid, or proposal. The preparation of any of these documents costs the supplier time and resources. The buyer must take this into consideration when preparing the solicitation so that unnecessary costs are not driven into the process.

Quotation or Bid – A quotation or bid from the supplier is an offer to sell. In public sector purchasing, a bid is an offer in a sealed-bidding process. In other forms of procurement, the offer may be referred to as a *proposal* or a *quotation*.

Proposal – In its simplest definition, a *proposal* is an offer made by one party to another as the basis for negotiations, prior to the creation of a contract.

Step 4: Buyer Evaluates and Selects a Supplier and Communicates the Choice to the Supplier.

Once the bids, quotes, or proposals are received from potential suppliers, the buyer evaluates them against the appropriate selection criteria and selects a supplier(s). The evaluation process can range from highly informal to highly formal depending on the dollars to be spent, the importance of the purchase to the organization, and the time available. Unnecessary costs can be incurred if the depth of the evaluation does not match the purchase. The potential suppliers must then be informed of the acceptance or rejection of their bid, quote, or proposal.

Bid Analysis Form – Bids are usually analyzed to compare their strengths and weaknesses. Although there is no uniform practice, some organizations use a bid analysis form to assist in analyzing bids or proposals (see Figure 7.4). Public sector purchasing, conversely, typically has strict rules for the evaluation of sealed bids. In any case, the intent is to eliminate any bias from the bidding and evaluation process.

Supplier Evaluation Matrix – Many organizations develop formal supplier evaluation matrices to assist in the objective analysis of existing or potential suppliers. The three critical components for an effective supplier evaluation form are criteria, weighting, and scoring. The criteria used to evaluate potential suppliers are typically technical quality, production capabilities, delivery, service, cost, and managerial capabilities. Once the criteria have been selected for a specific purchase, the buyer or sourcing team must determine the appropriate weight for each criterion. For example, for Purchase A the weighting for quality may be 60 percent, service 20 percent, delivery 10 percent, and cost/price 10 percent. Due to the different circumstances surrounding Purchase B, the weights may be quality 30 percent, service 50 percent, delivery 15 percent, and cost/price 5 percent. Once the weights have been established, a scoring system must be developed to assist the purchaser in accurately assessing and comparing different supplier's capabilities. Figure 7.5 is an example of a supplier evaluation matrix.

FIGURE 7.4
Bid Analysis Form

TELEPHONE BID RECORD			VENDOR			VENDOR			VENDOR		
DATE	BY	PURCHASE REQUISITION	QUOTED BY		BID AMOUNT	QUOTED BY		BID AMOUNT	QUOTED BY		BID AMOUNT
QUANT.	DESCRIPTION										
	TOTAL										
	DELIVERY TIME										
	TERMS										
	F.O.B. POINT										

101422-9 2/80

FIGURE 7.5
Key Supplier Evaluation Matrix (example)

FACTORS	A Importance to our Performance (1-Not Essential) (2-Essential) (3-Critical)	B Supplier Actual Performance (1-Not Acceptable) (2-Good) (3-Very Good)	C Variance (A-B)
Product Quality			
Product Delivery			
Customer Service and Support			
Total Cost of Ownership			
Design Capabilities			
Future Technology Development			
Management Leadership			
Human Resources			
Total Quality Maturity			
Financial Strength			
Safety Consideration			
Annual Expenditures			
Other Organization Specifics			
SCORE	_____	_____	_____

Purchase Order – A purchase order (PO) is used by purchasing to formally contract with suppliers (see Figure 7.6). For this reason, the PO is an important form for purchasing. Common information that appears on most purchase orders includes the supplier, price, quantity, product description, shipping and billing information, delivery date(s), payment terms, and date of order. With the expansion of

FIGURE 7.6
Purchase Order

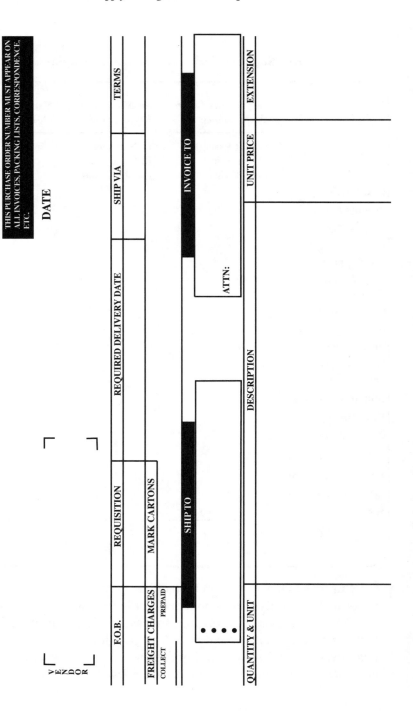

information technology and electronic commerce, most organizations have automated the issuance of the purchase order. The spectrum of such applications is great, ranging from a purchase order generated on a word processor to an online order transmitted over an extranet. These changes have had a profound effect on the document signifying the commitment to purchase. For example, changes to the Uniform Commercial Code have been proposed to make electronic signatures carry the same weight legally as handwritten signatures.

Step 5: Supplier Communicates Acceptance of the Order

After notifying the chosen supplier, the supplier's representative should acknowledge its acceptance (or rejection) of the award, and a formal document such as a contract should be executed.

Acknowledgment – The supplier communicates its acceptance of the purchase order by sending an acknowledgment either manually or electronically. This sets up a bilateral agreement, as long as the terms of the acknowledgment are not substantially different from those of the purchase order. In the past, the acknowledgment often presented a problem to the buyer because he or she had to follow up with the supplier to be sure the order was received and acknowledged without substantive changes. E-commerce has made it possible to confirm that an order has been received and acknowledged in a matter of seconds.

Contract – A contract is a written (or oral) agreement between two or more competent parties that defines a job or service to be performed and that is legally enforceable. The offer and acceptance process can occur in either direction. The seller can make the offer and the buyer can agree to it, or the buyer can make the offer and seller can agree to it. There is a growing effort in the United States to simplify the language of contracts and use "plain English" whenever possible. Ernest G. Gabbard, director of corporate procurement and contracting at Allegheny Teledyne, offers these suggestions for drafting "a simplified, comprehensive contract in plain English:"[5]

1. Outline the overall document before you begin writing. This will allow you to picture how the various clauses interrelate, ensure that all issues are covered, and eliminate redundancy.
2. Use a checklist of subjects to be addressed to ensure that all substantive issues are covered. Include only enough language to provide adequate coverage of the subject; avoid "generic" clauses intended to cover all circumstances.

3. Use "definitions" sparingly to avoid the necessity for the reader to flip back to the definitions section to understand a term or clause.
4. Use descriptive headers and subheads to divide the document into manageable, identifiable sections.
5. Group related clauses together to ensure a cohesive flow of rights and responsibilities.
6. Abbreviate sentences to facilitate comprehension by the reader.
7. Replace jargon and legalese with clear, concise statements. The need for clarity should be balanced with the need to ensure that all rights and responsibilities are adequately documented.
8. Use tables and appendices carefully. These are valuable tools for contract drafting; however, caution must be exercised to avoid redundancy and/or inconsistency.
9. Review the document after drafting to determine if it can be further simplified and/or abbreviated. Then have a third party review the document with the same goal.
10. Meet with the other contracting party(ies) to resolve all questions and agree that each subject is covered in the simplest, clearest manner possible.

Step 6: Communicate Special Needs to the Supplier

Change orders are used to modify or cancel purchase orders that have been issued. Some organizations use special change order documents, while others use their standard purchase order with "Change Order" printed or stamped on it. Because the purchase order is the written evidence of a contract, it is appropriate that all changes to the purchase order must also be in writing. Again, e-commerce has improved the process, by making it possible to send and receive acknowledgement of a change almost instantly. Thus, there is less temptation to make a change informally and delay issuing the confirming documentation until a more convenient time.

Step 7: Communicate Status or Fulfillment of the Order

Communication between the buyer and seller doesn't end with the order. Communication may be initiated by either party to communicate the status of the delivery or receipt of the materials.

Advanced Shipping Notice – This document is either faxed or e-mailed from a supplier to a purchaser to confirm the correct shipment of specific items and their quantities. This gives advance confirmation and planning information to personnel at the customer location.

Tracer Requests – If materials are late or lost, the buyer may request that a tracer be used to track the shipment's location and determine its estimated arrival time. Tracing production and shipment status is one of the greatest benefits of electronic communication. When a record of the delivery progress is maintained in an electronic file, anyone with authority to access the information (including the customer) can check the order's status at any time.

Receiving Documents – Receiving documents (also known as *receivers* or *receiving reports*) are used to indicate that a shipment of goods has arrived. They notify departments such as purchasing, production control, inspection, and accounts payable about the shipment. They also alert the appropriate individuals when there is a problem with the shipment. Often, the receiving document is one of the designated copies of the purchase order. In the case of an electronic system, the receiving report is another piece of information to be added to the file that the supplier and customer are maintaining.

Inspection Documents – Inspection documents differ from receiving documents in that they are used to record whether the goods conform to the organization's requirements. These forms typically specify the type of inspection used (for example, 100 percent inspection) and the results of that inspection (for example, 20 percent defective). Many non-manufacturing organizations do not have a centralized inspection process; inspection is the responsibility of a receiving function. In such cases, the receiving report and the inspection document may be the same.

Notice of Nonconformance – A notice of nonconformance informs the supplier that the material supplied did not meet the agreed upon specifications. Such a notice will normally specify what action the buyer is taking and/or it will request specific supplier action.

Quality Performance Documentation – Many organizations develop forms for documenting the quality of suppliers' performance and communicating this information to the suppliers. While no standard documentation exists, the idea is to compare actual quality performance to the quality specifications established up front through the mutual agreement of buyer and supplier. Those in the organization with managerial responsibility for quality assurance will choose the appropriate quality control processes, develop or implement the means for measuring quality, and facilitate the communication (such as an improvement process) with the supplier.

Material Return Form – This form is used to notify suppliers and in-house departments, such as purchasing and inventory control, that goods must be returned. The reasons for returning items may include over-shipments, rejections, or damaged goods. Material return forms are created in many different ways, but in all cases the intent is to authorize the shipment of goods from the customer back to the supplier.

Surplus Equipment Documentation – Purchasing departments are often asked to dispose of (or sell) surplus capital equipment or recyclable raw materials. The documentation used is similar to that used to sell other goods, and it would include a description, specifications, quantity, availability, and sometimes the asking price. Some organizations have begun listing such goods for sale using the Internet, and in some cases, the goods are offered to the highest bidder in an online auction.

Step 8: Communicate Approval for Payment

Once the goods have been received, or the service delivered, payment can be made. The supplier may communicate a request for payment by issuing a paper or electronic invoice to the buying organization. In some organizations or instances, approval to make the payment must be issued in the form of a check request (paper or electronic). In other organizations, payment is made automatically based on the terms of the contract.

Invoice – The invoice is the bill for the goods or services provided that is generated by the supplier and communicated to the buyer either by regular mail or e-mail. In some cases, an invoice is not needed. In an electronic purchasing system, payment may be authorized automatically when the receiving department acknowledges receipt of the materials in the computerized system. In a process improvement called *evaluated receipts*, some companies have instituted a two-way match between the purchase order and the receiver, which eliminates the need for the invoice.

At BHP Hawaii, a subsidiary of Australia's Broken Hill Proprietary, a reengineering effort led to a plan that includes using automation to eliminate all invoices that go through the purchasing department. This action, along with reducing the supply base and reducing inventory levels, is expected to cut purchasing costs by 5 to 10 percent.[6]

Payment by Electronic Funds Transfer – If electronic funds transfer (EFT) is used, the payment will be made electronically.

Motorola ISG, for example, deployed a program that implemented EFT with the approximately 150 suppliers who constituted more than 95 percent of the procurement activity. From the buyer's perspective, EFT electronically deposits funds in the supplier's designated account on the terms agreed to in the contract. This eliminates the expense of writing and mailing checks. The supplier benefits by receiving its funds automatically, thereby eliminating the need for mailing invoices and ensuring that the supplier consistently receives its funds on the exact terms negotiated.[7]

Payment by Check Request – In some organizations, the buyer needs to issue a check request form to authorize the accounts payable function to pay the invoice. In a manual system, typically a three-way match of PO, receiving document, and invoice is required before a check may be issued. In an electronic system, the check request step is programmed into the software so that confirmation of receipt initiates the check writing process. Using a two-way match, which compares POs and receipts or POs and invoices, simplifies the process, eliminates waste, and reduces process costs.

Step 9: Communicate Information for Managing Supplier Relationships

For each type of buyer-supplier relationship, it must be determined what information should be kept, how it should be stored, and what it will be used for. Purchase history and price records are a commonly used form of documentation. Supplier performance scorecards are also useful in assessing and documenting supplier performance.

Purchase History and Price Records – A purchase history and price record provides the buyer with easily accessible information that may be useful when preparing a new solicitation or a purchase order, or to develop price trends and forecasting.

Supplier Rating System – Many organizations develop formal systems for evaluating and rating suppliers' performance, which generally involves quality, service, delivery, and price. Rating formulas vary depending on the nature of the item being purchased, the quality required, and the competition within the supplying industry. Effective supply management requires regular tracking and reporting of supplier performance. Communication between the buyer and the supplier is critical to the success of the relationship. Figure 7.7 is a sample scorecard for evaluating supplier performance.

FIGURE 7.7
Supplier Performance Scoring Criteria

Quality

Item	Grade	Criteria
Rejected and nonconforming	4	No rejected or nonconforming shipments.
	3	Up to 5% of shipments nonconforming.
	2	>5-10% of shipments nonconforming.
	1	>10-20% of shipments nonconforming.
	0	>20% of shipments nonconforming.
Process capability, data/samples	4	Less than 1% outside control limits and samples/data received for all shipments.
	3	Up to 5% outside limits and 90-99% of shipments have samples/data.
	2	5-10% outside limits and 80-90% of shipments have samples/data
	1	10-20% outside limits and 70-80% of shipments have samples/data.
	0	More than 20% outside limits and <70% of shipments have samples/data.

Delivery

Item	Grade	Criteria
Quantity	4	All correct quantities (within tolerance).
	3	Up to 5% shipments incorrect (within tolerance).
	2	>5-10% shipments incorrect (within tolerance).
	1	>10-20% shipments incorrect (within tolerance).
	0	>20% shipments incorrect (within tolerance).
Time	4	All shipments on time (within tolerance).
	3	Up to 5% of shipments outside tolerance.
	2	>5-10% of shipments outside tolerance.
	1	>10-20% of shipments outside tolerance.
	0	>20% of shipments outside tolerance.
Paperwork	4	No missing lot numbers, packing lists, invoice errors, or other required documentation
	3	Up to 5% of shipments have errors.
	2	>5-10% of shipments have errors.
	1	>10-20% of shipments have errors.
	0	>20% of shipments have errors.
Shipment condition	4	All shipments received in expected condition.
	3	Up to 5% of shipments have damaged pallets, inadequate packaging or damaged cartons.
	2	>5-10% of shipments are damaged as above.
	1	>10-20% of shipments are damaged as above.
	0	>20% of shipments are damaged as above.

Continuous Improvement

Item	Grade	Criteria
Corrective	4	Nonconformance Action Report/Supplier's response and implementation action within 30 days.
	3	Nonconformance Action Report/Supplier's response and implementation within 31-60 days.
	2	Nonconformance Action Report/Supplier's response within 30 days,
	1	Nonconformance Action Report/Supplier's response witin 31-60 days.
	0	No response within 60 days.
Cost, lead time, lot size reduction	4	Major reduction in unit cost, lead time, amd lot size.
	2	Minor reduction in unit cost, lead time, and lot size.
	0	No reduction in unit cost, lead time, and lot size.

Source: Industrial Products Corporation (IPC) Case found in Leenders, M.R. and H.E. Fearon. *Purchasing and Supply Management*, 11th ed, Richard D. Irwin, Chicago, IL, 1997, pp. 256-257.

The shift in supply management from a transaction-oriented function to a relationship-oriented one has led to an interest in developing new ways to manage supplier relationships. At Charles Schwab, a "dealkeeper" position was created to analyze, interpret, and report on supplier relationships and performance issues. Beverly Mackay, vice president of procurement services for Charles Schwab, described the creation of the national contracts area at the company. "We recognized that we were working extremely hard on the front end of a 'deal,' with the negotiations, sourcing, and internal needs," Mackay said. "But we also realized that there was a gap on the other end, once the contract was in place, in terms of formal follow-up and feedback with the supplier." The documentation used by the dealkeeper includes traditional report cards, financial audits, and interactions with internal customers that lead to formal reports on supplier relationships. The goal is not just to report on the status quo, but to determine where and how the relationship should go in the future.[8]

Elements of Form Design and Management

Form or document design, and the management of documentation, can impact both the efficiency and effectiveness of the acquisition process. There are a number of issues to consider, including the medium, the organization of the information and user instructions, document control and retention, cost implications, and the information system used by the organization.

Available Media

The available media for operational documents range from standard paper to paperless systems. The appropriate media depend on such factors as the use of the form, cost, timeliness, ultimate disposition, and even the image the organization wishes to project.

Organization of Information

The way information is organized on a document is important to its success. The information should be kept to the necessary minimum. Superfluous information detracts from the needed information. Another element for creating successful forms is to make it easy for the user to enter information. This is most often accomplished with check marks next to appropriate responses, as opposed to a fill in the blank format. It is also important to keep the information on the form in a sequence that is logical or that makes sense.

Electronic documents have many advantages, including instant updates and distribution, no obsolescence, and fields blocked to prevent errors. Bar coding, which has the same advantages, is used in many places to automate the transfer of data onto the documents. Texas Instruments' (TI) online catalog system for MRO items uses bar coding. At the supplier's warehouse, a package label that includes a bar code and the employee's location is generated. When the supplier's warehouse employee picks and packs the box, scanning the bar code indicates order completion and produces the appropriate shipment and billing notice. This process reduces errors in purchase order number and item number mismatches. TI's system compares the shipment document to the outbound order, and if the data are correct, the system creates an invoice and sends it to accounts payable as approved for payment. Accounts payable then vouchers the amount for the next payment cycle.[9]

Figure 7.8 depicts the uses and contribution of electronic purchase systems to the step-by-step acquisition process.

An example of good information capture is the cash register system used at most large grocery stores. Each item being purchased has a bar code that allows the assignment of its identity and price. When the bar code is scanned by the cashier, an itemized sales slip is generated for the customer. At the same time, the store's receipts, inventory, and sales records are updated automatically. The only physical activity to record the transaction in four separate files is the scanning of the bar code. Contrast this with the task of completing a tax form, in which the taxpayer is required to gather information from dozens of sources and complete a variety of calculations to enter a single figure onto one line on the tax form.

Instructions

If possible, instructions for using a document should be provided on the document itself. The instructions need to be concise and clear for everyone who will be using the document.

FIGURE 7.8

Steps in Purchasing Cycle: Examples of the Potential Contribution of a Computerized Purchasing System

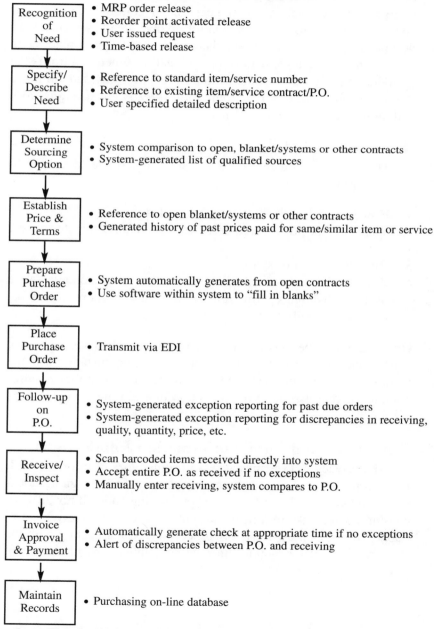

Recognition of Need	• MRP order release • Reorder point activated release • User issued request • Time-based release
Specify/ Describe Need	• Reference to standard item/service number • Reference to existing item/service contract/P.O. • User specified detailed description
Determine Sourcing Option	• System comparison to open, blanket/systems or other contracts • System-generated list of qualified sources
Establish Price & Terms	• Reference to open blanket/systems or other contracts • Generated history of past prices paid for same/similar item or service
Prepare Purchase Order	• System automatically generates from open contracts • Use software within system to "fill in blanks"
Place Purchase Order	• Transmit via EDI
Follow-up on P.O.	• System-generated exception reporting for past due orders • System-generated exception reporting for discrepancies in receiving, quality, quantity, price, etc.
Receive/ Inspect	• Scan barcoded items received directly into system • Accept entire P.O. as received if no exceptions • Manually enter receiving, system compares to P.O.
Invoice Approval & Payment	• Automatically generate check at appropriate time if no exceptions • Alert of discrepancies between P.O. and receiving
Maintain Records	• Purchasing on-line database

Source: Ellram, L. and L. Birou, *Purchasing for Bottom-Line Impact: Improving the Organization through Strategic Procurement*, Irwin Professional Publishing, Burr Ridge, IL, 1995, p. 135.

Document Control

Document control is important in any organization or bureaucracy. In larger organizations, this function is often centralized. In smaller organizations, someone in each department controls that particular department's documents. Such control involves the key elements of design, user determination, standardization, and appropriate stock levels. An important element of operational document control is the periodic review of all documents to ensure uniformity and eliminate the risk of obsolescence. Electronic forms greatly enhance this work and, in fact, eliminate much of it.

Retention Periods

The four standard questions to ask to determine how long to retain information are:

1. How long will the information be needed?
2. What are the legally required periods, if any, for storing the forms?
3. What is the cost of storage?
4. What will be the availability when the information is to be retrieved (who has permission, what is the procedure for authorization, how will it be retrieved)?

Often, retention periods are a result of compromises between cost, convenience, need, and legal requirements. The organization with the records must get approval from the agency or party that requires retention before assuming that retention in electronic media will be acceptable.

Privacy Act and Public Information Implications

The Privacy Act restricts access to some types of information. It is important to understand these restrictions when designing documents and systems. In governmental purchasing, most (if not all) purchasing documents are a matter of public record and are subject to public view. Legal advice is often necessary when dealing with the Privacy Act and the public information implications of document design and management.

Cost Implications

The amount of money it takes to print a supply of documents is only a fraction of the total cost. Many other cost areas are related to operational documentation. One of these is the time needed to fill out the document. Other costs are due to storage and the time needed to distribute the document (including copies). Another cost relates to the speed of information access, particularly if the document is poorly designed. Costs also result from errors in design or document completion. These errors can amount to substantial costs to the organization, and many of these costs can be eliminated through reengineering the acquisition process and developing an efficient electronic system with effective online documents. The principle to be applied is that the information should be captured only once and automatically transferred as needed without transcription, which introduces the opportunity for errors.

Printed vs. Electronically Generated Forms

There can be a large difference in the costs of operating a purchasing system that is computer based versus a manual system that uses printed forms. A key difference is the time and effort involved in accessing files and sending the information. Electronic information can later be retrieved for sorting and analysis in ways that are easier than paper-based information.

The advantages of computerized purchase systems also apply to the generation of forms. Probably the most commonly used computer-generated form in purchasing is the purchase order. A purchase order data file can be used to efficiently process purchase orders and to provide numerous reporting and status activities. Almost any form can lend itself to computer applications. Many computer-generated forms are used in a paperless system, where the form itself is viewed and used only on a computer screen.

Compatibility with Equipment

If information is captured or stored in various electronic systems, these systems must be able to exchange the information or move it to a central file for manipulation or analysis. Serious oversights can result in the inability of one function or department's system to "talk" to another department's system. Enterprise resource planning (ERP) involves a set of applications that helps to manage and automate a business. These applications include finance, human resources, manufacturing and logistics, and supply chain management. When successfully implemented, enterprise resource planning systems may eliminate many interface problems. Major suppliers of ERP systems include SAP, Baan, PeopleSoft, Oracle, Lawson, and J.D. Edwards.

Periodic Review

As discussed earlier in this chapter, documents should follow and flow from the development of an efficient and effective acquisition process. As processes change, it is necessary to review operational documents (paper and electronic) and ask if they enable or hinder the efficiency and effectiveness of the purchasing process.

Role of Information Systems

Information technology (IT) is an "essential enabler" to business process reengineering.[10] The same can be said for IT's role in streamlining and improving the operational side of the supply function, as well as in creating opportunities for improved information flows up and down the supply channel. This is one of the greatest opportunities for cost reduction and process improvement in the supply chain. Two principles should be applied:

- Capture the data just once, when it is first created. Then transfer it electronically whenever needed. This avoids all transcription errors and saves time.
- Streamline the process first, then the documents that support the process. An automated system managing the wrong, or unnecessary, information is a travesty. This is often referred to as "paving the cowpaths."

Key Points

1. Information and relationship management are vital to the effective execution of the purchasing and supply management function. Communication tools and techniques, both verbal and writ-

ten, may distinguish highly effective supply managers and supply organizations from less effective ones.

2. Documents, whether in paper or electronic form, are vital to the flow of information within and across organizations. While the form of documents may vary, proper design and application of documents can substantially improve the speed and effectiveness of information exchange.

3. The order fulfillment process is frequently a key to ensuring customer satisfaction. Optimize this process by making it as simple and straightforward as possible. Then put into place the documents needed to capture, transfer, and retain the information to support the process.

4. Certain types of information are legally required to be in writing. Use of the proper method of capturing, recording, and retaining this information can make the difference between winning and losing in the event of litigation.

5. Because the main purpose of a document is to communicate, document design should be guided by the same rules as any other form of communication, including using clear and concise language, avoiding ambiguity, and allowing for clarification. In addition, documents should "fit" with organizational, marketing, financial, and operational strategies.

6. Document design and control must consider not only the initial communication purpose of the document but also such factors as cost, who needs access to the information, limitations on access, retention, and compatibility with equipment and systems.

Questions for Review

1. Why is it important to focus on process?
2. What are the key functions served by a document?
3. Why do strategies flow down from the corporate level to the divisional and functional levels?
4. Why is it important to track supplier performance?
5. How is an evaluation matrix used to select the best overall supplier value?
6. What are the advantages of electronic documents over paper versions?

Endnotes

1. Hammer, M. and J. Champy. *Reengineering the Corporation*, 1st edition, HarperBusiness, New York,1993, p. 39.
2. Leenders, M.R. and H.E. Fearon. *Purchasing and Supply Management*, 11th edition, Richard D. Irwin, Chicago, 1997, p. 132.
3. Duffy, R.J. "Before and After," *Purchasing Today®*, November 1997, pp. 38-39.
4. Fearon, H.E., D.W. Dobler, and K.H. Killen. *The Purchasing Handbook*, McGraw-Hill, New York, 1993, p. 259.
5. Gabbard, E.G. "Doing Things the Write Way," *Purchasing Today®*, October 1999, p. 8-9.
6. Karoway, C. "Reengineering in Action," *NAPM Insights*, February 1995, p. 38.
7. Limperis, J. "Vendor-Benders: How To Assure That Your Supplier Relationships Are Collision Proof," Proceedings of the 1997 NAPM International Purchasing Conference, NAPM, Tempe, AZ, 1997, p. 454.
8. Duffy, R.J. "Trail Blazing," *Purchasing Today®*, April 1999, p. 47-48.
9. Bulkeley, M. "Express Buying Made Simple," *NAPM Insights*, May 1994, p. 10-11.
10. Hammer and Champy, 1993, p. 44.

CHAPTER 8

PERFORMANCE TRACKING
AND IMPROVEMENT

*How does a manager know when the department and
staff are doing a good job?*

Chapter Objectives

- To identify the reasons and methods for evaluating performance at the department and individual level
- To identify key factors in performance evaluation
- To show why it is important to align performance metric systems with organizational and functional plans at both the strategic and operational level

Organizational Expectations of Purchasing

One of the major functions of management is to evaluate and control the performance of an activity. The purchasing department or supply function is certainly no exception. Criteria for evaluating purchasing and supply department performance and individual staff performance must be developed. Also, a system for comparing actual performance to these criteria or standards must be developed and used. Two of the more challenging questions facing supply managers are:

- What should be measured?
- How should it be measured?

Chapter 2 addressed developing and implementing strategic and operational plans that outline the goals and objectives of the department. The department's goals and objectives should then drive the behavior of the department staff. Individual performance should be linked to the achievement of departmental goals, which in turn should contribute to the achievement of organizational goals and objectives. The supplier community has been described as the "extended enterprise." In this context, the performance of the suppliers under the leadership of the supply management team is a critical element of the enterprise's overall results.

To be effective, the performance evaluation and reward system must align with the goals and objectives of the organization. For example, if a major organizational initiative is continuous quality improvement but the individual buyer is evaluated and rewarded primarily for cost reductions, then the buyer may be more concerned with cost reductions than quality improvements. Unless credit is given for reducing the cost of quality, the means used by the buyer to achieve the necessary cost reduction may work against the ability of the purchasing and supply function to contribute to the overall organizational goal of quality improvement. If top management wants buyers to help the organization achieve its goals and support its mission, behavior that leads to attaining organizational goals needs to be recognized and rewarded. Developing a flexible performance evaluation system that can be adjusted to accommodate changes in strategic plans is a difficult task for human resources managers.

Congruence with Organizational Objectives

To determine departmental or functional effectiveness in meeting organizational needs, the mission of the organization and the specific objectives of the purchasing operation must be understood. Chapter 2 of this volume discussed the importance of aligning functional or departmental strategies with organizational strategies. Once the organizational mission is understood, those in the supply function can perform tasks that contribute to organizational goals. For example, the specific objectives of a purchasing function may be described as obtaining maximum value, prescribed quality, and continuity of supply in keeping with the organizational objectives of continuous improvement and quality. Benchmarks can be established to measure the impact of the departmental efforts. Much emphasis is placed on cost/benefit analysis. The purchasing department is expected to carry its weight in the organization. Fortunately, there are many ways, such as cost, quality, technology, and speed, that the supply base can contribute to achieving organizational goals. This makes the purchasing function's added value and, in the private sector, contribution to profit possible to document. Other ways that supply managers can contribute to organizational goals, such as through the quality of supplier relationships, may be more difficult to measure. These "softer" measures may actually contribute more to organizational success, but because of the difficulty in documenting and measuring them, they may be left out of the appraisal system.

Congruence with Supplier and Customer Objectives

Just as the objectives of purchasing should align with organizational objectives, purchasing objectives must also align with supplier and customer objectives. The buying organization's structure needs to facilitate the flow of information between customers and purchasers. This may be accomplished through cross-functional sourcing teams or through the efforts of individual buyers.

Concepts of the Purchasing and Supply Function

There are differing perspectives on the basic concept of the supply function. Historically, the function has been seen as a profit center or a cost center. More recently, supply management has been seen as the function responsible for bringing supplier capabilities to bear in fulfilling the organization's mission. The perception of the function affects the expectations placed on those in the function by all levels of management in the organization. The performance measurement system used to evaluate individuals in the function and the function itself, may reflect the overall perspective of the function. Because measurement is a key motivator of individual behavior, measurements must encourage the desired behaviors. For example, if only purchase price variance (the difference between actual prices paid and a preset standard or estimate) is measured, the price will be targeted for improvement, possibly at the expense of other key performance elements, such as quality, delivery, and leadtime.

Purchasing as a Profit Center

Some companies have designated business units that must compete for and sell their services to other groups within the company and, in some cases, to other companies. In such organizations, the purchasing and supply function is often considered to be part of "shared services" or "corporate services." There are many variations on how this concept is applied. For example, a purchasing department may charge other departments for its services. In the extreme, this concept moves procurement into its own corporation that must compete for the company's purchasing business. An example of this practice is the agreement by United Technologies Corporation (UTC) to use the IBM electronic procurement system to place its requirements for general (expense related) procurement purchases. UTC believes that implementation of the e-procurement system created by IBM for its own buying was the most cost effective way for UTC to automate its purchasing process.

Purchasing as a Cost Center

In many organizations, the purchasing and supply function is seen as a cost center because it does not generate revenue. Purchasing is believed to cost the organization money. While there are many arguments against this perspective, it is still common. The major weakness of this perspective is that it ignores the potential contribution to the enterprise of a well-structured and well-managed supply base.

Purchasing as an Independent Center

Another view of the supply function is as an independent center that markets its services to internal customers. Internal customers may use the organization's purchasing services or choose to purchase some other way. This is similar to the cost center approach in that it assumes a transactional relationship with all suppliers and misses the opportunity for tapping supplier capabilities.

Department or Function Performance Appraisal

A macro-level assessment of the supply function can serve many purposes. This assessment includes:

- Determining the effectiveness of department management
- Measuring performance trends over time (improvements or deterioration)
- Determining if value is being added or if a contribution is being made to the achievement of organizational goals
- Providing incentives for improvement
- Establishing rewards, such as raises or bonuses
- Determining resource allocation for the next time period

The factors that the purchasing manager may wish to rate include the skills and knowledge of personnel, the appropriateness of the organizational structure, the scope and accountability of each job, the departmental plans, policies, procedures, and so forth. These factors influence the department's performance and are, therefore, useful indicators of capability.

Measuring Improvement or Deterioration

Measurement can provide evidence of improvement or early warning signals about deterioration of performance. This allows managers and buyers to either use the success of improvement as leverage in internal negotiations or to take corrective action if performance is slipping in some area.

Providing Incentives for Improvement

Measurement also has a built-in incentive. Purchasing personnel constantly witness the impact of the competitive environment. Well-established and accepted measurement of continuous performance criteria generally provide an objective means of improvement.

Determining Resources Needed for Improvement

Measurement can also provide the data needed to argue for the allocation or reallocation of resources to achieve needed improvements. Changes in a variety of factors (for example, sales, product mix, manufacturing capacity, and raw material prices) will create the need to allocate or reallocate resources. Measurements need to be relevant and flexible to help predict these changing needs and to suggest appropriate responses.

Determining How Much a Process Adds Value

Many activities have been conducted for many years simply because they were never examined for improvement. Today most areas of the organization are subject to analysis to reduce, realign, or eliminate activities that no longer add value. This, of course, requires some level of agreement about what adds value to the organization.

Steps in Department-Level Evaluation

A process for performing a department-level evaluation should start with a review of the alignment of the department's objectives with those of the organization. Next, the criteria for success and the appraisal factors should be identified. A process for planning and conducting a department evaluation is explained in the following sections.

Identify Departmental Objectives

When a manager develops a system to evaluate the performance of any department, the logical starting point is an analysis of the department's objectives. As discussed in Chapter 2, departmental objectives should flow from and be aligned with the objectives of the organization. Once departmental objectives have been defined, the organizational structure and the responsibilities assigned to each work group should be examined to determine the impact each operating activity has on the attainment of departmental objectives. This procedure normally discloses the critical activities in the operation where evaluation and subsequent control are most important.

Analyzing departmental objectives in a purchasing department reveals one unfortunate fact: Most of the critical points at which evaluation and control should be affected lie in a single function — buying. Each purchaser has a range of extremely variable activities under his or her jurisdiction. Moreover, an examination of the basic responsibilities of each buyer reveals that performance in most areas is difficult to express quantitatively. Thus, the nature of the purchasing function makes it difficult to establish workable performance standards.

Many organizations have adopted a broad approach to the evaluation and control of purchasing activities. Most organizations attempt to establish performance targets (standards) for the measurable secondary factors that contribute to attainment of primary buying objectives. Recognizing that a single factor may not provide an accurate indication of creative buying performance, most organizations develop a crosscheck that measures several factors that relate to the same primary objective. For example, buying performance relative to the price objective can be checked from two standpoints:

- Actual prices paid can be compared with target prices.
- Targets for cost savings resulting from negotiation and from value analysis can be established and actual savings can be compared with these targets.

Thus, two measurements provide a crosscheck on the attainment of the same primary objective — price. A similar approach can be used in evaluating buying performance relative to each of the other basic objectives of the department and buyer.

Unfortunately, these "easy to quantify" measures often lead to over-emphasis on objectives like price and an under-emphasis on more strategic activities, such as contributions to developing and maintaining end-customers through effective buyer-supplier relationships.

Identify Criteria for Success

The criteria for success must be established for each task that is to be measured. Performance evaluations are meaningless unless the individuals managing and working in the department know up front what constitutes success and how the degree of success or failure will be determined.

Identify Appraisal Factors

Areas of appraisal may be related to tactical operations (day-to-day), commodity management (strategic), and the integration with product or market creation (strategic and technical). While many factors can be considered when evaluating a purchasing department's performance, typical appraisals consider one or more of the following factors.

Contributions to Profitability and Success of Core Activity – Contributions to profitability are a primary concern in a business. Government agencies and institutions are concerned with total value and the maximization of resource utilization. It is difficult to measure how the supply management function contributes to these results. Customer satisfaction, cost, quality, and speed are all key areas of attention for tracking the suppliers' contributions to the organization's goals.

Customer Satisfaction – Feedback from user departments or internal customers, as well as external or end customers, can be a good source of data on how well the purchasing department is functioning and serving its customers. Feedback can be obtained informally or through structured questionnaires and surveys. The decision about what information to collect and how to collect it depends on the costs associated with data collection as well as the benefit of having the knowledge. If no concrete plan exists for using the information to increase efficiency or effectiveness, it may not be worth the data collection and analysis costs.

External Customers – In many organizations, purchasing does not have direct contact with external or final customers. However, knowing and understanding the final customer is one of the best ways for purchasing personnel to align their activities more closely with organizational goals. Supply managers need to develop a process for learning about external customers' needs and wants. Honda of America Manufacturing follows the philosophy that it is, in part, serving as a conduit by which suppliers deliver value to the Honda customers.

At United States Cellular Corporation, purchasing personnel do not interact directly with external customers. The customer satisfaction program, Operation Satisfaction, which is driven by operations and marketing, is based on direct customer feedback drawn from telephone interviews. Purchasing receives Operation Satisfaction reports and modifies its programs based on the information gathered. For example, purchasing personnel work with the product planning department personnel on modifications or changes driven by subscriber equipment comments about service, equipment, or technology.[1]

At Steelcase, Inc., in Grand Rapids, Michigan, purchasing personnel have direct contact with external customers who often request sourcing involvement. Customers may attend presentations on Steelcase's sourcing practices and receive information on the latest materials. The sourcing group can inform customers of Steelcase's efforts to control costs. The contacts also give the sourcing group the chance to benchmark and get new ideas from final customers.[2]

Internal Customers – Measuring the satisfaction of internal customers can be instrumental in improving the performance of the purchasing department and the individuals in the department. Finding out how internal customers view the role of purchasing in the organization can also help purchasers to understand why internal customers behave as they do when working with purchasing. When a writer for *Purchasing Today*® asked a group of internal customers how purchasing can improve its relationships with internal customers, six items emerged:[3]

- Make sure other departments are aware of purchasing's procedures and requirements, along with the value purchasing can bring to the process. Offer to "teach" other departments in a question-and-answer session.
- Develop a familiarity with the issues and constraints that other departments face. What special needs or requirements do they have? What can purchasing do to help meet those needs?
- If a department seems to continuously make last-minute or unreasonable requests of purchasing, find out why. What can purchasing do? Can purchasing work with the department to help change this?
- Keep individuals from other departments informed throughout the procurement process.

- "Sell" purchasing's services to other departments. What can purchasing do for internal customers? Are internal customers aware of what purchasing can offer?
- Show and share some successes that other departments have had in working with purchasing. Can individuals from these departments offer testimonials?

Timeliness of Actions – One of a purchasing department's primary responsibilities is to support operations or the satisfactory completion of the organization's tasks. Three measurements that indicate how effectively this responsibility is fulfilled for a production or retail operation are:

- Percentage of overdue orders
- Percentage of stock-outs caused by late deliveries
- Number of production stoppages or lost sales and customers caused by late deliveries

Depending on the need and purpose of evaluation, these data can be categorized by material classification, supplier, or buyer.

In a government or service industry the focus will be on cycle time or supplier leadtime. For example, if the maintenance of a police or emergency vehicle is not completed on schedule, the consequences can be serious. If operating room supplies are not delivered as promised, a hospital may be unable to meet scheduled surgical needs.

It is obvious that a number of performance factors can be measured to appraise buying proficiency. These factors differ in importance among organizations, depending on the nature of the business and the materials purchased. Each organization selects the measures that are most useful and cost-effective for its own situation.

Material and Service Costs – Five techniques provide cross-checks on the reasonableness of the prices paid for materials:

- Standard or target prices can be established for major materials. Prices actually paid can then be charted against the target figures to display any significant differences. Another basis of comparison would be a materials budget using standard price data.

- An organization can develop its own average "price paid" indices for major classes of materials. The trends of such price indices are valuable guides in assessing the effectiveness of performance. If developed on a comparable basis, these indices can also be charted against national commodity price indices published by the Bureau of Labor Statistics, the Department of Commerce, and others. This comparison will reveal cases in which an organization's costs are rising at a greater rate than market prices during an inflationary period.
- Periodic cost savings figures can be charted for savings arising from such activities as negotiation, value analysis, design and material changes, supplier suggestions, supplier changes, packaging improvements, and transportation cost reduction projects.
- If an organization engages in forward buying activities, gains and losses from these activities can be periodically reported to determine forecasting effectiveness.
- A report of the percentage of purchase orders that are issued without firm prices provides another basis for evaluating and controlling costs.

The preceding measurements can be classified and subclassified in ways to pinpoint the causes of the problems they reveal.

Material and Service Quality – Once material or service specifications have been established, the most direct measure of quality performance is the number of delivered materials or services that are rejected or found unacceptable by inspectors and customer departments. The number of such items is compared with the total number of items received, and the defect rate is expressed as a *percent defective*. Because even a small percentage can be a significant and unacceptable rate of defects, many organizations track defects in parts per million (ppm). To understand the significance, note that 1 percent defective is equal to 10,000 ppm. Many manufacturers have found that customers demand defect rates of 100 ppm or less. To check on the improvement of quality specifications, the purchasing manager can also review the value analysis reports dealing with design or service changes and material substitutions. The same concepts apply to service purchases.

Supplier Reliability – Five measurements can be used to indicate the reliability of major suppliers:

- Percentage of late deliveries or late completion of services and percentage, or ppm, of rejected items, further analyzed and classified by supplier, buyer, and so on
- Percentage of orders in which incorrect materials were shipped or incorrect services were provided
- Percentage of orders in which incorrect quantities of materials were shipped or incorrect number of service calls were performed
- Percentage of orders in which split shipments were made or where it was necessary to accept partial completion of the service on the due date
- Quality and reliability of transportation service offered by various carriers

Supplier Development – Suppliers impact a significant part of cost, and their failure to perform must be considered in the search for maximum value. The more reliable the supplier, the less costly it is to deal with the supplier's organization. It is difficult to measure the costs an organization incurs from poor supplier performance, but some of the sources of such costs are expediting, inspecting and sorting, reworking, returning defective goods, missing customer promises, and filing warranty claims. Many astute purchasing teams have begun to work closely with key suppliers to improve both supplier and customer processes to attack these sources of unnecessary costs.

For example, on October 8, 1998, Nordstrom, Inc., a fashion specialty retailer, announced a partnership with Streamline, Inc., an online leader in the consumer direct marketplace. The deal included a $28.8 million investment in Streamline so that the company could accelerate its national growth strategy and strengthen "the ability of both companies to capture the enormous market opportunity for consumer direct services, which is expected to exceed $60 billion by the year 2005. Nordstrom may provide merchandise offerings through Streamline in the future."[4]

Order Quantity and Inventory Effectiveness – Purchasing's failure to buy the right quantity (that is, the quantity that keeps the operation functioning, yet minimizes the money tied up in inventory investment) jeopardizes the cost structure or misuses resources that might be better used elsewhere. Four measurements for evaluating how well purchasing invests funds are:

- A chart showing target and actual inventory levels in the aggregate and by major classifications along with a chart showing inventory turnover rates for the same material classifications. When analyzed together, these charts point out imbalances between inventory carrying costs and material acquisition costs.
- A report of "dead stock" materials carried in stores, resulting from overbuying or less-then-planned use. Inventory may be measured in "days-on-hand" to indicate the effective rate of turnover.
- The number of stock-outs and production stoppages, or customer orders not filled, attributed to underbuying.
- A list of supplier stocking arrangements that have been negotiated, along with an estimate of resulting inventory savings.

Creativity and Value Creation – Value creation is becoming an important factor in the success of organizations. The degree to which creativity and value can be obtained from suppliers is something that purchasing can facilitate.

Deciding what to measure is the first step in developing a performance appraisal system. Margaret Williams, C.P.M., director of supplier management, reports that at Tandem Computers, Inc., in Cupertino, California, measures are tailored to the specific situation.

> Tactical procurement measures include: obtaining material to meet MRP forecasts; maintaining inventory level and turn goals; and ensuring suppliers perform to basic standards of on-time delivery, flexibility, quality, basic competitive pricing, and support. In the strategic arena, measures include supplier and commodity strategy at the product development stage. Commodity managers are responsible for the core commodities — representing 80 percent of the purchase dollars — from development through the end of life cycle. The managers and their teams own and are meas-

ured on how they achieve competitive cost allocation and quality products and develop supplier relationships. Finally, supplier performance measures are included in the overall evaluation of purchasing. Clearly, our performance is directly related to our suppliers' performance. When our suppliers succeed, we succeed; when they fail, we fail. Our Tandem products typically reduce in price from 10 percent to 30 percent each year. It doesn't take a rocket scientist to figure out what challenges the commodity teams must live up to. Our cost reduction efforts must meet or exceed those reductions for us to improve or maintain margins.[5]

Internal Audits

A purchasing audit is a comprehensive, systematic, independent, and periodic examination of an organization's purchasing environment, objectives, strategies, and activities. It is used to identify strengths and weaknesses and to develop a plan of action to improve purchasing performance. Regular and unbiased feedback is needed, and an audit is one way to gather this information.

Often, audits are conducted by outside consultants to ensure the objectivity and independence of judgment. They are, however, also conducted internally. A drawback to this may be hesitancy on the part of the auditors to be critical of performance, even when it is justified.

Process Benchmarking

Process benchmarking refers to the search for organizations that perform the "best" in a particular area and the examination of their processes for the purpose of emulating them. In other words, process benchmarking answers the question: "How are we doing compared to other leading-edge organizations?" The answer to this question should push an organization toward the development of best practices for its own operations.

Before initiating process benchmarking, several questions need to be answered, including:

- Is the organization willing to make a major change? Unless all parties agree that the current situation is unacceptable, change may be difficult to foster.
- Is the expected improvement worth the expenditure?
- Are the results important to the organization?
- Does the process impact a critical success factor?
- Have all investigations related to this process been completed? Have all other alternatives been explored?
- Has the organization begun measuring the current process?
- Does the organization know the major cost components and service factors of its process?
- Is the organization willing to wait for a benchmarking study to be completed before implementing any changes?
- Is the organization willing to reveal information about its own processes to outside organizations?

Process benchmarking may involve dividing the functions of an organization into several modules to be analyzed as independent processes. Such a study may find, for example, that one organization has the best order processing, another has the best inventory control, and so on.

The mission of the Center for Advanced Purchasing Studies (CAPS) — a non-profit organization affiliated with NAPM and the Arizona State University College of Business — is to help organizations achieve competitive advantage by providing them with leading-edge research and benchmarking information to support the evolution of strategic purchasing and supply management. CAPS has been conducting industry wide, and some governmentwide, purchasing performance process benchmarking studies since 1986.[6] Figure 8.1 lists the industries for which CAPS has conducted benchmarks and the date(s) of the studies. To date, more than 25 industries have been examined, some three or four times thus providing trend analysis opportunities. The CAPS benchmarking studies include data on a set of standard benchmarks, as well as benchmarks of specific interest to the members of the industry-based ad hoc committee. Figure 8.2 lists the standard benchmarks used in all of the CAPS purchasing performance benchmarking studies.

FIGURE 8.1
CAPS List of Industries that Have Been Benchmarked

Aerospace/Defense Contracting (1997 report, 1996 data)

Appliance (1992 report, 1990 data

Automotive (1997 report, 1996 data)

Banking (1999 report, 1997 data)

Beverage (1999 report, 1997 data)

Carbon Steel (1999 report, 1997 data)

Chemical (1999 report, 1997 data)

Computer/Telecommunications Equipment (1998 report, 1997 data)

Department of Energy Contractors (1999 report, 1998 data)

Electrical Equipment (1998 report, 1996 data)

Electronics (1996 report, 1995 data)

Engineering/Construction (1999 report, 1997 data)

Food Manufacturing (1999 report, 1997 data)

Higher Education (1997 report, 1995 data)

Investment Recovery (1999 report, 1997 data)

Life Insurance (1997 report, 1996 data)

Machinery (1998 report, 1997 data)

Mining (1999 report, 1997 data)

Municipal Governments (1997 report, 1996 data)

Paper (1999 report, 1997 data)

Personal Care Products (1997 report, 1995 data)

Petroleum (1998 report, 1997 data)

Pharmaceutical (1998 report, 1996 data)

Semiconductor (1997 report, 1995 data)

State/County Governments (1998 report, 1997 data)

Telecommunications Services (1998 report, 1997 data)

Textiles/Apparel (1999 report, 1997 data)

Transportation (1998 report, 1997 data)

Source: Center for Advanced Purchasing Studies, Cross-Industry Comparison of Standard Benchmarks, 1999, www.capsresearch.org.

FIGURE 8.2
CAPS Standard Cross-Industry Benchmarks

1. Purchase dollars as a percent of sales dollars
2. Purchasing operating expense dollars as a percent of sales dollars
3. Cost to spend a dollar (purchasing operating expense dollars as a percent of purchase dollars)
4. Purchasing employees as a percent of company employees
5. Sales dollars per purchasing employee
6. Purchase dollars per purchasing employee
7. Purchase dollars per professional purchasing employee
8. Active suppliers per purchasing employee
9. Active suppliers per professional purchasing employee
10. Purchase dollars spent per active supplier
11. Purchasing operating expense dollars per active supplier
12. Change in number of active suppliers during the reporting period
13. Percent of purchase dollars spent with minority-owned suppliers
14. Percent of purchase dollars spent with women-owned suppliers
15. Percent of active suppliers accounting for 90 percent of purchase dollars
16. Purchase order cycle time (in days)
17. Percent of purchase transactions processed through electronic commerce
18. Percent of services purchases handled by the purchasing department
19. Percent of total purchases handled by the purchasing department
20. Average annual training hours per professional purchasing employee
21. Percent of purchase transactions processed via procurement card

Source: Center for Advanced Purchasing Studies, www.capsresearch.org.

Exercising Management Control in Response to Results

Evaluation should be an ongoing process, a catalyst for improvement in the purchasing function, and a means of validating performance to management's expectations. Once the results of a performance appraisal are obtained, management must be sincere in its efforts to find the root cause and to correct the problems identified through the appraisal. Otherwise, the entire performance appraisal process will serve no useful purpose. Measuring performance is only half the battle. Deciding what to do with the results of the measurement and how to do it is the other half.

Conflict Resolution Skills

Conflict resolution is a model for resolving disagreements. The model starts with the assumption that the parties involved in the conflict are stuck and need to get unstuck. It is a non-judgmental model in that neither side is assumed to be inherently wrong, bad, or evil. Supply managers need to develop a conflict resolution strategy for dealing with issues that arise out of performance appraisals or audits. The following seven-step checklist may help in the development of a conflict resolution strategy:[7]

1. Resolve internal conflicts.
2. Forgive the other person.
3. Listen to what the other party needs.
4. Set priorities — needs and wants.
5. Discuss the situation calmly.
6. Come to a mutually agreeable solution.
7. Follow up to see how things are going.

Non-Defensive Problem Solving

Dr. W. Edwards Deming (1900-1993), in his quality absolutes, notes that a major obstacle to process improvement is employee fear, which often arises from the common practice of determining "who did it" when a mistake occurs. Deming notes that even when human error is the apparent source of a problem, most often something in the system or process led to the person's error. Therefore, it is necessary to seek the root cause behind the error and eliminate the source of this root cause. This is called *mistake-proofing*. If problem solving can be focused on searching for the root cause rather than placing blame, non-defensive problem solving can occur.

Corrective Action Process

The corrective action required will vary depending on the magnitude and root cause of the problem. In general, the process will include establishing timeframes for improvement, prioritizing the steps in the improvement plan, and conducting a cost/benefit analysis to determine the appropriate level of resources to allocate to the corrective action plan implementation.

Establishment of Timeframes – It is necessary to establish timeframes for corrective action. This may take the form of a due date, along with milestones and timeframes leading up to full implementation of the corrective action. The manager must be clear about the purpose of the corrective action. In some cases, the first step may be to take the time to determine the root cause of the problem and then develop an action plan for dealing with the root cause. In other cases, interim measures may be taken to deal with symptoms of the problem while a plan is developed to address the root cause.

Prioritization – Whatever the process, prioritizing the steps in the implementation plan is critical. This process should include an understanding of the resources needed for the action and their availability.

Cost/Benefit Analysis – Corrective action must be cost effective, given the expected benefits if the action is undertaken. A comparison of resources (people, time, equipment, money, and so on) and the expected value should be performed. The ability to quantify the value of the benefits achieved is paramount, and in most process improvements this benefit is in the form of saving people's time. Therefore, one of the most commonly used methods of quantifying the savings is through activity-based cost analysis.

Evaluate Staff Performance

The success or failure of each purchasing employee is in some part determined by the department's processes, policies, and procedures, especially the performance measurement system. Performance standards must be established for each buyer to provide guidelines for appropriate behavior and to clarify the expectations of management. There must also be a clear link between meeting or exceeding standards and the reward system in the organization.

Determine Employee Objectives

The objectives for each employee should flow from the strategy of the purchasing/supply department (which should be aligned with both business unit and corporate strategy) (see Figure 2.2 in Chapter 2). Richard L. Mooney, C.P.M., a purchasing consultant, suggested applying Pareto analysis to determine the 20 percent of tasks performed by an individual that are expected to account for 80 percent of the beneficial impact on the employee's overall performance.[8] Performance standards should be established for these *A* tasks, and metrics should be developed to determine the degree to which the standards have been met.

Another common approach is to flow down objectives from top levels of management. At each level the objectives are determined by what the individual can accomplish that supports or contributes to the next level achieving its defined results. As more work is performed in teams, the individual's objectives are determined by how he or she can contribute to the success of the team. This is determined by breaking down the team's work into individual roles and responsibilities. These then become the individual's objectives and potential contributions to team results.

Management by Objectives (MBO), which was discussed in Chapter 4, is an objective-setting process that depends on mutual agreement between the individual and the supervisor. Together they identify objectives, establish goals, define evaluation criteria, and measure results.

Determine Criteria for Success

The criteria for success must be established for each task that will be measured. Performance evaluations are meaningless unless the individual knows up front what constitutes success and how the degree of success or failure will be determined.

Determine Appraisal Factors

How does a purchasing manager determine the factors of an employee's performance that should be evaluated? Each purchasing management group must choose the factors that are related to its specific responsibilities. Typically, measures include both quantitative and qualitative factors. While there is no standard set of factors that fits every organization or situation, some commonly used metrics are shown in Figure 8.3.

FIGURE 8.3

Factors in Purchaser or Supplier Performance Assessment

Cost Measures
- Actual costs compared to: historic (standard) cost, target costs, cost-reduction goal, benchmark costs
- Total cost of acquisition compared to total cost of use
- Inventory levels, inventory costs
- Improved cash flow

Quality Measures
- Actual quality compared to: historic quality, specification quality, target quality
- Quality improvement compared to: historic quality, quality-improvement goal

Delivery Measures
- Actual delivery compared to: promised delivery, window (that is, two days early to zero days late)
- Actual delivery for rush orders compared to promised delivery
- Actual delivery frequency compared to promised delivery frequency
- Actual delivery compared to specified delivery

Service Measures
- Responsiveness to internal customers
- Accuracy of record keeping
- Ability to work effectively with teams
- Responsiveness to changing situations
- Administrative costs/cost reduction
- Participation/success of supplier-certification program

Service Measures (applied to suppliers)
- Receptiveness to partnering/teaming

Service Measures (applied to purchasers)
- Quality, development, and certification of supplier base
- Organizational, cross-functional development

Source: McGinnis, M.A. "Building Better Performance Measures," *NAPM Insights*, May 1995, p. 52-53. Used by permission.

Types of Performance Assessment Systems

Performance measurement systems typically fall in one of four categories, efficiency-oriented, effectiveness-oriented, multiple-objectives oriented, or naïve.[9]

Efficiency-Oriented

For the supply function, efficiency measures include material cost reductions, number of purchase orders processed per employee, and dollars purchased per buyer. These metrics are often the focus of performance measurements because they are easy to quantify. However, if the organization is concerned with continuous improvement or reducing total cost of ownership, efficiency measures may drive individual behavior away from the stated organizational goal. If an individual is going be measured and rewarded based on material cost reductions, this knowledge may drive the individual to make decisions that will lead to a high performance evaluation. This may lead to frequent supplier switching or an over-emphasis on price or other behaviors that will not contribute to the organization's attainment of its strategic goals of continuous improvement or lowest total cost of ownership.

Effectiveness-Oriented

Managers may move to an effectiveness-oriented system in which the performance goals relate to the purchaser's contributions, for example, to profit and the quality of buyer-supplier relationships. Measuring along these lines may bring the performance evaluation system into alignment with the strategic goals of the organization, but figuring out how to measure and quantify performance becomes an issue. Also, while effectiveness is a desirable goal, most managers want their employees to be effective in the most efficient way possible. If an individual is measured strictly for effectiveness, it may mask an inability to manage all of the tasks that the job entails.

Multiple-Objectives Oriented

A multiple-objectives system may be used to measure performance on both efficiency and effectiveness. The dilemma with this type of system is that the measures may conflict with one another, leaving the individual to try to decide which behavior(s) will actually be rewarded. For example, buyers may be measured on material cost reductions and the quality of buyer-supplier relationships. To attain material cost reductions, the buyer might switch suppliers frequently, cut corners on factors such as quality, or engage in behaviors that alienate supplier personnel. The buyer may bring home material cost reductions, but the quality of supplier relationships may deteriorate, and costs may be driven into the entire acquisition process.

Balancing the demands for both efficiency and effectiveness is the challenge faced by each individual in supply management and each manager who is charged with evaluating performance. Focusing on total cost of ownership rather than on material cost reductions is one example of a way to balance the two. By measuring total cost of ownership, intangible factors, such as the cost of doing business with one supplier versus another, can be included in the analysis. Developing short- and long-term goals so that all parties evaluate performance in the context of the overall contribution to the strategic objectives of the organization can also help employees balance efficiency and effectiveness.

Naïve

If supply personnel are told that their performance will be monitored and evaluated, but they are given no goals or metrics, this is a naïve performance measurement system. There are serious hazards to using this approach because individuals are left to try to decide for themselves what behaviors will be valued and rewarded by the organization. The lack of direction may leave individuals confused when making decisions and have severe consequences for organizational performance. While this approach is not used by progressive organizations, it is used in some organizations.

Data Gathering Approaches

Once a performance measurement system has been put in place, means must be established for gathering objective data to be used in the assessment. Data gathering techniques include interviews and feedback, team or peer input, self-assessment, internal customer input, and supplier input.

Conduct Interviews and Give Feedback

Performance reviews are usually conducted as face-to-face interviews between the supervisor and the employee. Supervisors often dislike this sort of activity for the following reasons:

- The supervisor's appraisal may differ from the subordinate's self-appraisal.

- Most supervisors find it difficult to carry out the appraisal in such a way that the reaction of the employee will be positive because the supervisors may lack the necessary interpersonal skills.
- Raters sometimes experience distaste for the critical analysis of another's performance and the conflict that sometimes results from a performance review.
- Supervisors receive few positive rewards from the performance review process.

Managers should keep in mind that there is a limit to an employee's tolerance for criticism. Most individuals probably feel they have some weaknesses or deficiencies and that they have not performed as well as they might have in some instances. However, when the criticism exceeds what the individual perceives to be valid (the "critical level" is exceeded), the individual may exhibit anger or tension. In such cases, communication difficulties compound rapidly and the chances for obtaining a useful outcome diminish.

For feedback to be effective, it should be as precise as possible. Managers should not speak in general terms, because what they are saying could be interpreted in a number of ways. Feedback should be timely and given shortly after incorrect performance or behavior has taken place. Also, feedback should be impersonal. Criticism of personal traits is especially likely to cause an emotional reaction. As a result, the nature of the performance deviation itself may be overlooked. Feedback should be obvious and clear, so that the individual is made aware of the information and can take corrective action when required. Feedback also should be given often to enhance the employee's understanding of his or her performance. This ensures that feedback is received early enough to identify problems in achieving goals.

Team or Peer Input

At times, feedback and review information can come in the form of team or peer appraisals. These approaches have been used for many years in the military and academia, as well as in industry. The firsthand knowledge that peers often have of each other's performance is the rationale for using such input. However, if competition exists, this type of rating may not be effective.

Peer Reviews – Because the impact of an individual's performance is felt by people beyond his or her immediate manager, it makes sense to seek input from multiple sources. First, measurement areas must be identified based on the goals and objectives of the organization and function. Data sources are determined by the manager and the individual to be reviewed. Data is then collected confidentially from these sources and aggregated by a third party, such as human resources. A self-evaluation may also be included in the data collection. The final report is then discussed by the manager and the individual.

Team Reviews – Team reviews are gaining importance in many organizations as the use of teams increases. The goal of team reviews is to gather input from all of the key stakeholders, such as team members, team leaders, managers, internal and external customers, and suppliers, regarding the degree to which the team has achieved its objectives. The team member review process is often conducted in a team meeting. Each team member is reviewed in a discussion with the whole team. Obviously, this process can quickly go awry unless team members have received adequate training in conflict resolution and collaboration. When team members have been carefully selected and trained to function effectively together, and when the reward system recognizes both individual and team accountability, the stage can be set for successful team reviews. Allocating the time and resources required to carry this process through effectively and efficiently presents a challenge for managers.

360-Degree Reviews – Some organizations are using a 360-degree review process. The goal of this approach is to get input from everyone an individual interacts with at work. Therefore, evaluations come from team members about each other's performance and the team leader's performance, from the team leader about each team member's performance, and from internal and external customers or suppliers. Obviously, one drawback of this approach is the time and resources needed to carry out this process in an effective, yet efficient, manner.

Self-Assessment
The advantage of self-assessment is that employees are in a privileged position to evaluate themselves with respect to job knowledge and performance. Such assessments foster development and less defensive appraisals. However, some employees may inflate ratings when making self-assessments, and they may attribute their problems or poor performance to their environment or to others, rather than to themselves. Conversely, other employees may underestimate ratings.

Either tendency will skew results and make it difficult for a manager to accurately assess and reward performance.

Internal Customer Input

At times, the purchasing manager may obtain useful performance appraisal data from the user departments with which each buyer has frequent contact. This information will tell the individual and the manager if the internal customer's needs are being met promptly, courteously, and accurately, with minimal problems and with responsiveness when problems occur. As with supplier input, internal customer input can be collected informally or formally through structured questionnaires and surveys.

Supplier Input

Supplier input is invaluable in providing individual purchasers with information about how they perform as customers. This information can be used to improve the department's and organization's relationships with suppliers. According to Cynthia S. Fuller, C.P.M., senior procurement specialist for Tennant Company, the steps in attaining useful supplier input are:[10]

1. Define the key items to survey.
2. Identify the key departments that interact with the organization's suppliers.
3. Determine which suppliers should receive the surveys.
4. Identify who will receive the feedback.
5. Use the results to make improvements.
6. Incorporate new items in future surveys.
7. Discuss results in a face-to-face session with the supplier.

Figure 8.4 shows a sample supplier survey that solicits input from the supplier about relationships with procurement, material controllers, quality assurance and inspection, and other personnel; supply quality updates provided by the buyer; and training the buying organization could provide to the seller.[11]

FIGURE 8.4
Sample Supplier Survey

	Excellent	Good	Average	Poor
I. OVERALL BUSINESS RELATIONSHIP	___	___	___	___

II. RELATIONSHIP WITH PROCUREMENT SPECIALISTS

1. How responsive are we in:
   - returning telephone calls?
   - accessibility?
   - problem-solving?
   - promtness for appointments?
2. How do you rate our overall professionalism?
3. How receptive are we to your ideas?
4. Rate our product knowledge.
5. How helpful are the annual business management sessions?
6. How clear are the communications with you?
7. What can we do to improve? _____

III. Relationship with other personnel

1. How receptive are we to your ideas?
2. How effectively do we communicate our needs/plans?
3. How realistic are our expectations of you?
4. How effectively do we use the resources you offer?
5. How do you rate our overall professionalism?
6. What can we do to improve? _____

IV. Relationship with material controllers

1. How clear is it to you as to when we want you to ship product?
2. Rate your understanding of our MRP/JIT reports.
3. How well are changes in ship date communicated?
4. How well do we adhere to your order policy?
5. How responsive are we in:
   - returning telephone calls?
   - accessibility?
   - promptness for appointments?
   - problem-solving?
6. How do you rate our overall professionalism?
7. What can we do to improve? _____

V. Supplier Quality Updates

1. How well do these meet your needs:
   - timeliness?
   - accuracy?
   - going to the right person(s)?
2. What is the value to you of:
   - overall updates?
   - quality-performance data?
   - delivery-performance data?
   - reliability-performance data?
3. How well do you understand our supplier qualification process?
4. How clearly are we communicating our expectations to you?

VI. Relationship with quality assurance and inspection

	Frequently	Occasionally	Seldom	Never
1. How often do you have contact with our quality assurance or inspection personnel?	___	___	___	___

	Excellent	Good	Average	Poor
2. How do you rate our overall professionalism?	___	___	___	___

3. What can we do to improve? _____
4. In addition to supplier quality updates, how useful is the quality data provided?
5. Can we provide more data or assistance? Please explain. _____

VII. What types of training support should we provide you?
❑ Problem-solving ❑ Reliability ❑ SPC ❑ JIT Other _____

Comment on what you consider to be our greatest strengths and weaknesses in doing business with your firm. _____

Strengths: _____

Weaknesses: _____

Other Comments: _____

Source: Fuller, C.S. "Measuring Performance Through Supplier Input," *NAPM Insights*, May 1995, p. 6.

Uses of Performance Appraisal Data

Performance appraisal data can be used to encourage employee accountability, determine compensation, make promotion decisions, promote personal and career development, foster employee morale, justify disciplinary action, recognize employees, and motivate performance improvements.

Employee Accountability

A constructive performance appraisal will identify for the employee the areas in which he or she has problems and will specify what he or she needs to do to correct them. The appraisal provides the employee with guidance on how to improve and makes him or her accountable for that behavior with a definite time span for improvement. In the appraisal, it is also important to identify and build on areas in which the employee is doing well.

Compensation

No department operates at its full potential for long if its salary structure fails to reward individuals in relation to their respective performance levels. A good performance appraisal program does not guarantee an equitable salary structure. It does, however, provide data that can be used in developing a sound compensation plan or in correcting an inadequate one.

Promotion

How do managers know which employees in their departments are likely to become candidates for the top jobs? They determine this by analyzing each aspect of an individual's performance record. It is imperative that such analysis be made using detailed and accurate written data. A well-designed appraisal program provides the required data.

Personal and Career Development

The most important benefit that can come from a constructive employee evaluation program is the information needed to stimulate and direct each individual employee's professional development. A supervisor's prime responsibility is to develop capable and effective personnel. The data provided by appraisals can be analyzed to determine each employee's strengths and weaknesses, and facilitate the development of a realistic professional improvement program for each individual.

Employee Morale

Every purchasing manager must develop a well-structured personnel performance appraisal program. Nothing is more disastrous to the morale of a department than the haphazard or inconsistent evaluation of employee performance.

Disciplinary Action

A well-designed employee performance appraisal program is a guide for disciplinary actions that are focused and fair and that provide direction for employee improvement.

Employee Recognition

Purchasers (as well as other staff) want to know that they will be compensated for their diligence. When departments reward their most effective workers, heavy workloads are viewed as an opportunity to win recognition, earn respect, and be included in the most interesting and high-profile projects. Most purchasers are motivated when their managers make them feel good about quality work through the acknowledgement of superb efforts. Many organizations have found that programs that allow purchasers to be recognized and rewarded for their performance benefit the entire organization.

Performance Improvement

One of the key purposes of staff appraisals is to motivate employees to improve their performance. Well-designed appraisal systems will provide each employee with the feedback and guidelines necessary to achieve higher levels of performance in the next measurement period. Employees should have the sense that continuous improvement applies to their efforts as well as to the efforts of suppliers.

Employee Performance Problems

Most organizations have work rules that, if violated, can result in various penalties, including dismissal. The following sections cover the aspects of employee performance problems.

Corrective Action Process

The principle of corrective action (sometimes called *progressive discipline*) means that management responds to a first offense with some minimal action, but subsequent offenses are met with more serious penalties, such as a layoff or discharge. Corrective action includes these steps:

1. Notice of the problem. The first step is to warn the employee about the problem. Usually, the warning is oral, but if the problem continues, a written warning is given stating the consequences of future offenses.
2. Identify the problem. The employee must be given sufficient time to demonstrate a change in behavior. This time period may be several months, depending on the problem.
3. Monitor progress. The manager should carefully monitor the progress of the employee and offer feedback (especially if positive behavior changes occur) to give the employee a sense of whether his or her actions are appropriate.

Types of Issues

A number of issues may arise in the workplace that require some form of corrective action, including performance problems; attitude, stress, and burnout; theft; substance abuse; ethical violations; attendance problems; and other illegal behaviors. In some situations, the rules and regulations under the Americans with Disabilities Act may apply.

Performance Problems – Performance is one of the main employee work problems. This may include frequent errors, oversights, sloppy work, slow performance (that is, failure to meet deadlines), or an inability to interact effectively as a team member. It can also include habitual lateness or missed days.

Attitude, Stress, and Burnout – Many employee performance problems can be linked to poor attitude, which can be caused by job stress and burnout. Many organizations have in-house counselors to help troubled employees change their attitudes toward their work and develop a more positive approach.

Theft – Incidents of employee pilfering, embezzlement, or theft are serious violations that may involve criminal proceedings as well as disciplinary action or dismissal.

Substance Abuse – Estimates of the percentage of workers affected by alcoholism run from 5 to 10 percent. A somewhat smaller percentage has problems with drug abuse. Many employers offer counseling and treatment for substance abusers, an expense that is frequently covered by employee benefit packages.

Ethical Violations – The opportunity for ethical violations, or the perception of them, is great in the supply management profession because of the dollar amounts involved. Most organizations have written ethics policies, as well as procedures for dealing with ethical violations.

Attendance Problems – Rules about work hours and absences from work should be clearly established and communicated.

Other Illegal Behaviors – Policies and procedures should be in place to deal with issues of illegal employee behavior, and it should be clear to employees how the organization will deal with behaviors, such as sexual harassment, possession of a firearm in the workplace, or substance abuse on the job.

Documentation

A first offense may warrant nothing more than a discussion with the employee. Any subsequent incidents of employee difficulties should be well documented by the manager, including the dates of incidents, warnings, meetings with the employee, and the nature of all manager-employee discussions.

Collective Bargaining Requirements

Collective bargaining is the process of negotiating a labor agreement between union representatives and employer representatives. The contract negotiated between union and employer representatives is called the *collective bargaining agreement*. The agreement sets forth the terms and conditions under which union members will offer their services to an employer. Such agreements usually have specific requirements for dealing with employees who are performing poorly. It is the responsibility of the manager to ensure that those requirements are met whenever he or she disciplines or dismisses a union employee.

Employee Assistance Programs

Employee Assistance Programs (EAP) are formal counseling programs aimed at assisting employees with problems due to such difficulties as personal or family crises, substance abuse, or emotional illness. Typically, such programs reside in or are connected to the employee's medical plan or human resources department. Such programs can assist in the general mental health of an employee, and they can also help improve communication and understanding between a superior and a subordinate.

Retraining

Retraining for new skills is important today, given the rapid changes in business and other organizations. Often retraining is required when there is a performance problem with an employee. The term retraining implies that training took place at some previous time. Determining why the retraining is necessary may help in being successful the second time around. Has something changed about the nature of the job task(s), the individual, or the performance expectations? Perhaps the initial training was weak and ineffective. If so, why put someone through the same process again? Perhaps the individual learns best in a hands-on environment, and the training was done in a classroom setting without the appropriate tools. Many people have received computer training without sitting in front of a computer and actually performing the operations. The learning environment (classroom, computer, on-the-job, and so on) needs to be considered. If performance expectations have changed, the employee may need to be engaged in a process that leads to an understanding of why his or her performance is inferior. If after retraining there is a realization that the person, the task, and the expectations are mismatched, then some other form of management action will be necessary. Chapter 5 discusses training issues and options in greater detail.

Key Points

1. Performance tracking is important in order to recognize and reward behaviors that lead to attaining organizational goals. A vital source of information regarding these behaviors is feedback from the internal and external customers of the purchasing processes.
2. The supply organization needs to be structured in a way that facilitates the flow of information between end customers and purchasers.
3. Measurement is needed to track trends in performance that will provide evidence of improvement or provide early warnings about deteriorating performance. Unbiased data should be captured at regular intervals as part of the normal functioning of the unit. In other words, information gathering should be built into the process.
4. Management's response to the information gathered from measurements is as critical as the measurements themselves. The information must be used to guide decisions and actions concerning organizational structure, individual development, and staffing needs.
5. Feedback must be as unbiased as possible. One method of assuring this is to gather information from several perspectives, as is done in 360-degree personnel evaluations.
6. The supply function is in a position to contribute substantially to the results desired by the organization, whether the desired result is profitability for a private-sector business or effective resource utilization for a not-for-profit organization.

Questions for Review

1. How have cross-functional sourcing teams been used to gain greater alignment of purchasing decisions with organizational objectives?
2. Why do managers want to track the performance of the supply management function? How does the tracking of performance motivate individuals to improve?

3. Why should managers identify key stakeholders when seeking to evaluate the performance of an organization? How do managers identify these individuals?
4. Why should purchasing be concerned with the satisfaction of internal customers? How should this be measured?
5. Why is benchmarking information desirable? Where is useful benchmarking information available?

Endnotes

1. Gill, P. "What We Do to Relate to the Final Customer: Keeping in Touch," *Purchasing Today®*, October 1997, p. 36-37.
2. Ross, J. "What We Do to Relate to the Final Customer: Teaching Them Teaches Us," *Purchasing Today®*, October 1997, p. 37-38.
3. "The Internal Customer Wish List," *Purchasing Today®*, October 1997, p. 34.
4. Nordstrom, Inc., "Nordstrom Announces Partnership with Streamline," Oct. 8, 1998, www.nordstrom.com.
5. McGinnis, M.A. "Building Better Performance Measures," *NAPM Insights*, May 1995, p. 50-53.
6. Center for Advanced Purchasing Studies (CAPS), 2055 E. Centennial Circle, P. O. Box 22160, Tempe, Arizona 85285-2160, 480-752-2277, FAX: 480-491-7885, www.capsresearch.org.
7. Smith, M. and R. Zelman, "New Models for Diversity and Conflict Resolution," *Purchasing Today®*, September 1998, p. 10.
8. Mooney, R.L. "Setting Employee Standards," *NAPM Insights*, May 1995, pp. 18-19.
9. Dumond, E.J. "Performance Measurement and Decision-Making in a Purchasing Environment," *International Journal of Purchasing and Materials Management*, Spring 1991, pp. 21-31.
10. Fuller, C.S. "Measuring Performance Through Supplier Input," *NAPM Insights*, May 1995, p. 6-7.
11. Fuller, 1995, p. 6.

CHAPTER 9

THE REPORTING PROCESS

*How does purchasing communicate the right information
to the right people?*

Chapter Objectives

- To identify the types of information needed by internal and external constituencies
- To explain different communication tools and the appropriate uses of each
- To discuss various data management techniques and the role of Internet-based communication

Reporting in the Information Age

This volume has discussed strategic planning at the corporate level, budgeting, leading and managing, hiring and retaining employees, instituting control mechanisms, developing policies and procedures, and implementing an appraisal and reward system. The final topic for consideration in managing the supply function is determining the who, what, why, when, where, and how of information reporting:

- Who: determining to whom information should be transmitted
- What: identifying supply management outcomes, activities, performance data, and other information that needs to be communicated
- Why: determining the interests of specific constituencies for certain information
- When, where, and how: deciding on the format and means of communicating relevant information

Who Needs to Receive Information?

Determining who needs to receive information is the process of identifying stakeholders in the supply management process. These stakeholders may be internal or external to the organization. Internally, supply managers must report information to two primary constituencies: the organization's leadership or management and fellow employees. Externally, four constituencies need to receive information: investors, suppliers, customers, and the community(ies) in which the organization operates. The needs and interests of these stakeholders may conflict in some instances and be congruent in others. The task of managing involves continually balancing the needs and desires of all the stakeholders and making decisions within a climate of varying degrees of uncertainty, incomplete information, and conflicting interests.

What Information Needs to Be Communicated?

The information to be communicated to each constituency depends on the needs and interests of that specific group. The needs and interests of the internal and external constituencies are discussed in the following sections. Figure 9.1 provides a synopsis of the information typically of interest to internal constituencies, the organization's leadership or management, and the employees.

FIGURE 9.1
Reporting to Internal Constituencies

WHO (the audience)	WHAT (is being communicated)	EXAMPLES
Top Leadership or Management of the Organization	Supplier performance	Price and cost trends, leadtimes, shortages, labor strife, cartel actions, new technology, mergers affecting the supply chain
	Performance to plan	Budgeted expenditures, headcount, savings plan, quality improvement, training
	Supply market conditions	Present and forecast raw material availability and cost, supplier capacities, mergers and acquisitions
Employees	Special supplier terms for employee purchases	Employee purchase discounts for personal computers
	Terms of certain supplier agreements affecting employees	Travel, services, utilities, temporary help, printing, and so on
	Policies and procedures relative to supply management	Ethics policy (the organization's commitment to treat suppliers fairly and honestly; rules about accepting gifts and gratuities)

The Organization's Leadership or Management

Top management generally is concerned with issues that may positively or negatively affect the overall organization, especially its profitability, market share, competitive advantage or stock price. When deciding what information to share with top management, it is good to ask, "Is this issue of high or low importance to the organization as a whole?"[1] The issue may be of utmost importance to the individual supply manager, but before presenting it to higher-level managers, the individual must assess the issue's potential impact on the whole organization. The organization's culture and especially the concerns of the manager to whom one reports are important. In some organizations, senior level managers want to know everything, and in other organizations managers delegate more. Individual managers also vary greatly in their perception of what they need to know. It is the responsibility of lower-level employees to understand and respond appropriately to both the individual manager's needs and to the culture of the organization.

To determine what information to share, review what the organization's leaders report to others through such documents as the annual report, periodic financial statements, or similar high-level status reports. The ways in which the issues discussed in these documents are affected by the performance of suppliers or the supply management function will determine the importance of reporting information to the organization's leaders. Also, the specific issues on which managers have requested information in the past must be given primary consideration. Some types of information that may be of interest to top management are supplier performance feedback, performance to plan, supply market conditions, schedule needs, new product plans, and expectations of key suppliers.

Supplier Performance – Topics of possible interest to top management may include price and cost trends, leadtimes, shortages, labor strife, cartel actions, new technology, or mergers affecting the supply chain.

Performance to Plan – How the supply function is performing relative to budgeted expenditures, headcount, savings plan, quality improvement, and training may also interest top management. At United Technologies Corporation, a key management reporting tool called STARS (Savings Tracking And Reporting System) is used to track all supply management savings projects. Project data is entered into an online reporting system by purchasing and finance personnel as it occurs at the divisions' operating sites. Reported savings become an essential part of quarterly executive reviews by each business unit. Senior management considers this information to be vital for projecting earnings in current periods.

Supply Market Conditions – One of the key roles of supply managers is remaining up to date on market conditions, including present and forecasted supplies. This may include raw material availability and cost, supplier capacities, mergers and acquisitions.

Employees

Employees of the organization are affected in many ways by the activities, processes, and procedures of the supply function. In some organizations, the purchasing or supply department is responsible for developing and negotiating employee purchase programs in conjunction with suppliers. Also, the terms and conditions of many contracts have an impact on employees' behaviors. For example, decisions that buyers make about travel companies, service providers, utilities, temporary help, and printing will affect the actions and behaviors of various employees in the organization.

Special Supplier Terms for Employee Purchases – In many companies and industries, suppliers offer the employees of the buying organization special terms for personal purchases. For example, Dell Computer offers employee purchase discounts to customers with more than 400 employees, as well as to employees of educational institutions. The Dell web page provides a contact phone number based on the size category of an individual's employer.[2]

Terms of Certain Supplier Agreements Affecting Employees – Many contracts negotiated by buyers directly affect the actions and behaviors of employees. For example, the organization may have contracts that require all organizational or institutional travel to be booked through a specific travel agency or with a specific airline. The same may be true for service providers, utilities, temporary help, or printing. The purchasing department management must have a mechanism in place for communicating these requirements, and the specific terms and conditions, to appropriate personnel.

Ethics Policy – Purchasing employees are in an especially vulnerable position when it comes to ethics, because they are making spending decisions. In addition, employees outside of the purchasing and supply function may engage in questionable behavior with suppliers. It is important for all employees of an organization to understand and abide by the ethics policies of the organization, especially the organization's commitment to treat suppliers fairly and honestly.

The external constituencies — suppliers, customers, investors, and communities — are also interested in the activities of the supply management function. Figure 9.2 provides a synopsis of the information that may be communicated to these groups.

FIGURE 9.2
Reporting to External Constituencies

WHO (the audience)	WHAT (is being communicated)	EXAMPLES
Suppliers	Performance feedback	Quality, delivery, leadtime, cost improvements
	Schedule needs	Forecast, quantity versus date, annual requirements
	New product plans	Specifications, quantities, production dates
	Key expectations of suppliers	Continuous improvement, competitiveness
Customers	Product or service improvements	Quality, delivery, leadtime, cost improvements
	Innovations in process or delivered value	Specifications — new features, advantages or benefits
	Faster response time	Accurate and predictable delivery dates
Investors	Cost and customer value improvements	Quality, delivery, leadtime, cost improvements, specifications
	Key supplier relationships	Strategic alliances that may (or do) significantly impact value
Communities	Supplier diversity programs	Percentage of annual spending awarded to minority — or women — owned businesses or small businesses
	Local and regional content	Percentage of end product that is composed of material made, mined, or assembled locally.

Suppliers

Supply managers must communicate efficiently and effectively with suppliers. The basic types of information that must be communicated to suppliers include performance feedback, schedule needs, new product plans, and key expectations.

Performance Feedback – Some method must be used to measure and evaluate supplier performance and to communicate this information to the supplier's representatives. Typically, the customer will track quality, delivery, and price or cost performance. Quality (the number of defects received) and delivery (the number of pieces delivered late, early, or short to requirement) are tracked in parts per million over a specified time period, usually quarterly or monthly. Price or cost performance is commonly tracked against either a historic price or a specified target cost. This may be done either on a line item basis or over a number of items, depending on the organization's needs. An important step in this process is the comparison of tracking information to the buyer's requirements and timely feedback to the supplier. More sophisticated systems also track suppliers' leadtimes and cost or performance improvement contributions, because these have become increasingly vital to organizational performance.

Schedule Needs – Suppliers must have accurate and timely information on forecasts, annual requirements, and quantity versus date required in order to plan their own activities. Suppliers complain that buyers often do not provide sufficient schedule information and do not update information they have already provided regarding changes in customer schedules.

New Product Plans – Specifications, quantities, and production dates must be communicated to suppliers. In many cases, key suppliers are brought into new product development teams through an early supplier involvement program. Pratt & Whitney Aircraft used this approach in the design of its PW6000 series aircraft engines. Suppliers were preselected (called Day-One-Suppliers) to participate in the design effort alongside the P&W engineers, beginning with the earliest design concepts. This collaborative design effort created opportunities for process improvements to quality, cycle time, cost, and simplicity of design.[3]

Key Expectations of Suppliers – It is critical for the buyer to ensure that the supplier understands the expectations of the buying organization. These expectations may be related to continuous improvement, competitiveness, or any other aspect of the buyer-supplier relationship or supplier performance.

Customers

Supply managers work directly with internal customers, but they must also keep their eyes on satisfying the end customers of the organization. A good approach for keeping the needs of the end customer in mind is to ask, "Is the information (and all activities necessary to collect, create, and distribute it) of value to the customer?" Often it is best to work backward to determine where the information will come from, how will it be collected, and what form will be of greatest value.

The supply manager must work internally with marketing personnel to determine the needs and desires of end customers. Then, supply managers must work with internal customers, such as design engineers, production, and new product development teams, to ensure that these needs and desires are designed into the products or services offered by the organization. In service industries, customer needs can also be satisfied, in part, by supplier performance. For example, when a customer uses an automated teller machine to complete a banking transaction, satisfaction will be affected by the quality of the display and the features of the supplier-provided ATM equipment. Some of the information that end customers will be interested in include product or customer service improvements, innovations in processes or value, and faster response time.

Product or Customer Service Improvements – Customers receive information about supplier innovations, such as new technologies and features, through a variety of channels. For example personal computer manufacturers have used the "Intel Inside" label to tell customers that an Intel brand microprocessor has been used by the PC manufacturer to enhance the performance and features of its machine. In this case, the choice of supplier is seen as a distinct marketing advantage.

Innovations in Process or Delivered Value – Suppliers often improve their processes or products, and the supply management organization wants to pass key information about these improvements along to customers. Dell Computer, for example, relies heavily on supplier innovations to trim delivery time in support of its direct selling model.[4] While the end customers may have little concern about the specific improvements, they are vitally interested in the resulting reductions in leadtime and cost.

Faster Response Time – In manufacturing, quick responses to customer demands can be a significant competitive advantage. One of the primary drivers of responsiveness is supplier leadtimes. Working with suppliers to improve processes and reduce cycle time can lead to a greater advantage with customers, who must be advised of the organization's improved ability to meet changes in demand.

Investors

Taking the investors' viewpoint means focusing on return on investment, future expectations, direction, control, and predictability. A company's annual report will typically identify the strategic goals of the organization and link them to areas of concern to investors. For example, in its 1998 annual report, Wendy's International, Inc., identified strategic initiatives undertaken in the past 12 months to improve shareholder value. The supply function at Wendy's contributed to the improvement of shareholder value though the consolidation of purchases with key suppliers. Another example is the considerable amount of coverage in the press about how various automobile manufacturers are working with specific fuel cell suppliers to develop hybrid power plants for future automobiles.[5] Investors are most interested in the success or failure of these efforts, because they may affect future sales and profit results.

Cost and Customer Value Improvements – Investors, like customers, may be interested in any improvements or innovations brought about through the efforts of supply managers. Anything that might be translated into a better investment opportunity will be of interest to investors.

Key Supplier Relationships – Relationships with key suppliers that have the potential to greatly impact value, such as strategic supplier alliances, will interest investors. For example, in the letter to shareholders in its 1998 annual report, Wendy's International, Inc., reported on two key supplier relationships:

- Consolidation of the national soft drink business with Coca-Cola, ensuring a long-term agreement with the No. 1 soft drink company in the world
- Consolidation of a major portion of the company's national food distribution network with Sysco Corporation and its Sygma subsidiary, ensuring improved service and valuable economies for the company and its franchised stores[6]

Communities

The members of the community in which the organization is located also have a stake in the activities and outcomes of the supply function. A potential for conflict exists because the interests of the community in which a company does business may not be congruent with the interests of other stakeholders, such as investors or customers. Two major areas of concern are supplier diversity programs and the local and regional content of purchased goods and services.

Supplier Diversity Programs – The members of the community or communities in which an organization has operations typically expect the organization to employ and do business with members of that community. Of particular interest is the effort of buyers to diversify the supply base based on the ownership of the supplier company. Because many minority- or women-owned businesses are small businesses, this effort has, at times, meant paying more for a particular good or service than what a higher volume supplier might have offered.[7] Reconciling these two seemingly divergent organizational goals, purchasing at the lowest total cost of ownership and supporting the local community, is an ongoing challenge facing supply managers everywhere. Many customers today seek to develop key suppliers to maintain the desired diversity and at the same time elevate supplier performance levels. This requires a commitment by the buying organization to help the supplier identify opportunities to improve and implement changes to achieve the improvement.

Local and Regional Content – Today's economy is global, but individuals, cities, and states may still put self-interest above the good of all humankind. This affects the decisions made by a buyer or supply manager in that local constituents may question decisions that send purchase dollars out of the town, state, or country. The civil disobedience and violence that erupted in Seattle, Washington, during the 1999 World Trade Organization talks is an example of how it is impossible to make trade decisions that please everyone. In trying to please the community after building its first manufacturing plant in the United States, Honda sought to develop a local supply base and gradually increased the U.S. content of its U.S.-made cars to a high percentage.[8]

How Will Information Be Communicated?

At times, news that will be heralded by one constituent group will be condemned by another. The ability to find common ground among different stakeholders is a valuable managerial skill. Deciding how and when information is communicated is critical to maintaining the balance among constituencies. How to communicate information may vary from constituency to constituency.

Top Management – When communicating to top management, it is important to speak the language of top management. This means putting information in terms of what top management cares about and understands, specifically financial results and the impact of the information on the organization's strategic plan. According to Barbara Donnelly, C.P.M., manager of strategic sourcing for Johnson & Johnson, the method of presentation should be tailored "to the culture of your company, and the preferences of top management."[9] For example, at Johnson & Johnson, directors provide project updates via e-mail, and then they make face-to-face presentations quarterly. In making a face-to-face presentation, Donnelly suggested using one visual per project with bullet points highlighting the key areas. "When reporting to the CEO, keep it simple," she said. "Anything you present to the CEO should be tied back into the organization's goals and objectives."

Another approach is to provide an executive overview or summary with supporting detail. This overview or summary should include the key point or central message along with supporting evidence. Before preparing the summary ask three questions: Why is this important? What is expected? How will it be measured, or how will progress be tracked?

The "bring solutions, not problems" approach is popular in many organizations. Many organizations operate under the philosophy that empowering employees means that decisionmaking is pushed to the lowest possible level. It is expected that the individual will take the initiative to solve problems and bring solutions to his or her manager. However, the danger is in creating an organization in which people let issues become problems to be solved, because this creates an opportunity to engage in a problem-solving effort that will be highly visible.

In *The Dance of Change*, Lotte Bailyn refers to this approach as "a formula for creating chronic crisis in organizations."[10] People are rewarded for solving problems, rather than for preventing problems. Crisis preventers or "lead users" do the behind-the-scenes work to solve problems before they get big. These people get things done and keep the place running with less expense, waste, and trouble than the more visible efforts of the problem solvers. In Chapter 8, the problem of measuring and rewarding the right behaviors was discussed. How to make problem prevention efforts more visible and reward the "lead users" is a challenging notion. For example, Bailyn described an engineer whose manager wanted to promote him because he held the unit together. Upper management, on the other hand, wanted to promote an engineer who was more highly visible and met their promotion criteria of individual deliverables, even though this individual was disruptive to team performance and wasted people's time.[11]

Employees – Information can be communicated to employees in a number of formats including policy and procedures manuals (print-based or online), face-to-face communications, and postings to internal Web sites. Technological innovations have made it easier to communicate information to groups of employees. Many organizations now rely heavily on Intranet systems to post information for retrieval and use by appropriate personnel.

Suppliers – Probably the most critical supply management communication is with suppliers. As described earlier, this includes clear expectations, performance reporting, and long-range planning information. Routine communication with suppliers, including day-to-day requirements and feedback, is increasingly accomplished using the Internet or intranets to achieve greater speed and ease of information transfer. This does not mean that face-to-face communication is obsolete. Rather, the buyer and supplier must decide what information requires face-to-face meetings, whose presence is required for an effective exchange, and what format these meetings should take. For example, many organizations send production requirements to suppliers via the Web, updating them whenever changes occur, daily or more frequently if necessary. Suppliers will acknowledge receipt of the latest information and their proposed delivery schedule in response. All of this is done as quickly as the data can be determined and entered into the record. For example, Dell Computer maintains a site strictly for suppliers to share information, such as product quality and inventory.[12] For long-range planning of new requirements, strategy setting, and negotiations, a meeting of the key individuals from both the customer and the supplier is advised.

Customers – Web sites are quickly becoming a primary means of reaching current or potential customers. All of the key supply management messages mentioned previously can be posted to the Web site for customers to access. Dell Computer creates a site for each major customer, which offers information of specific value to that customer, and Dell provides secure access to the site for that customer only.[13]

Investors – Many organizations are using the Internet to communicate with investors. For example, Wendy's International, Inc., maintains an investor Web site at www.wendys.com that enables visitors to obtain in-depth, instant, and ongoing information in an easy-to-use format about Wendy's, Tim Hortons, and company-related activities. Site visitors are provided with a comprehensive overview of the company, including financial comparisons of Wendy's and its competitors. Additionally, Wendy's reports that the company has taken a leadership role in the restaurant industry by enabling online visitors to sign up to automatically receive company and earnings news releases via e-mail. According to Frederick R. Reed, chief financial officer, "Wendy's is dedicated to providing consumers and investors various ways to easily obtain important information they need to better understand the company and to make informed investment decisions."[14]

While supply information is not the primary focus of these Web sites, relevant supply information, such as new supplier alliances or technologies, can be posted and reach investors through this medium. For example, IBM devotes a section of its site (www.ibm.com) to news and discussions about business partners. It is also used to communicate about IBM services that are available to small and minority businesses and to encourage these businesses to become potential suppliers to IBM.

Community – Information of interest to the wider community, which typically includes employment levels, diversity objectives, and investment information, is communicated through company press releases, and it can also be found on company Web sites. Again these communication vehicles can disseminate supply-related information, such as local contract awards and expansion or construction plans, to these constituencies.

Effective Presentation Techniques

As stated in Chapter 5, effective communication skills were identified by employers as the top requirement for new hires. The oral and written presentation skills of employees can affect how well or how poorly information is transmitted, received, and understood. Educators, parents, and employers are concerned that many people lack rudimentary reading, writing, and speaking skills. The avalanche of information that is available because of technological advances has increased the demands placed on individuals in terms of communication skills. Information is so plentiful that people must prioritize their reading, assess the accuracy or validity of sources of information, and develop the ability to sort relevant information from irrelevant information. For example, an Internet search for information on a specific topic may yield hundreds, if not thousands, of hits or possible sources. The individual must be able to narrow the search and to quickly determine which sites are likely to be most relevant and reliable.

Individuals need to be concise and direct in their communications to ensure that important information is received by those who they wish to inform. It is not sufficient merely to send the information; it must also be seen as having value to the recipient. In addition, the sender must develop techniques for determining that the meaning was accurately received. Being a good listener and a good interrogator are important skills in effective communication.

Oral Communication

A number of presentation techniques are available. Figure 9.3 identifies some of the advantages and disadvantages of each. First, information can be presented either orally or in writing. Either approach can be formal or informal, depending on the circumstances and purpose of the communication. If oral communication is the chosen means of transmission, the speaker must decide if the presentation should be formal or informal. A formal presentation may include visual aids, such as electronic slides, transparencies, or videos. The level of formality may affect the attire of the speaker and audience, the language used in the delivery of the information, and the structure of the presentation, such as when and how questions are handled. An informal presentation may take place at the office or workstation of the sender or receiver of information, or at a neutral spot. The language, mood, and structure of the conversation may be informal and involve more give and take between speaker and listener(s).

FIGURE 9.3
Presentation Techniques

Form	Advantages	Disadvantages	Best Applications
Oral	Speed, ease	No permanent record unless taped	Quick information exchange
Written	Permanent record, privacy	Slow, need to file and recover	Legal agreement
E-mail	Speed, simplicity, record if needed	Informal	Information exchange in the absence of other party
Internet	Global access	Post and retrieve	Marketing information
Intranet	Privacy, targeted audience	Limited access	Policies, organization charts, periodic reports

Written Communication

If written communication is chosen, the writer must again decide if a formal or informal approach is required, and then choose the format or structure of the message. Transmission methods for written communications include writing a report, sending an e-mail message, or writing a letter or memo.

E-mail Communication

According to a 1999 survey of 915 U.S. businesses conducted by Watson Wyatt Worldwide, a global management consulting firm, e-mail usage has jumped 37 percent between 1994 and 1999.[15] Ninety percent of the companies represented in the survey reported using e-mail to communicate with employees. However, only 50 percent say it is more effective than traditional communication tools, such as meetings and publications. E-mail makes regular communication easier and faster, but not necessarily better. Many people are inundated with e-mail messages on a daily basis. Learning to sort incoming messages according to some categorization system, such as ABC analysis, is critical from a time management standpoint. Also, many people lack the ability to communicate the simplest information in a concise, clearly written message. Some blame the informality and impersonal nature of e-mail for these problems. Others look to training employees in basic writing skills and online etiquette. E-mail's advantages of speed and immediate availability assure its place in organizational communication. The key is to identify the times and places when e-mail is an appropriate means of communication.

Intranet and Internet Communication[16]

An intranet is an Internet-based internal Web site. Many purchasing and supply departments have developed intranet sites for gathering and disseminating information, linking with external resources via the Internet, and accessing online supplier catalogs. According to Andy Icken, materials and services manager with Exxon Company, U.S.A., "Electronic catalogs maintained by our suppliers will reduce our internal maintenance costs, reduce their publishing costs, and provide more comprehensive and timely product information."[17]

Typically, the first step in intranet development for a purchasing department is to create a site that includes organizational charts of the purchasing function, corporate purchasing policies and procedures, and updates on major initiatives and projects being undertaken by the supply function. This information is posted on the intranet and retrieved by other employees.

Many managers have gone beyond this stage to create intranets that increase the efficiency of the supply function's activities. For example, at specialty chemical manufacturer Rohm and Haas, the purchasing department linked its intranet to Internet resources such as the Thomas Register, published commodity pricing, and used equipment sources. It also listed corporate suppliers for office supplies, computers, and laboratory equipment, and created online catalogs for internal customers to use to order online. Suppliers send summary bills with cost center details directly to Rohm and Haas' general ledger.[18]

According to Michael Masciandaro, procurement process and systems manager for Rohm and Haas, the greatest benefit of the intranet has been keeping departments from multiple divisions informed about decisions. The decision-support applications created by the purchasing department help purchasers see what they purchased and from whom. Users can access information about suppliers to compare and rank pricing at different locations. Even though a transaction may take place locally, the source selection decision can be made in light of what is happening throughout Rohm and Haas' worldwide operations. Not only does this access to information help in negotiations, it also brings the divisions together and allows the purchasers to act as one entity. The intranet applications for the Rohm and Haas purchasing department include the following:[19]

- Links to published commodity pricing, used equipment information, and other Internet-based resources
- Links to approved suppliers' online catalogs for office supplies, computers, and lab equipment so that employees can purchase online
- Decision-support applications that allow users to view purchasing activity on a "real-time" basis

At the construction services and site remediation company Fluor Daniel Hanford, the first purchasing information to be posted on its intranet was organizational directories and points of contact for the purchasing and materials management processes. Today, nearly 10,000 customers and employees in dozens of Hanford facilities access information about suppliers and purchasing procedures, as well as information posted by other departments, such as warehousing, accounts payable, human resources, and safety. According to Michael Taylor, acquisition specialist with Fluor Daniel Hanford, the greatest benefit has been the consolidation of information into one location. Intranet applications for the purchasing department at Fluor Daniel Hanford include:[20]

- Organizational directories and points of contact
- A directory of suppliers' telephone numbers, with links to their Web sites, when available
- Contact information for site services, such as pesticide application or hazardous material disposal
- Policy and procedure manuals with instructions and forms that are linked back to the "controlling" procedure, including guidance documents for writing statements of work, invoice reviews, and technical evaluation proposals
- Training documents on contract administration, federal regulations, and contract terms
- Links to government agencies and legal references

Data Management Techniques

Technology is driving the supply chain management movement, and one of the critical roles of technology is its implications for information management and information processing. As a communications tool, technology is revolutionizing the way people think about and carry out work. The Internet provides an excellent tool for company-to-company communication. According to Richard M. Vanatsky, a manager in Andersen Consulting's Industrial Products Practice, "The Internet has vast potential to facilitate the technique of collaborative planning, the process of sharing and collaborating on demand forecasts and production schedules with your supplier. By working jointly on future schedules, suppliers can synchronize their own production and sourcing operations with those of their customers and, therefore, improve service levels and eliminate redundant inventory from the supply chain."[21]

Data Warehousing and Data Mining[22]

A *data warehouse* stores data from disparate systems so that it can then be readily and easily retrieved from a single point of access. Unlike enterprise resource planning (ERP) systems, which are designed around transactions, data warehouses are designed around subjects (for example, orders filled per month and customer demographics). A data warehouse may be integrated with online analytical processing (OLAP) tools, thereby providing increased usability and query performance. The initial step in creating a data warehouse is for users in each department to identify the data that the information systems designers should include in the warehouse. Historical data is inserted in the warehouse in the appropriate format, and then new data is collected by the online transaction processing (OLTP) system and transferred to the data warehouse.

Data mining is the process by which decision makers query the data warehouse. Innovations in data warehouse systems include the use of a natural language query system. This means that the user can make queries in plain English. The system translates everyday English into the systems query language and processes the queries. Combining online analytical processing (OLAP) tools with the data warehouse's user-friendly interface will lead to greater and easier data mining, and possibly, better decisions. Intranets can be used to bring information from global operations to one easily accessible location, thus serving as an easy-to-use data mining interface.

At General Electric Company, data warehousing and data mining are integral parts of using the corporate intranet to better manage indirect and MRO purchases. The company's Enterprise Sourcing and Payables-Integrated Indirect Service includes three components:

- The purchasing service with the Trading Process Network (TPN) as the backbone
- The payment settlement process
- The strategic sourcing data warehouse[23]

All three components are linked via the GE intranet with external links to the marketplace via the Internet and EDI.

The software used in the system is critical to the end user in terms of the decision-support capabilities. The software can be highly flexible or specific, and in turn, it can be either easy or difficult to use. If the software is highly flexible, users can write their own queries and perform their own analysis. Specific software provides preformatted, unchangeable reports. If a user is making periodic decisions, preformatted reports may be sufficient. However, if the user is looking for patterns or strategic business advantages, flexible queries may be a better solution.

Conclusion

This volume has attempted to convey the critical importance of the purchasing and supply management function to the success of the organization, whether the organization is a manufacturer, a process industry, a service business, or a private or a public institution. Given the vital role of the supply function, it is critical that expert and enlightened leaders guide purchasing and supply. This volume has defined the roles and responsibilities incumbent with this leadership. This has been difficult in light of the profound changes taking place in how work is accomplished due to the rapid advances in technology, in particular the Internet. This discussion should serve as a valuable guide, while at the same time offering readers the opportunity to apply the lessons they learn in a constantly changing environment.

Key Points

1. Supply managers must identify key stakeholders, or constituencies, both internal and external to the organization. Internal constituencies include top management and the organization's employees.
2. The information provided to each constituency should be tailored to the needs and interests of that group. These interests may, at times, conflict. Balancing the needs and interests of different constituencies requires the work of skilled communicators.
3. The Internet and organizational intranets provide faster communication and a broader distribution of information to each constituency. New data management techniques allow for real-time access to data, flexible queries of stored information, and customized reporting.

Questions for Review

1. Who are the key constituencies to whom the management of the supply organization must report information?
2. What information should be reported to each constituency?
3. How should the information be communicated to each constituency?
4. How can an intranet be used by the supply management function to communicate internally with users and externally with suppliers?

Endnotes

1. Mauffette-Leenders, L., J.A. Erskine, and M.R. Leenders, *Learning with Cases*, Richard Ivey School of Business, London, Ontario, 1997, p. 42.
2. Dell Computer Corporation, "Medium and Large Businesses, Employee Purchase Program," www.dell.com.
3. Sam Farney, United Technologies, 1999.
4. Dell, M. "Collaborating in a Connected Economy, The Power of Virtual Integration," June 24, 1998, www.dell.com.
5. http://216.51.18.233/fct/goingon.html, Jan. 30, 2000.
6. Wendy's International, Inc., "Letter to Shareholders," 1998 *Annual Report*, p. 1.
7. Leenders, M.R. and H.E. Fearon. *Purchasing and Supply Management*, R.D. Irwin, Chicago, 1997, p. 542.
8. Honda of America Manufacturing. "Investing in America, Overview of Manufacturing and Assembly," www.hondacorporate.com.
9. Wining, L.C. "Straight to the Top," *Purchasing Today®*, February 1997, p. 8.
10. Bailyn, L. "Integrating Work and Personal Life...in Practice," in Senge, P., A. Kleiner, C. Roberts, R. Ross, G. Roth, and B. Smith, *The Dance of Change*, Currency/Doubleday, New York, 1999, p. 99.
11. Bailyn, 1999, p. 99-100.
12. Dell Computer Corporation, "Dell FactPak, What Sets Us Apart," www.dell.com..

13. Dell, M. "Direct Connect", Aug. 25, 1999 (speech).
14. Wendy's International, Inc., "Wendy's Announces Significant Upgrades to Investor Web Site," Nov. 23, 1998, www.wendys.com.
15. "How Effective Is E-mail in the Workplace?," *Purchasing Today®*, September 1999, p. 4.
16. This section was paraphrased from Masciandaro, M. "Intranets in Action: Rohm and Haas," and Taylor, M. "Intranets in Action: Fluor Daniel Hanford," *Purchasing Today®*, April 1998, pp. 31-32.
17. Karoway, C. "Superior Supply Chains Pack Plenty of Byte," *Purchasing Today®*, November 1997, p. 34.
18. Taylor. 1998, p. 31.
19. Masciandaro, 1998, p. 31.
20. Taylor, 1998, p. 32.
21. Karoway, 1997, pp. 33-34.
22. This section was paraphrased from Clark, D. and T. Miller. "Dust Off the Data in Your Warehouse," *Purchasing Today®*, July 1999, p. 19-20.
23. Cafiero, W.G. and R.M. Rowe. "Using a Corporate Intranet for Indirect and MRO Purchases: A General Electric Case Study," *Proceedings of the 1998 NAPM International Purchasing Conference*, NAPM, Tempe, AZ, 1998.

APPENDIX

EQUAL EMPLOYMENT OPPORTUNITY LAWS AND REGULATIONS

During the 1960s and 1970s, legal and social changes influenced organizations' policies and practices in administering personnel functions. In effect, the federal government created an umbrella of regulations that surround and permeate all the personnel programs and practices discussed in this volume. The major thrust was directed at preventing discrimination against various groups of employees. Key regulatory actions are the Federal Civil Rights Act of 1964 (specifically Title VII), Executive Order 11246 in 1965, the Age Discrimination Act of 1967, and the Equal Employment Opportunity Act of 1972.

Federal Civil Rights Act, Title VII

Title VII of the 1964 act makes it illegal to discriminate among employees on the basis of race, religion, color, sex, or national origin. It focuses on discrimination with regard to any employment condition, including hiring, firing, promotion, transfer, compensation, and admission to training programs. The original act gave the Equal Employment Opportunity Commission (EEOC) the responsibility to try to effect compliance by means of conferences with the groups involved, conciliation, and persuasion. If these efforts failed, EEOC could ask the attorney general to bring suit against the organization.

Equal Employment Opportunity Act

In 1972, the Equal Employment Opportunity Act (EEOA) was passed to provide a series of amendments to Title VII, expanding its coverage and strengthening its enforcement. Coverage was extended to virtually all organizations with 15 or more employees. The EEOC was given the power to file lawsuits against offending organizations.

Affirmative Action

Another significant provision of the EEOA requires organizations to take "affirmative action" to move toward achieving a work

255

force that accurately reflects the composition of the community. In other words, an organization must compare its employment, by department and by job level, with data on the availability of talent in the relevant labor market. In each case, the organization must then attempt to achieve a work force comprised of approximately the same percentage of the various minority groups (including women) that exist in the available labor market. The enactment of this provision is an extension of Executive Order 11246, issued in 1965, which required organizations doing business with the government to prepare a written affirmative action plan to accomplish this same result.

The development of a sound written affirmative action program is seen as a way for an organization to fulfill its social responsibility. In addition, some companies today view affirmative action as a preventive approach to minimize the possibility of problems with the EEOC and also possible legal actions. Such a plan can be developed using a three-step approach:

1. Determine the jobs in which any group is under-represented, and appraise the availability of that group in the labor market.
2. Set numerical integration goals for increasing the representation of that group in those jobs.
3. Specify the actions to be taken to attain the goals.

In most organizations, the responsibility for developing policies and procedures for complying with EEO regulations is assigned to the personnel department. An effective purchasing manager, however, should initiate actions to work closely with the human resources department in this regard, because his or her human resources management activities must be designed to fit within the framework of these legal requirements.

Americans with Disabilities Act[1]

Court rulings that pertain to employment discrimination based on a disability are abundant, and at times, confusing. For a manager, two areas of particular importance are writing job descriptions and ensuring appropriate on-site accommodations. A key tool in determining what an employer needs to do under the Americans with Disabilities Act (ADA) lies in defining essential job functions. Generally, a function is essential when the position exists to perform the function, there are a limited number of employees available who could perform the function, or the function is highly specialized (29 C.F.R. § 1630.2(n)(2)).

Job Descriptions – Courts rely on job descriptions when determining if individuals with disabilities are qualified to perform the essential functions of a position. Therefore, employers should be certain that the wording of job descriptions is accurate in listing the essential functions (that is, integral duties) of a position. Human resources professionals should be available to work with managers to determine if a function is essential and to help word job descriptions appropriately. The courts have ruled, however, that essential job functions do not have to be listed in job descriptions. For example, functions such as regular attendance and the ability to handle stress and get along with supervisors and co-workers are so basic to all jobs that they do not need to be listed in the job description.

For example, an appeals court ruled that performing job tasks without offending customers was an essential function of a grocery store bagger (*Taylor v. Food World*, 133 F.3d 1419 [11th Cir. 1998]. If essential functions are listed, they may be changed for business reasons, such as increasing production standards to improve competitiveness (*Milton v. Scrivner*, 53 F.3d 1118 [10th Cir. 1995]). Although attendance is not considered an essential job function in the EEOC enforcement guidelines on reasonable accommodation and undue hardship, most courts have held that reliable job attendance is. The ADA does not typically protect persons who have erratic, unexplained absences, even if those absences are a result of a disability (*Waggoner v. Olin Corp.*, 169 F.3d 481 [7th Cir. 1999]). However, in at least one case (*Cehrs v. Northeast Ohio Alzheimer's Research Center*, 155 F.3d 775 [6th Cir. 1998]) the court ruled that uninterrupted job attendance is not an essential job function because a leave of absence is a reasonable accommodation.

On-Site Accommodations – The 1990 Americans with Disabilities Act provides for equal opportunity for all persons in the areas of employment, public services and accommodations, and telecommunications. According to the Job Accommodation Network (JAN)[2] run by West Virginia University, job accommodations are usually not expensive, and they may be as simple as rearranging equipment. For example, providing a drafting table, page-turner, and pressure sensitive tape recorder for a sales agent paralyzed from a broken neck cost about $950. Changing a desk layout from the right to the left side for a data entry operator who had a shoulder injury cost nothing. Using an articulating keyboard tray to alleviate strain of repetitive motion and carpal tunnel syndrome cost $150. In fact, 80 percent of the job accommodations suggested by JAN cost less than $500. Appropriate accommodations can reduce workers compensation and other insurance costs, increase the pool of qualified employees, and create opportunities for persons with functional limitations.

Sexual Harassment

Sexual harassment is any kind of sexual behavior that is unwelcome or inappropriate for the work place. Sexual harassment can include verbal harassment (that is, derogatory comments or dirty jokes under some circumstances), visual harassment (that is, derogatory or embarrassing posters, cartoons, and drawings), physical harassment, and sexual favors (that is, sexual advances and confrontations involving sexual demands). In the work place, sexual harassment can come from the owner, supervisor, manager, lead person, foreperson, a co-worker, or a customer.

Title VII of the Civil Rights of 1964, which strictly prohibits sexual harassment, applies to any company with more than 15 employees in an industry affecting interstate commerce. Title VII classifies sexual harassment claims into two categories: quid pro quo and hostile work environment.

Quid Pro Quo Sexual Harassment – Quid pro quo sexual harassment takes place when a supervisor or someone with authority over a person's job demands sexual favors from that person in exchange for assistance in being promoted, hired, or retained. The demand for sexual favors can be direct, for example, "If you go to bed with me, I will make sure you keep your job or get a raise," or it can be implied from unwelcome physical conduct, such as touching, grabbing, or fondling.

Hostile Work Environment – A hostile work environment has been created if the sexual harassment unreasonably interferes with a person's work performance or creates an offensive or intimidating work environment. In order to have a claim for a hostile work environment, the employee must be able to prove that there was more than one incident of harassment. The employee may also have to show that the sexual conduct was unwelcome. Being the butt of sexually charged jokes or pranks, being grabbed or whistled at, sexual advances, requests for sexual favors, or other verbal, visual, or physical conduct of a sexual nature can create a hostile work environment and can qualify as sexual harassment. Conduct that makes the work place sexually charged does not need to be directly aimed at the person being harassed in order for it to be actionable. For example, being subject to pornographic posters or pictures or profanity can create a hostile work environment.

Preventing Sexual Harassment – An organization can minimize the number of sexual harassment claims by:

- Drafting and publicizing an anti-sexual harassment policy
- Implementing a procedure for employees to follow if they feel they have been the victim of sexual harassment
- Conducting companywide sexual harassment prevention training programs

Managers at all levels in an organization have an individual, and collective, role and responsibility for creating and fostering a work environment that motivates performance. Dysfunctional work places are easily created when managers shirk this responsibility. The costs associated with work environments filled with fear, abuse, and disrespect are immeasurable. Talent is lost as people, sickened by the pervasive climate, leave or refocus their time, energy, and efforts on more rewarding and validating areas of their lives.

Responding to Claims of Sexual Harassment – Once an employer knows or should know about sexual harassment, it is the duty of the manager to take immediate and appropriate corrective action. An employee who believes she or he is being sexually harassed at a job, should report the harassment (preferably in writing) to a supervisor or manager as soon as possible. The complaint should include the facts involving the sexual harassment and the effect the harassment is having on the employee's ability to perform her or his job. The employer's response must be reasonably calculated to end the harassment. If earlier discipline did not end the harassment, more severe discipline is required. The employer may be held liable if he or she knew or should have known about the harassment but failed to take any prompt remedial steps to stop the harassment.

If an employee's claim meets the legal requirements for proof, the employee may: stop the harassment, recover lost wages and other job-related losses (that is, promotions or favorable work status lost because of the sexual harassment), obtain compensation for personal injuries (that is, physical, mental, and emotional injuries), obtain punitive damages against the harasser(s) and/or the organization, recover attorneys' fees and costs, and make reforms within the company or entity held liable for sexual harassment.

Endnotes

1. The information in this section was drawn from Fram, D. *ADA Compliance Guide*, Thompson Publishing.
2. Job Accommodation Network, West Virginia University, P.O. Box 6080, Morgantown, WV, 26506-6080, janweb.icbi.wvu.edu.

AUTHOR INDEX

SUBJECT INDEX

Membership Application

National Association of Purchasing Management, Inc.

Members are encouraged to join a local affiliated association. To obtain information on the affiliated association closest to you and dues information, please call NAPM Customer Service at 800/888-6276 or 480/752-6276, extension 401. Applications can also be submitted via the Internet at www.napm.org.

Please check the appropriate box:

❑ New Member   ❑ Past Member   NAPM ID Number (if known)

❑ I am replacing the following current member in my organization (If replacing a current member, send completed application to the affiliate.)

Member Name _____   NAPM ID# _____

Dr. Mr. Mrs. Ms. Miss _____

(please circle)   First Name   MI   Last Name

Title (required) _____   Organization (required) _____

Please check the preferred mailing address:

❑ BUSINESS   ❑ HOME

City	State	ZIP Code

City	State	ZIP Code

Country _____ Postal Code   Country _____ Postal Code

E-Mail _____   E-Mail _____

(____) _____   (____) _____   (____) _____

Business Phone Number**   Fax Number**   Home Phone Number**

**For international numbers, please include country and city codes.

Date of Birth (optional): ____/____/____

Industry Code (choose a 3-digit code from the list provided on page two of this application): ____ ____ ____

Number of employees at your location (please check one): ❑ under 100 ❑ 100-249 ❑ 250-499 ❑ 500-999 ❑ 1000+

Education (check highest level completed): ❑ High School ❑ Associate's ❑ Bachelor's ❑ Master's ❑ Other_____

❑ Student (estimated graduation date): _____

Are you a C.P.M.? ❑ Yes ❑ No   Are you an A.P.P.? ❑ Yes ❑ No

Do you hold other professional designations? If so, please list:_____

Would you like to serve on a committee? ❑ Yes ❑ No

Are you involved in sales? If so, explain: _____

MEMBERSHIP TYPE: Please select one of the options below. See back for option details.

Option I	Option II
❑ **Regular Membership** – Includes National and local affiliate benefits. I choose to become a member through (please provide affiliate name):	❑ **Direct National Membership** – Includes National benefits only. Does not include affiliate benefits.
_____	NAPM Dues: $ 270.00
For dues information and District/Affiliate code, contact NAPM Customer Service at 800/888-6276 or 480/752-6276, extension 401.	Administrative Fee: $ 0.00
	TOTAL: $ 270.00
District/Affiliate Code (Code provided by NAPM): ___ ___ / ___ ___ ___	**Method of payment (U.S. Funds Only):**
Annual NAPM/Affiliate Dues: $ _____	❑ Personal Check ❑ Organization Check
Administrative Fee: $ 20.00	❑ VISA ❑ MasterCard ❑ American Express ❑ Diners Club
Affiliate Initiation Fee: $ _____	Charge Card# _____
Other: $ _____	Exp. Date ____/____ Amount to be Charged $ _____
TOTAL: $ _____	Cardholder Signature _____

NAPM members receive *Purchasing Today*® magazine as a $12 portion and *NAPM InfoEdge* as a $12 portion of the national membership fee.

I agree to abide by the *NAPM Bylaws*, *Principles and Standards of Purchasing Practice*, and *Statement of Antitrust Policy*, as stated on the back of this application. A copy of the *NAPM Bylaws* may be obtained by writing or calling NAPM Customer Service at the address and telephone number listed below.

_____   _____

Signature   Date

RETURN TO:	APPROVALS FOR AFFILIATE/NAPM USE ONLY	
	NAPM _____ Date _____	51
	Affiliate _____ Date _____	SMKS4
	Other _____ Date _____	

NAPM Use Only

Amount $_____   Approval #_____   Date Entered _____   Initials _____

NAPM, P.O. Box 22160, Tempe, AZ 85285-2160 • 800/888-6276 or 480/752-6276, extension 401 • Fax 480/752-2299

Regular Membership

Regular Membership is when an individual chooses to join an Affiliated Association and National. Each Affiliated Association will set the annual dues for its local membership, which will include National dues.

Any individual that chooses this type of membership will receive discounts on both National and Affiliate levels.

OPTION II

Direct National Membership

Direct National Membership is when an individual chooses to join the National level of NAPM only. The annual dues are $270.

This membership allows for discounts on the National level of products and services only.

OPTION III

Volume Discount Membership

With NAPM's Volume Discount Membership, organizations with 50 or more purchasing employees nationwide can save substantially on their membership dues. This category is available to organizations as well as governmental entities of every level and type.

The discount schedule is as follows:

Number of Members (nationwide)	Discount on Dues (without meals)
50-99	10%
100-249	20%
250 and over	30%

Volume Discount Membership is arranged through your organization or government entity. Volume Discount members and all necessary information will be provided to NAPM headquarters by one individual from each organization/entity. NAPM will invoice your organization/entity for the correct amount of dues, and forward the affiliate portion to the affiliate. Any individual with Volume Discount Membership will receive the benefits of belonging to an affiliate and the National Association.

For more information contact NAPM at 800/888-6276 or 480/752-6276, extension 3111.

Principles and Standards of Purchasing Practice

LOYALTY TO YOUR COMPANY
JUSTICE TO THOSE WITH WHOM YOU DEAL
FAITH IN YOUR PROFESSION

From these principles are derived the NAPM Standards of Purchasing Practice.

1. Avoid the intent and appearance of unethical or compromising practice in relationships, actions, and communications.

2. Demonstrate loyalty to the employer by diligently following the lawful instructions of the employer, using reasonable care, and only authority granted.

3. Refrain from any private business or professional activity that would create a conflict between personal interests and the interests of the employer.

4. Refrain from soliciting or accepting money, loans, credits, or prejudicial discounts, and the acceptance of gifts, entertainment, favors, or services from present or potential suppliers that might influence, or appear to influence, purchasing decisions.

5. Handle confidential or proprietary information belonging to employers or suppliers with due care and proper consideration of ethical and legal ramifications and governmental regulations.

6. Promote positive supplier relationships through courtesy and impartiality in all phases of the purchasing cycle.

7. Refrain from reciprocal agreements that restrain competition.

8. Know and obey the letter and spirit of laws governing the purchasing function and remain alert to the legal ramifications of purchasing decisions.

9. Encourage all segments of society to participate by demonstrating support of small, disadvantaged, and minority-owned businesses.

10. Discourage purchasing's involvement in employer-sponsored programs of personal purchases that are not business-related.

11. Enhance the proficiency and stature of the purchasing profession by acquiring and maintaining current technical knowledge and the highest standards of ethical behavior.

12. Conduct international purchasing in accordance with the laws, customs, and practices of foreign countries, consistent with United States laws, your organizational policies, and these ethical standards and guidelines.

NAPM Antitrust Policy

It is the express policy and intention of NAPM to comply at all times with all existing laws, including the antitrust laws, and in furtherance of this policy, no activity or program will be sponsored or conducted by or within NAPM or any association affiliated with NAPM which in any matter whatsoever will represent or be deemed a violation of any existing law, including the antitrust laws. This statement of policy will be implemented by the publication of the "Principles for Antitrust Compliance," "Standards for NAPM Activities," "Standards for Membership and Professional Self-Regulation," and "Standards for Conduct and Use of Surveys" which are available to all members of the association upon request.

Dues, contributions, or gifts to this organization are not tax-deductible charitable contributions for income tax purposes. Dues may, however, be deductible as a business expense.

Return to local affiliate association or:
NAPM
P.O. Box 22160
Tempe, AZ 85285-2160
Or fax application to 480/752-2299

STANDARD INDUSTRY CODES (SIC) — If you have responsibility for more than one industry, please use only the one three-digit code representing the major activity of the company, division, or plant for which you work. (Write the three-digit code on the reverse side of this form in the appropriate space.)

AGRICULTURE, FORESTRY, AND FISHERIES
010 Agricultural production - crops
020 Agricultural production - livestock
070 Agricultural services
080 Forestry
090 Fishing, hunting, trapping

MINING
100 Metal mining
120 Bituminous coal/lignite mining
130 Oil and gas extraction
140 Nonmetallic minerals, except fuels

CONTRACT CONSTRUCTION
150 General building contractors
160 Heavy construction contractors
170 Special trade contractors

MANUFACTURING
200 Food and kindred products
210 Tobacco manufacturers
220 Textile mill products
230 Apparel/other textile products
240 Lumber and wood products
250 Furniture and fixtures
260 Paper and allied products
270 Printing and publishing
280 Chemicals and allied products
290 Petroleum and coal products
300 Rubber and miscellaneous plastic products
310 Leather and leather products
320 Stone, clay, and glass products
330 Primary metal industries
340 Fabricated metal products
350 Machinery, except electrical

360 Electric/electronic equipment
370 Transportation equipment
380 Instruments and related products
390 Miscellaneous manufacturing industries

TRANSPORTATION, COMMUNICATION, AND UTILITY SERVICES
400 Railroad transportation
410 Local/interurban mass transit
420 Trucking and warehousing
430 U.S. Postal Service
440 Water transportation
450 Transportation by air
460 Pipelines, except natural gas
470 Transportation services
480 Communication
490 Electric, gas, and sanitary services

WHOLESALE AND RETAIL TRADE
500 Wholesale trade - durable goods
510 Wholesale trade - nondurable goods
520 Building materials/garden supplies
530 General merchandise stores
540 Food stores
550 Automotive dealers/service stations
560 Apparel and accessory stores
570 Furniture/home furnishings stores
580 Eating and drinking places
590 Miscellaneous retail

FINANCE, INSURANCE, AND REAL ESTATE
600 Banking
610 Credit agencies, except banks
620 Security commodity brokers/services
630 Insurance carriers

640 Insurance agents, brokers/services
650 Real estate
670 Holding/other investment offices

SERVICES
700 Hotel/other lodging places
720 Personal services
730 Business services
750 Auto repair, services/garages
760 Miscellaneous repair services
780 Motion pictures
790 Amusement/recreation services
800 Health services
810 Legal services
820 Educational services
830 Social services
840 Museums/botanical, zoological gardens
860 Membership organizations
870 Engineering/accounting/related services
880 Private households
890 Miscellaneous services

GOVERNMENT
910 Executive, legislative/general
920 Justice, public order, and safety
930 Finance, taxation, and monetary policy
940 Administration of human resources
950 Environmental quality/housing
960 Administration of economic programs
970 National security/international affairs

NONCLASSIFIABLE
999 Nonclassifiable establishments